PROCLAIMING *A* REPUBLIC

Ireland, 1916
and the National Collection

Darragh Gannon

With contributions by
Sandra Heise, Brenda Malone & Pádraig Clancy

IRISH ACADEMIC PRESS

First published in 2016 by
Irish Academic Press
10 George's Street
Newbridge
Co. Kildare
Ireland
www.iap.ie

In association with the National Museum of Ireland
www.museum.ie

© Darragh Gannon, 2016

978-1-911024-48-4 (Paperback)
978-1-911024-45-3 (PDF)

British Library Cataloguing in Publication Data
An entry can be found on request

Library of Congress Cataloging in Publication Data
An entry can be found on request

1.11 BELUM.W2013.29. Ulster Provisional Government Proclamation (1913)
© National Museums Northern Ireland. Collection Ulster Museum.
2.25 Courtesy of the Curran family.
8.1, 8.2, 8.3, 8.7, 8.8, 8.9 © National Library of Ireland
8.5 © RTÉ Archives
8.6 © Lensman Photographic Agency
8.16 Courtesy of Peter Figgis

Front cover image: Design by Yvonne Doherty.

Back cover image: A public notice issued by General John Maxwell on 2 May 1916. HE:EWT.465

Front flap image: Ammunition and instructions from James Connolly were hidden in this secret compartment of a book. HE:EW.499a

Back flap image: The 'Plough and the Stars' flag, flown from the Imperial Hotel during Easter Week. HE:EW.2362

Previous page: i The remains of the Imperial Hotel building on Sackville Street, after Easter Week. HE:EW.3798

Opposite page: ii *Leabhar na hAiséirghe*, detail from the 'Sixteen men' page. HE:EW.79

Design by Yvonne Doherty

Typeset in Baskerville 11/15 pt

Printed and bound by Gráficas Castuera, Spain

museum
National Museum of Ireland
Ard-Mhúsaem na hÉireann

The names here
of
The Sixteen Men.

Pádraig mac Piarais.
Tomás mac Donncada.
Tomás Ó Cléirig.
Seósaim M. Pluingcéid.
Eamonn Ó Dálaig.
Mícéal Ó hAnnracáin.
Liam mac Piarais.
Seán mac Giolla Brígde.
Concobar Ó Colbáird.
Eamonn Ceannt.
Mícéal Ó Meallain.
Seán S. mac Aoda.
Tomás Ceannt.
Séumas Ó Congaile.
Seán mac Diarmada.
Ruaidrí mac Asmuint.

Who is this
that cometh
from Edom: with dy'd
garments fro
Bozrah? Th
that is glor
in his appa
travelline
the garmer
of his stre
wherefore
thou red i
ap

iii
The 'Irish Republic' flag flown over
the Prince's Street corner of the
GPO during Easter Week.
HE:EW.3224

CONTENTS

Acknowledgements

A book of this scale opens as many acknowledgements as it does pages. I am, first and foremost, indebted to Conor Graham and Irish Academic Press for their steadfast belief in this project. Conor has provided unerring support and necessary perspective throughout this process and for that I am most grateful. I would like to specially acknowledge Fiona Dunne, IAP Managing Editor, whose continued patience and professionalism helped deliver this book to completion. Thanks are also due to Myles McCionnaith IAP Marketing and Editorial Executive, and to Linda Longmore, Guy Holland and Amanda Bell who successively copy-edited, proofed and indexed the manuscript.

This book is, above all, a testament to the National Museum of Ireland and its staff. I would like to express my sincere thanks and appreciation to Director Raghnall Ó Floinn whose vision for the Museum's 'Proclaiming a Republic: the 1916 Rising' exhibition and trust in my writing a book on same made this publication possible. Thanks are also due to Head of Collections Rolly Read for his continued support of the project. I am most grateful to Audrey Whitty, Keeper of the Art and Industry division, who has championed this publication assuredly from concept to completion. I would like, further, to reserve special acknowledgment for Sandra Heise whose unsparing confidence in my contribution to the Museum's 2016 programme, and this publication in particular, has offered me once in anyone's lifetime opportunities. I am forever indebted to her for those memories. Thanks also to my Art and Industry division colleagues Jennifer Goff, Lar Joye, Sarah Nolan and Alex Ward for their encouragement and collegiality throughout my time at the Museum.

Extracts of the exhibition text appear in certain paragraphs of the book. I would like to acknowledge the contributions of Sandra Heise, Brenda Malone and Pádraig Clancy to the original exhibition text, and for their support of my writing this follow-up publication. Sandra Heise has solely authored a fascinating study of Art Ó Murnaghan and Leabhar na hAiséirghe ('the Book of the Resurrection') in Chapter 8 entitled 'The National Memorial'. A note of thanks is also due to Raghnall Ó Floinn, Audrey Whitty and Sandra Heise for their generous giving of time and thought to review the manuscript as it was being prepared.

This project has truly been a collaborative experience. The Museum's Photographic Department, namely Valerie Dowling and Richard Weinacht, have supplied the images for this volume (unless otherwise stated). They have been responsive and resourceful throughout, working beyond expectations to ensure that this book was ready for publication. I thank them for their commitment to this project. The Museum's Design Department, further, have been instrumental in bringing this publication to reality. Michael Heffernan and Darko Vukšić have skilfully carried out digital restoration on images for the publication while John Murray, in addition, has expertly produced the map contained within. The beautiful page-by-page design of this book, finally, is the signature of Yvonne Doherty. Yvonne has worked tirelessly on this project from first to final day, formatting text, positioning images and perfecting the presentation of the entire publication. It reads as much her book as it does mine. The Museum's staff overall have been immensely helpful throughout. Special thanks in this regard are due to Seamus Lynam (Services), Ann Daly and Maureen Gaule (Marketing), Emer Ni Cheallaigh (Documentation) and David McKenna and Paul Harrison (IT).

Within the academy I have had the privilege of working closely with Anna Bryson, Vincent Comerford, Enda Delaney, Roy Foster, Marian Lyons, Seán McConville and Ian Speller over the years. I thank them for their encouragement and for their inspiration to ask questions where there are answers. I have been fortunate to have enjoyed academic discussion and debate with many other scholars on the subject of this book including John Borgonovo, Mel Farrell, Dion Georgiou, Richard Keogh, Ann-Marie Kilgallon, Georgina Laragy, Eve Morrison, Conor Mulvagh, William Murphy, Daithí Ó Corráin, Justin Dolan Stover and Barry Whelan. A flavour of those coffeed conversations can be found within these pages.

Family and friends have helped me through the writing of this book. I thank, in particular, my longest suffering friends: Seán Atkinson, Stephen Carragher, Mark Donnelly, John Fallon, Ivor Keane, John McGinnity and Edward Tynan. I thank also my brother Conor, sister Grace and extended family for understanding my lengthy absence. My parents, Jim and Paula, have been the very foundation on which this study was written. When ideas became sentences they were there, when ideas did not become sentences they were there. I thank them dearly. My final thanks are to Yulia. I have found over sixty thousand words to account for one hundred and fifty years of Irish history but I am lost to find any which adequately convey my appreciation for your support over the last five months. This book is dedicated to you, and to my parents, for everything.

Darragh Gannon, 29 September 2016

Foreword

The year 2016 has witnessed an astonishing level of interest and engagement by the public in the events surrounding the Easter Rising of 1916. Exhibitions, lectures, re-enactments and commemorative ceremonies have been held across the country and abroad, along with new commissions in art, theatre, music, television and film, augmented by books (to be numbered in the hundreds), newspaper columns and special supplements. In contrast to previous commemorations, which focused on the main protagonists, both military and political, the focus in 2016 has been the foregrounding of the experiences of individuals – the ordinary soldiers, policemen, rebels and civilians (men, women and children) – caught up in the events of Easter Week, 1916, as participants, casualties or witnesses.

Today, the Museum's Easter Week collection is in a unique position to tell these stories, given its range and depth, and its full potential has been realised for the first time in the Museum's current exhibition 'Proclaiming a Republic: the 1916 Rising'. In its first five months, the exhibition has attracted over 125,000 visitors. The overwhelming feedback from the public has been positive; visitors have been moved by their experience. This is testament to the power of objects to evoke a range of emotional responses, whether it be their encounter with the type used to print the Proclamation and the 'Irish Republic' flag raised over the GPO, the objects associated with the 15-year-old Charles D'Arcy who was 'killed in action' on the first day of the Rising, or the rugby ball pressed into service by the internees at Frongoch, Wales, to play Gaelic football. Some, such as the anti-Home Rule salt cellar in the shape of an egg 'laid at Westminster in 1912 but won't hatch in Ulster' still resonate to this day.

iv
Staff of the National Museum of Ireland, including Ellen Prendergast (centre), prepare for its 1941 exhibition on the 1916 Rising.

The National Museum of Ireland's unrivalled Easter Week collection of objects and documents has been a valued resource for researchers of the period and has also played a key role in commemorative exhibitions since the first display of 'relics' of 1916 was mounted as part of the 31st International Eucharistic Congress, which was held in Dublin in 1932. This modest exhibition was shown alongside a major exhibition of Early Christian Irish art curated by the then Director, Adolf Mahr. Mahr objected to the display of this historical material, arguing that it was 'neither scientific nor artistic not illustrating antiquity or industry'. However, the exhibition went ahead thanks to the perseverance of Nellie Gifford-Donnelly, and the material displayed forms the core of the Museum's Easter Week collection. Ironically, Mahr's predecessor as Director of the Museum, Count George Noble Plunkett (father of Joseph Mary Plunkett who was married to Nellie Gifford-Donnelly's sister, Grace), was stripped of his position because of his involvement in the events of Easter Week as was Liam Gógan, assistant keeper of Irish Antiquities at the time, who took it upon himself to close the Museum on Easter Monday. Gógan was later to be reinstated and was eventually to take charge of the Museum's Easter Week collection as Keeper of Art & Industry. A debt is owed to Gógan and to his successors as curators in charge of the historical collections in the Art and Industrial Division, most notably Gerald A. Hayes-McCoy, Oliver Snoddy, Michael Kenny and Sandra Heise for augmenting, curating, researching, publishing and displaying the collections: the Easter Week collections have been the subject of exhibition at the Museum on no less than eight occasions.

v
Count George Noble
Plunkett.
HE:EWL.227.91

I would like to congratulate Darragh Gannon for producing such a worthy companion volume to the exhibition, and for his dedication in completing the text following his work on the exhibition. Darragh was assisted by the deep knowledge and expertise on these collections of Sandra Heise, Assistant Keeper in the Art and Industrial Division, and of Brenda Malone and Pádraig Clancy, curatorial researchers on the exhibition. The design and layout was produced in-house and is the work of Yvonne Doherty, Graphic Designer, assisted by John Murray, Senior Graphic Designer, Michael Heffernan and Darko Vukšić, while most of the photographs were newly commissioned from Bryan Rutledge and Peter Moloney under the supervision of Valerie Dowling, Senior Photographer, with digital imaging support by Richard Weinacht. I would also like to thank Audrey Whitty, Keeper of Art & Industry, for her support. I am grateful to Conor Graham, Publisher, Irish Academic Press, for his continued support for this project.

The exhibition associated with this publication was the work of an incredibly dedicated in-house team drawn from across the Museum – curators, conservators, education and outreach staff, facilities, graphic design, photography, IT, marketing and retail. We are indebted to our lenders – The Imperial War Museum, the Royal Collections and the Royal Society of Antiquaries of Ireland – for their support, to the OPW for continued assistance in the installation of the exhibition and to the Department of Arts, Heritage, Regional, Rural and Gaeltacht Affairs through the 1916 Commemorations Unit for financial support.

Raghnall Ó Floinn
Director
National Museum of Ireland
October, 2016

Introduction

It has been a long 2016. The centenaries of the 1916 Rising, executions at Kilmainham, Cork and Pentonville prisons, internment at Frongoch, and the Battle of the Somme (Thiepval, Guillemont, Ginchy) have spanned a breathless series of commemorative events across Ireland and the Irish world. The state's comprehensive 'Ireland 2016' programme re-remembered '1916' to the centenary generation through seven strands of public engagement: state ceremonial, historical reflection, *an teanga bheo*, youth and imagination, cultural expression, community participation, global and diaspora. The scale of commemorative fervour and participation revealed itself in the capital on 27 and 28 March on the occasions of the Irish State's 1916 Rising parade and RTÉ's three hundred-venue 'Reflecting the Rising' event respectively: over one million people were 'out' in Dublin during Easter Week 2016. Such popular expression of interest in '1916' is historic. It need not be. History must have a place in Ireland's future too. The extraordinary public engagement with Irish history in 2016 itself confers a mandate upon government to secure its role in the cultural, educational and heritage life of the country. This would be a legacy to be remembered by the generation of 2066.

Culture, education and heritage have defined the commemorative experience at the National Museum of Ireland. Its extensive 1916 programme included a series of talks with writer in residence Dermot Bolger at the Museum of Decorative Arts & History, Collins Barracks, and the Museum of Country Life, Turlough Park; the development of an online learning resource ('1916 object stories') for primary and post-primary schools; and the curation of 'Roger Casement: voice of the voiceless', a display of international effects at the Museum of

vi

(Opposite page)
The pocket watch of Seán Mac Diarmada given by him to his friend, Barney Mellows, at Kilmainham jail hours before his execution.
HE:EWL.110

Natural History and the Museum of Archaeology. Over one million people visited its four sites between January and September 2016. The centrepiece of the National Museum of Ireland's centenary calendar, however, has been 'Proclaiming a Republic: the 1916 Rising'. Housed in the Riding School at Collins Barracks, this exhibition uniquely reveals the physical realities of life in Ireland before, during and after the events of Easter Week in the form of three hundred objects, articles and images. It has been the largest display of 1916 material in the history of the institution. *Proclaiming a Republic: Ireland, 1916 and the National Collection*, builds upon this landmark exhibition, bringing the National Museum of Ireland's artefacts out of their physical displays and making the case for their presentation as exciting 'new' historical sources for understanding Ireland's 1916 experience.

The objects of the 1916 Rising have not been subject to sustained historical analysis. Institutional catalogues of '1916' artefacts are the customary form of museum publication. The National Museum of Ireland itself has published extensive guides to both its 1966 and 1991 exhibitions.[1] Michael Kenny's superb stand-alone volume *The Fenians: photographs and memorabilia from the National Museum of Ireland*, further, has illustrated an iconography of 'Fenianism', prefacing the 1916 Rising.[2] Beyond the institution, meanwhile, John Gibney's *A history of the Easter Rising in 50 objects* has provided snapshots of the Rising's material culture in the 'biography of objects' tradition.[3] However, as Toby Barnard has observed, 'the study of material culture involves more than listing and classifying the materials that survive from the past. It has to concern itself with attitudes and ideas.'[4] The concept of material culture as products of political thought has been initially explored within a collection of essays edited by Joanna Brück and Lisa Godson, entitled *Making 1916: material and visual culture of the Easter Rising*. Contributors treated variously of the tricolour flag, half-proclamation, Castle Document and photographs from the *Catholic Bulletin*, among other topics. There is much of value in this exploratory volume but the essays contribute discrete, not complete, analyses of the Rising's objects.[5] This study, conversely, explores the 1916 Rising across an entire collection of objects and artefacts: the National Museum of Ireland's Easter Week collection.

The Easter Week collection is one of twenty-two thematic holdings assembled under the auspices of the Art and Industry Division at the National Museum of Ireland. It was first established in 1935 with the purview of the 1916 Rising and the wider 'revolutionary period'. Within a decade the Easter Week collection comprised a full 4,275 artefacts. The vast majority of these (77 per cent) were gifted to the Museum by donors. Other items were either loaned to the Museum (16 per cent) or purchased by the Museum (7 per cent).[6] However, acquisition figures alone do not capture the collection culture associated with the Easter Week material. This archive was a quintessential Art and Industry Division collection. Writing on the Museum's three divisions (Antiquities, Art and Industry, Natural History) in the 1960s, Director A.T. Lucas commented: 'In the Art Division acquisition of material is highly selective.'[7] The development of the Easter Week collection across the twentieth century has been in keeping with this curatorial approach. The historical significance of objects was a critical factor in the selection process. Reviewing the effects of Joseph Plunkett loaned by his widow Grace Gifford-Plunkett, Keeper G.A. Hayes-McCoy recommended against acquiring ten of the twenty-three items (including his cigarette case, leather slippers and a lock of his hair): 'they are purely personal items, adding nothing to historical knowledge, and they should be retained in the family'.[8] Originality was a key criterion. Irish Minister Plenipotentiary to the United States Robert Brennan was one of many donors who offered complete runs of early-twentieth-century journals and newspapers. Responding to his submission, Museum and Archives Assistant Tomás Ó Cléirigh only committed to accepting the file on 'seeing precisely what we have, what lacunae exist and how best to set about completing them'.[9] Many donors of print material already acquired were directed towards the National Library of Ireland.[10] The authenticity of the objects, most importantly, was carefully ascertained before being accepted for the Easter Week collection. This frequently involved detailed correspondence with the donor, the presentation of supporting evidence and, occasionally, peer review on the part of leading academics and contemporaries. Discussing this rigorous process in relation to the provenance of Seán Heuston's rosary beads in 1937, then Keeper Liam Gógan affirmed:

'Obscurities of this kind are bound to interpose themselves at this distance from the events involved and it is only by such means as the present that they can be removed.'[11] The acquisition of objects for the Easter Week collection continues into the present. As of 2016 it houses over 15,000 artefacts.

The Easter Week collection is a 'comprehensive' archive, consisting of objects, textiles, metalwork, memorabilia, prints and ephemera. Its holdings restore the history of Ireland, 1916, to tangible, contemporary experience. Many of 1916's well-documented events are physically represented within the collection's iconic materials. These include an original Proclamation printed at Liberty Hall in the early hours of Easter Monday morning (signed by its compositors and printer), the 'Irish Republic' flag flown over the GPO during Easter Week and the last letters and personal effects of those executed at Kilmainham jail following the Rising. The presence of unique narrative-artefacts adds weight to accounts submerged within the historical record. Successive hotel bills itemise Joseph Plunkett's journey across Europe to wartime Germany, a 'Votes for Women' badge evidences the idealism displayed by Francis Sheehy-Skeffington on his arrest and execution in Dublin, while a darkened nun's veil illuminates the realities of Liam Mellows' escape from Galway after the Rising. Other items add depth of character to figures previously consigned to two-dimensional biography: Thomas Clarke's razor, Patrick Pearse's spectacles, Countess Markievicz's wristwatch. The collection, moreover, embodies the daily life of the past, hidden by history. Everyday objects such as the Sinn Féin piggy bank, Unionist salt cellar, the Jacob's Biscuit Factory garrison chessboard, internees' prison biscuits and the tricoloured bow-tie instance the lives and times of those who lived through this period. All of these objects, and hundreds more, are incorporated into an exploration of Ireland's 1916 experience for the first time. This book also integrates artefacts from complementary holdings within the Museum's Art and Industry Division: the Arms and Armour, Ceramics and Historical collections. The concentration and combination of '1916' artefacts across their catalogues extends to them the title of Ireland's 1916 National Collection.

Objects and artefacts like any other primary source are characterised by inherent bias. The select material presented to the

Museum is, by its very nature, a conscious representation of a past event, period or individual to the historical record on the part of the donor. Such artefacts must be critiqued and contextualised in order to be treated as historical sources. Scholars of material culture indeed have long warned against the 'fetishisation' of objects. They have also, however, begun to reconceptualise the significance of source material. Traditional approaches within the field framed material deposits as purely illustrative of current political, cultural and social values.[12] More recent studies, however, have positioned artefacts as both subjects and objects of historical change. Scholars such as Arjun Appadurai and Igor Koptyoff have proposed an exploration of the 'social life' of artefacts, the different meanings attached to objects by individuals as the context of the object changes.[13] Others such as Alfred Gell have gone further, suggesting that artefacts possess 'agency' i.e. that objects, materials and print matter can, of themselves, influence political thought and action.[14]

This book integrates these and other perspectives on material culture into the study of Ireland's 1916 experience. Chapter 1 addresses the significance of the 1916 Proclamation to both contemporary and commemorative Ireland. Chapter 2 profiles the campaigns by nationalists and unionists to (re)define national identity during the period of Union, with particular focus on objects as signifiers of 'banal nationalism'. Chapter 3 recreates the world of Easter Week in real-time as it was experienced by both combatants and civilians, investigating the impact of flags, uniforms and weaponry on perceptions of the ongoing conflict. Chapter 4 accounts for the surrender of rebel positions in Dublin and elsewhere in Ireland. Chapter 5 marks the fifteen executions which followed the Rising, through last letters and personal effects, and weighs their impact on public opinion. Chapter 6 captures the daily existence of Irish internees and prisoners removed to British detention centres, discussing the palliative effect of artefacts on life behind barbed wire. Chapter 7 charts the evolution of Irish political life between the 'Sinn Fein rebellion' and Sinn Féin Convention in October 1917, critiquing fashionable material as carriers of political change. Chapter 8, finally, explores the legacy of the 1916 Rising through practices of commemoration, memory and history, with particular focus on the National Museum of Ireland's exhibitions and collections.

POBLACHT NA H EIREANN.

THE PROVISIONAL GOVERNMENT
OF THE
IRISH REPUBLIC
TO THE PEOPLE OF IRELAND.

IRISHMEN AND IRISHWOMEN : In the name of God and of the dead generations from which she receives her old tradition of nationhood, Ireland, through us, summons her children to her flag and strikes for her freedom.

Having organised and trained her manhood through her secret revolutionary organisation, the Irish Republican Brotherhood, and through her open military organisations, the Irish Volunteers and the Irish Citizen Army, having patiently perfected her discipline, having resolutely waited for the right moment to reveal itself, she now seizes that moment, and, supported by her exiled children in America and by gallant allies in Europe, but relying in the first on her own strength, she strikes in full confidence of victory.

We declare the right of the people of Ireland to the ownership of Ireland, and to the unfettered control of Irish destinies, to be sovereign and indefeasible. The long usurpation of that right by a foreign people and government has not extinguished the right, nor can it ever be extinguished except by the destruction of the Irish people. In every generation the Irish people have asserted their right to national freedom and sovereignty ; six times during the past three hundred years they have asserted it in arms. Standing on that fundamental right and again asserting it in arms in the face of the world, we hereby proclaim the Irish Republic as a Sovereign Independent State, and we pledge our lives and the lives of our comrades-in-arms to the cause of its freedom, of its welfare, and of its exaltation among the nations.

The Irish Republic is entitled to, and hereby claims, the allegiance of every Irishman and Irishwoman. The Republic guarantees religious and civil liberty, equal rights and equal opportunities to all its citizens, and declares its resolve to pursue the happiness and prosperity of the whole nation and of all its parts, cherishing all the children of the nation equally, and oblivious of the differences carefully fostered by an alien government, which have divided a minority from the majority in the past.

Until our arms have brought the opportune moment for the establishment of a permanent National Government, representative of the whole people of Ireland and elected by the suffrages of all her men and women, the Provisional Government, hereby constituted, will administer the civil and military affairs of the Republic in trust for the people.

We place the cause of the Irish Republic under the protection of the Most High God, Whose blessing we invoke upon our arms, and we pray that no one who serves that cause will dishonour it by cowardice, inhumanity, or rapine. In this supreme hour the Irish nation must, by its valour and discipline and by the readiness of its children to sacrifice themselves for the common good, prove itself worthy of the august destiny to which it is called.

Signed on Behalf of the Provisional Government,

THOMAS J. CLARKE,
SEAN Mac DIARMADA.   THOMAS MacDONAGH,
P. H. PEARSE,   EAMONN CEANNT,
JAMES CONNOLLY.   JOSEPH PLUNKETT.

1

THE PROCLAMATION

'IRISHMEN AND IRISHWOMEN ...' The opening sounds of the 1916 Proclamation are remembered nostalgically in twenty-first century Ireland as the first words of the Irish State. Idealistic, articulate and inclusive, the address has become symbolic of the document in full, inspiring popular appropriation across modern Irish history. The Proclamation, in turn, has acquired an almost biblical status within Irish society, serving as referential text to a wide spectrum of social, cultural and political campaigns. It has, to some extent, outdated the 1916 Rising of which it was born. This process is not unique to Irish history. In the near aftermath of the American Revolution, historian Garry Wills has observed, 'the Declaration [of Independence] had already begun to live as a "conservative" symbol of past action'.[1] The Proclamation of the Irish Republic was similarly 'conserved' in twentieth-century Ireland, dislocated from the context and controversies of the 1916 Rising. In 1923, President of the Executive Council W.T. Cosgrave cited the Proclamation's committment to Ireland's place 'among the nations' during his speech in Geneva on the occasion of Ireland's admission to the League of Nations.[2] During the Dáil Éireann debates over the Statute of Westminster in 1931, Fianna Fáil T.D. Seán Lemass evoked the 'old tradition of nationhood' in his remarks, criticising the Cumann na nGaedheal government's continued faith in British foreign policy.[3] Meanwhile, Taoiseach Éamon de Valera's speech on neutrality in 1945, directed towards Winston Churchill, again invoked the 'dead generations'.[4] The Proclamation was presented as a touchstone of Irish national identity in the age of The Republic. American President John F. Kennedy was guided to the Proclamation at Arbour Hill in 1963 while former French President Charles de Gaulle was introduced to the Proclamation on his visit to the National Museum of Ireland in 1969.[5] The Irish State's self-representation through the 1916 Proclamation evidently made an impression on international statesmen. Nelson Mandela, Deputy President of the African National Congress, quoted the Proclamation's 'cherishing all the children of the nation equally' in his 1990 speech to Dáil Éireann,[6] while, at a St. Patrick's Day ceremony at the White House in 2016, American President Barack Obama described the Proclamation as 'a daring document', 'ahead of its time' and a 'visionary statement'.[7]

The Proclamation has been central to the Ireland 2016 commemorative programme. Its oration by Captain Peter Kelleher of the Irish Defence Forces outside the GPO underpinned a full spectrum of ceremonies across Ireland on 27 March. At a Mansion House symposium one day later, President Michael D. Higgins signified the Proclamation in 2016: 'its emancipatory call is certainly one that still resonates strongly with us, a century later'.[8] This was reflected by its integration into national and international commemorative spaces.

As part of the state's 'Flags for Schools' initiative, members of the Irish Defence Forces were designated to deliver the national flag, and

1.0
(Previous page)
This original Proclamation was owned by Dr Kathleen Lynn who fought in the 1916 Rising. Its authenticity was confirmed by its printer, Christopher Brady, and compositors, Michael Molloy and Liam Ó Briain, who signed their names to the document.
HE:EWL.2

recite the Proclamation, to each of Ireland's 3,200 primary schools between January and March. Primary and secondary school children, meanwhile, were encouraged to compose a 'Proclamation for a New Generation', using the 1916 document as a foundation.[9] On 15 March, Proclamation Day was marked at educational institutions across Ireland. Each bespoke programme was to be centred on a public reading of the original Proclamation and presentations of the many 'new'.[10] The Proclamation, was also the subject of considerable scholarly attention. Trinity College Dublin staged a full one-day symposium entitled 'The 1916 Proclamation in its national and international context', while it was also foregrounded during academic colloquia at the Royal Irish Academy, National University of Ireland Galway, the University of Oxford and Glucksman House, New York University. Copies of the Proclamation, meanwhile, adorn exhibitions at the National Print Museum, the General Post Office and the National Library of Ireland. Significantly, however, the National Museum of Ireland's new exhibition 'Proclaiming a Republic: the 1916 Rising' exhibits an original Proclamation, signed by its three printers Christopher Brady, Michael Molloy and Liam Ó Briain.

Debate over the Proclamation has, inevitably, filtered out into the public domain. The central issue, philosophically, was the continuing relevance of the 1916 Proclamation to contemporary Ireland. Intellectual positions were taken. A full year before the centenary, University College Cork historian, John A. Murphy, charged that twenty-first century Ireland remained 'starry eyed' about the Proclamation without fully understanding its concepts and claims. He drew particular attention to contemporary misinterpretations of the phrase: 'cherishing all the children of the nation equally'. The Proclamation, Murphy concluded, was a 'nineteenth century document' and should be assayed in that context alone.[11] The Princeton University scholar Philip Pettit countered that the Proclamation provided Ireland with a republican 'manifesto that can guide us today'. Drawing on European republican traditions of democratic, personal and national freedoms, Pettit argued that the Proclamation should be understood from a contemporary 'neo-republican' perspective.[12] Diarmaid Ferriter, meanwhile, has suggested that the centenary commemoration should provide an occasion to give more thought both 'to the context for the original' and its 'subsequent use and misuse' in modern Ireland.[13]

Questioning the relevance of scripture to the present is a sign of a healthy body politic and is to be encouraged, particularly over the commemorative course. However, it is important to recognise that Ireland is not alone in asking fundamental questions of founding documents. The eighth hundreth anniversary of the Magna Carta in 2015 prompted unprecedented public interest in the evolution of this 'Great charter' of legal rights and a debate over the continuing relevance of its articles in modern Britain, given that the majority had already been repealed under parliamentary legislation.[14] The Houses of Parliament, consequently, established a Commons Select Committee to consider the composition of a 'new Magna Carta', in consultation with the British public.[15] Conversely, the Declaration of the Rights of Man and of the Citizen, issued during the French revolution in 1789, is considered so intrinsic to the relationship between state and society in France, that the constitution of the Fifth Republic, its current constitution, states that the principles of the Declaration still have legal value.[16] The Proclamation sought to locate the Irish Republic 'among the nations'. Perhaps we can locate commemorative discourse on the Proclamation similarly.

Contemporary relevancies notwithstanding, the Proclamation of the Irish Republic has much to reveal in its historical context. What were the contributions of author(s), compositors and printers to the making of the Proclamation? What was its impact on the Dublin of Easter Week? How, potentially, was it read in the Ireland of 1916? The names of Thomas J. Clarke, Seán Mac Diarmada, Thomas MacDonagh, P.H. Pearse, Éamonn Ceannt, James Connolly and Joseph Plunkett underwrite the 1916 Proclamation. What did they give their names to?

MAKING THE PROCLAMATION

The Proclamation was printed at Liberty Hall through the night of Easter Sunday–Monday, 23–4 April 1916, by Michael Molloy, Liam Ó Briain and Christopher Brady. These three men had been in the

1.1
Christopher Brady, Liam
Ó Briain and Michael
Molloy – the printer and
compositors of the 1916
Proclamation, *c.*1935.
HE:EW.53

collective employ of James Connolly since 1915, tasked with the weekly publication of his radical socialist journal *The Workers' Republic*. Though not aware of the existence of the Military Council or its plans for Easter Week, they were acquainted with its individual members, who had, by the spring of 1916, become familiar visitors to Liberty Hall. It was to this location, on Good Friday, 21 April, that Connolly summoned Brady, Ó Briain and Molloy for Easter Sunday morning, without explanation. The latter, alone, was asked to acquire additional print materials for the occasion. Molloy borrowed extra type from a Capel Street printer named William West accordingly.[17] On arrival at Liberty Hall at 9.00 a.m. on Easter Sunday, the three men were met by Connolly and Thomas MacDonagh, who presented them with an original manuscript of the Proclamation and the task of printing it.[18] Molloy, Brady and Ó Briain accepted the responsibility.

The authorship of the Proclamation remains uncertain. The manuscript itself has not survived and we are thus dependant on the printers as witnesses for signature identification. Patrick Pearse, on their accreditation, emerges the most likely candidate. Liam Ó Briain distinctly remembered the text looking 'entirely legible, the script being upright and almost perfect, without any changes or corrections', a description agreed with by the other compositors.[19] Brady, further, was certain that it was not in Connolly's longhand, 'as I was familiar with his scrawl'.[20] On interview with the printers and inspection of the signatories' respective papers, meanwhile, Joseph Bouch ruled out Thomas MacDonagh as a written contributor.[21] Calligraphically, Pearse appears to have been the sole creator of the original manuscript.

It is not clear if the Proclamation was, in fact, signed by the seven signatories. Those in Liberty Hall on Sunday 23 April 1916 are in dispute over the matter. Liam Ó Briain averred that the Military Council's names were on the original manuscript which he received from MacDonagh: '[they] were in the same handwriting as that throughout'.[22] Michael Molloy, however, maintains that he witnessed the signing of the Proclamation that morning at Liberty Hall.[23] It appears unlikely that the Proclamation manuscript was in fact 'signed' by each of the Military Council. W.T. Cosgrave recalled that Éamonn Ceannt stated categorically that he had not signed the document.[24] Moreover,

1.2
An armed guard of the Irish Citizen Army patrol the front of Liberty Hall, September 1914.
HE:EW.707

the British authorities were unable to use the Proclamation as evidence in the courts martial of the leaders, as a signed document was not found in the possession of the rebels or indeed at the heavily searched Liberty Hall.[25]

Reviewing the laborious process behind the production of the Proclamation, Charles Townshend has adjudged its very completion a 'minor epic of printing'.[26] It is difficult to disagree with such an analysis. The three-man team were constrained by immense pressures of time, security and machinery. The emergency meeting of the Military Council had already decided to reschedule the Rising for the next morning, Easter Monday; printing the Proclamation had an immediate deadline. This urgency was exacerbated by concerns over potential discovery. Liberty Hall had been raided by the Dublin Metropolitan Police only one week previously and MacNeill's public countermanding order heightened suspicions of an eleventh-hour intervention on the part of the Dublin Castle authorities.[27] Molloy, Brady and Ó Briain, subsequently, would strain over the making of the Proclamation surrounded by an armed guard of the Irish Citizen Army. Brady carried an automatic pistol in his pocket.[28]

The most formidable difficulty facing the compositors, however, lay in the printing process itself. Neither their machinery nor materials were adequate for an undertaking of this scale. The Liberty Hall printing press was an old, dilapidated Wharfdale Double-Crown model. Christopher Brady had great difficulty in maintaining even inking, at one point using several bricks as a means to weight the machine's rollers.[29] The compositors also faced shortages of type which frustrated their attempts to produce the Proclamation to specification. The document, consequently, had to be printed in two halves, with the team meticulously typesetting the top half first. When that section was printed, the lower half was typeset and impressed onto the half-finished sheets.[30]

1.3
The small brass shooter used to lock type on the press which printed the Proclamation.
HE:EWL.114

1.4
Printing type from Liberty
Hall.
HE:1998.29 (Allen)

The limited supply of double-line Great Primer type, their default font, forced further improvisation. In the absence of sufficient type the team fashioned fonts from the remaining Liberty Hall stocks. This is particularly evident in the varying styles of the letter 'e' throughout the document.[31] Most markedly, perhaps, Brady converted a capital 'F' into a makeshift 'E' in the title section ('TH<u>E</u> PEOPLE … ') using a piece of sealing wax. This exhaustive process was further complicated by the poor quality of paper available to the printers, which resulted in the fainting and smudging of text.[32]

1.5
Title: there is a makeshift
'E' in the title section
('TH<u>E</u> PEOPLE … ').

Line 13: visible on
the letter 't' in 'the' is
smudging of ink.

Line 32: the 'e' is upside
down in the word 'the'.

Line 36: note the missing
space between the words
'worthy' and 'of'.

THE PEOPLE

not extinguished the **the** **worthyof**

Finally, at approximately 1.00 a.m. on Easter Monday, the compositors completed their undertaking. They had wrenched out a full 2,500 copies of the Proclamation.[33] Neither Christopher Brady, Liam Ó Briain or Michael Molloy were recognised by the Military Pensions Board for their work on the Proclamation.[34]

PERFORMING THE PROCLAMATION

The Proclamation of the Irish Republic was read aloud by Patrick Pearse at 12.45 p.m. on the afternoon of Easter Monday. Less than one hour earlier, the General Post Office had been seized by approximately 150 rebels and the Rising begun. Sackville Street, already busy with Bank Holiday wayfarers, was now knotted with crowds curious as to the chain of events which had already transpired. Pearse paced between the portico of the GPO and Sackville Street, surveying the attendant audience and waiting for the opportune moment.[35] When his 'supreme hour' did arrive, however, it proved somewhat anti-climactic. Dressed in green military uniform and military hat, Pearse addressed the crowds near the front of the GPO, flanked by Clarke and Connolly.[36] Present at

1.6
Patrick Pearse addressing a crowd of Gaelic League members at Dolphin's Barn, Dublin, in August 1915. He was to read the Proclamation wearing the same military uniform.
HE:EW.173

the oration was acquaintance and admirer Stephen McKenna: '[Pearse was] very pale ... very cold of face ... for once his magnetism had left him ... [I] felt sad for him'.[37] Another bystander recounted with more than a hint of irony: 'somebody was reading a manifesto in the sincere, dignified style of Pearse'.[38] Though he was recognised by the crowd of one hundred or more, their reaction to his address was a mixture

The front of the GPO
just after the 1916 Rising.
It was here that Patrick
Pearse read out the
Proclamation.

of muted cheer and quiet murmuring. Diarmuid Lynch believed the
scene provided 'an index to the denationalised state of Ireland'.[39] More
prosaically, perhaps the front of the GPO provided an inauspicious
setting for a performance of the Proclamation. The document itself
prompted a more enthusiastic response. Upon the three signatories'
return to the GPO, the previously reticent crowd rushed forward to
view the text posted along the front of the building. Excerpts of the
Proclamation were read aloud and this time passed through the crowd
more evenly, to a warm reception.[40]

The impact of the Proclamation during Easter Week is an underexplored subject. In his memoir, Seán T. O'Kelly recalled a collection of the rebels assembling outside the GPO to hear Pearse's oration: 'We went back into the GPO and discussed what had happened, all of us deeply impressed by the importance of the occasion and the seriousness of the implication of the proclamation that had just been read.'[41] However, this does not appear to have been the pervasive experience. Fellow garrison members Oscar Traynor and Eamon Bulfin were completely unaware of these scenes.[42] Indeed it is notable how few GPO veterans discuss the Proclamation in statements to the Bureau of Military History or Military Pensions Board. The influence of the Proclamation proved to be even more remote at other garrison locations.[43] This appears to have been a communication oversight on the part of the Military Council. Pearse was certainly determined that the rebels in Ulster would be aware of the Proclamation and its provisions before carrying out their orders on Easter Monday, urging the Tyrone-bound Ina Connolly to: 'Read it, study it and try to remember what is written and then you will be able to tell the men of the north.'[44] He had also insisted that the Proclamation be read at Tara.[45] Volunteers elsewhere in Leinster, Munster and Connacht do not appear to have encountered the Proclamation during the Rising.

The Proclamation appears to have made an underwhelming impression on Dublin opinion during Easter Week. Bands of people continued to descend on the Sackville Street area on Easter Monday afternoon, in search of information and intrigue. Copies of the Proclamation were pasted liberally along the street's buildings and monuments, drawing immediate attention. Reactions, however, were somewhat subdued. The young medical student, Ernie O'Malley, surveyed the scene at Nelson's Pillar: 'Some looked at it with serious faces, others laughed and sniggered.'[46] The playwright Joseph Holloway was similarly underwhelmed, recording in his journal: 'It was a long and floridly worded document full of high hopes.'[47] The real-time impact of the Proclamation, however, may also have been stunted by its limited circulation within the capital. Initial batches were sold by enterprising news boys.[48] Seán T. O'Kelly, and a handful of willing volunteers, were then tasked by James Connolly with posting the remaining copies

1.8
Seán T. O'Kelly
succeeded in sending an
original Proclamation to
his mother during Easter
Week. She received it in
the post one week later.
It now sits in Leinster
House.
HE:EW.2049

throughout the city on Easter Monday afternoon. Separating himself from the others, who remained close to Sackville Street, O'Kelly tracked arduously through Westmoreland and Dame streets before eventually running out of material on Grafton Street.[49] The Proclamation, accordingly, appears to have had limited visibility in areas south of the Liffey. Indeed it is notable how few eye-witnesses from this part of the city made reference to the Proclamation. Joseph Holloway, who walked through Mount Street, Merrion Square and Nassau Street that afternoon, eventually chanced upon a copy of the Proclamation near O'Connell Bridge.[50] Restricted to the vicinity of St Stephen's Green, meanwhile, the poet and novelist James Stephens, did not encounter a copy of the document over the entirety of Easter Week.[51] Indeed the 'Proclamation' most commonly referred to in contemporary accounts of the Rising was the declaration of martial law by the British authorities.[52] This public notice was widely distributed across the capital, most noticeably in the *Irish Times*, the only city newspaper to go to print between Tuesday and Thursday.[53] The Proclamation of the Irish Republic, conversely, was first printed in full by the national press on 5 May and the provincial press on 6 May, in the swim of the executions of rebel leaders.[54] It is entirely plausible, therefore, that the idealism, sincerity and integrity of the Proclamation, being widely read now for the first time, may have been important in turning the tide of public opinion.

EXPLAINING THE PROCLAMATION

1.9
(Opposite page)
The proclamation of
martial law for Dublin city
and county, issued on 25
April 1916.
HE:EWL.243b

The Proclamation of the Irish Republic, traditionally viewed as prose, has been described by both Charles Townshend and Fearghal McGarry, more recently, as a poem.[55] Reading the Proclamation in this manner effects a more sonorous text. As the French poet Charles Baudelaire once exhorted 'always be a poet, even in prose'.[56] Yet Baudelaire's invocation also has interpretative significance. Being a poet, and therefore understanding poetry, involves creative engagement with title, structure, tone and theme. The inculcation of meaning in poetic form was particularly apparent to the signatories of the Proclamation, three of whom, Pearse, Plunkett and MacDonagh, composed poetry. Reading the 1916 Proclamation as a poem, thus, might help to reappraise its historical meaning.

G. R.

A PROCLAMATION

Regulations to be observed under

MARTIAL LAW

I, Major-General, the Right Hon. L. B. Friend, C.B., Commanding the Troops in Ireland hereby Command that

(1) All persons in Dublin City and County shall keep within their houses between the hours of 7.30 p.m. in the evening and 5.30 a.m. on the next morning, on all days till further notice; unless provided with the written permission of the Military Authorities; or, unless in the case of fully qualified medical practitioners or medical nurses in uniform in the discharge of urgent duties.

(2) All persons other than members of His Majesty's Forces or Police, or acting in aid of said forces, who are seen carrying arms, are liable to be fired upon by the military without warning.

(3) All persons shall give all information in their possession as to stores of arms, ammunition, or explosives, or of the movement of hostile bodies to the nearest military authority, or to the nearest police barracks.

(4) All well disposed persons are hereby warned and advised to keep away from the vicinity of all places where military operations are in progress, or where hostile bodies are moving, and persons that enter such areas do so at their own risk.

Dated at Headquarters, Irish Command,

Park Gate, Dublin. 26th April, 1916.

L. B. FRIEND,
Major General, Commanding Troops, Ireland.

In his penetrative analysis of the Proclamation, Liam Kennedy has alluded to the apparent incongruity of its title: 'the choice of the term "proclamation" for the document is curious, being associated with established authority, particularly that of Britain'.[57] Entitling the document as such, it has been suggested, was a symbolic homage to Robert Emmet, who had issued a 'Proclamation of an Irish Republic' in 1803.[58] The titles certainly bear similarity of presentation. Emmet's heading '*The Provisional Government*' is underset 'to THE PEOPLE OF IRELAND', making it comparable to the legend of the 1916 Proclamation.

1.10
The proclamation issued by Robert Emmet during the 1803 rebellion of which 10,000 were circulated. Emmet read extracts of the proclamation to the Dublin public on 23 July 1803.
HH:1949.36

The influence of Emmet in the presentation of the document is certainly consistent with his historical influence on several members of the Military Council, most notably Patrick Pearse.[59] However, Emmet's Proclamation, more generally, does not provide a structural blueprint for the 1916 Proclamation. The 'Proclamation of the Ulster Provisional Government' presents an alternative interpretation. Issued by Ulster unionists at the height of the Home Rule crisis, copies were posted throughout Belfast in September 1913. It remains, nonetheless, less conspicuous than the Ulster Covenant in historiographical comparisons with the 1916 Proclamation.[60] There are, however, marked similarities. Both documents were produced to announce a 'Provisional Government'. The unionist document, accordingly, is headed 'Ulster Provisional Government' and thinly underlined underneath. The republican document is formatted similarly. The unionist address 'TO ALL WHOM IT MAY CONCERN' is centred underneath the header, similar to 'TO THE PEOPLE OF IRELAND' in the 1916 Proclamation. The latter, meanwhile, closely adheres to the spatial presentation of the names of the Ulster Provisional Government, which are prefixed by the signature 'ON BEHALF OF THE CENTRAL AUTHORITY' and are listed aligned to the bottom right of the Proclamation. Although longer in content than the Ulster Proclamation, the Proclamation of the Irish Republic had commensurate purpose of creation, analogous title and comparable presentation. Moreover, substantive parts of the republican text refer directly to unionists. In its structural composition, therefore, the 1916 Proclamation may have been partially framed as a documentary riposte to the 1913 Proclamation.

In his analysis of the Proclamation, Liam de Paor has commented: 'The Proclamation is primarily a declaration of war.'[61] This may not be representative of the document in its entirety. Nonetheless, a First World War leit-motif is identifiable in the text with the use of phrases such as 'summons her children to her flag', 'gallant allies in Europe' and 'this supreme hour'. As F.S.L. Lyons observed, the allusion to German military support exposed the signatories to accusations of high treason and Ireland, potentially, to the European conflict.[62] The tone of the Proclamation, moreover, is suggestive of First World War heroic idealism. In his seminal study, *The Great War and Modern Memory*, Paul Fussell has identified a lexicon of 'high diction', which emerged in the Victorian period but was more widely contemporaneous to the First World War.[63] The Proclamation is replete with such language: 'gallant', 'comrades', 'allegiance', 'Most High God', 'valour', 'august'. These betray an idealised image of the European conflict unspoiled by the biting realities of the First World War and its poets. The 1916 Proclamation was a document of its time.

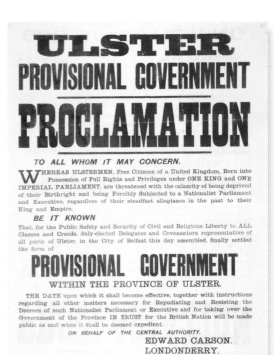

1.11
The 'Proclamation of the Ulster Provisional Government' issued in September 1913.

2

BEFORE THE RISING

Every historian examining the period of Union faces a crisis of national identity. The Acts of Union effected, from 1 January 1801, a United Kingdom between Great Britain and Ireland. The state of the Union thus constituted the overarching framework for understanding the British experience between 1801 and 1922.[1] Its four nations offered alternative perspectives. Identities such as 'Britishness', 'Englishness' and 'Irishness', according to intellectual and cultural historian, defined and defied the legal bind of the United Kingdom of Great Britain and Ireland.[2] As a pivotal moment in the eventual fracturing of this legislative relationship, the 1916 Rising represented a significant conflict between state and

2.0
(Page 16)
The Black Raven Pipe
Band of Lusk, Co. Dublin,
in 1915.
HE:EW.3523

2.1
The early leadership
of the Irish Republican
Brotherhood.
HH:1952.8

nation. Was it a crisis of national identity? In a seminal study on nationalism and national identity, Michael Billig has forcefully argued: 'crises do not create nation states as nation states … daily the nation is indicated or flagged in the lives of the citizenry. Nationalism, far from being an intermittent mood in established nations, is the endemic condition.'[3] The proliferation of material culture in Ireland presented tangible evidence of such 'banal nationalism'. The National Museum's Easter Week collection, thus, can present afresh the ideologies, identities and influences which generated the 'making of' the 1916 Rising.

'In so far as such things can be dated' Tom Garvin has suggested 'the Irish revolution started with the founding of the IRB in 1858'.[4] The Irish Revolutionary Brotherhood, later the Irish Republican Brotherhood, was an oath-bound secret society established by former Young Irelander James Stephens. Its American 'sister' organisation the Fenian Brotherhood, later Clan na Gael, was formed by fellow Young Ireland veteran John O'Mahony. Their avowed aim was the realisation of an independent Irish republic. The IRB, by its very inception, claimed to be the provisional government of Ireland. This self-legitimation, what Matthew Kelly has termed the 'Fenian ideal', was predicated on the historic Irish nation, not the actual governance of power enshrined by the Act of Union.[5] The IRB's alleged members, known fraternally as Fenians, were committed to using violence to achieve this political reality. In the wake of the failed 1867 rebellion in Ireland, the term 'Fenianism' came to denote Irish political violence and political subversion more broadly, as defined by partisan institutions of Church and state.[6] Although the IRB's alliance with the Land League and Home Rule League suggested a 'New Departure', local acts of violence during the Land War were often injudiciously ascribed to 'Fenianism'.[7]

Lazare Carnot's famous injunction that 'revolutionaries are not born, they are made' militates against investing 1858 with equal historical importance as the birth year of Thomas Clarke. In so far as such things can be dated, Thomas Clarke's revolution started with his induction into the IRB in 1878. Within two years he had become the centre of the Organisation's Dungannon circle before emigrating to America. Here he found Fenians of bearded vintage: John Devoy, Thomas Francis Bourke and Jeremiah O'Donovan Rossa. In 1883 he volunteered to participate in O'Donovan Rossa's dynamite campaign in Great Britain but was arrested in London before he could detonate his device.[8] He would serve fifteen years in Pentonville prison, unrepentant.[9] Charles Townshend's personification of the arch-Fenian captures Clarke's stoic radicalism: 'an inspirational sense of character-building, a posture of self-respect, and the repudiation of servility'.[10] Meeting Clarke following his release from Pentonville in 1898, P.S. O'Hegarty was struck by this 'embodiment of Fenianism, an impregnable rock'.[11] Writing to his wife Kathleen in 1900, Thomas Clarke admitted: 'A fellow can do nothing but keep on churning his wrath.'[12] His recourse to rebellion was Fenian-congenital.

2.2
Thomas Clarke was born on the Isle Wight to Irish parents on 11 March 1858. Having spent his early childhood in South Africa, Clarke's family moved to Dungannon, Co. Tyrone, in 1865. Here he was educated at St Patrick's National School.
HE:EW.966

2.3
The razor gifted to Thomas Clarke by Kathleen following his prison release in 1898. Emblematically, he would use it every day until Easter Monday 24 April 1916.
HE:EWL.193

2.4
Engraved on this walking
stick are the names of
Nationalist political
leaders. As the object is
rotated they can be read:
O'Connell, Butt, Parnell,
Biggar, Davitt, Devlin,
Dillon, [T.P.] O'Connor,
Harrington.
HH:1976.1

By the turn of the century, however, several of his fellow 'brothers' had joined the Irish Parliamentary Party.[13] The historiographical imperative by one eminent scholar to place the fenians 'in context' has done much to texture later interpretations of 'fenianism'.[14] R.V. Comerford's influential formulation, 'patriotism as pastime', embedded Fenian activity in the associational cultures of mid-Victorian Great Britain and Ireland.[15] The development of the Gaelic Athletic Association in the late nineteenth century, narrowly depicted in some studies as a vehicle for IRB machinations, has been viewed by Mike Cronin as significant of wider contemporary influences such as muscular Christianity and manliness.[16] Matthew Kelly's scholarship has illuminated republican political thought through Fenian prose and song.[17] Owen McGee, meanwhile, has framed the IRB as an alternative secular, liberal party in a pre-democratic Ireland.[18] This 'democratisation' of the IRB has prompted suggestions of a more latent republican disposition within Nationalist Ireland than has heretofore been allowed.[19] Recent appraisals of nationalist political culture in Ireland, moreover, have accounted for a spectrum, rather than a dichotomy, of attitudes on politics and political violence. The Manchester Martyrs were honoured by the Irish Parliamentary Party and its constituency organisation the United Irish League, while its more openly sectarian affiliate the Ancient Order of Hibernians (AOH) regularly engaged in street violence. Nationalist leaders such as Daniel O'Connell and Charles Stewart Parnell, meanwhile, carried firearms.

Historically O'Connell and Parnell have been perceived as nationalist leaders of an Irish 'constitutional tradition', or what Alan Ward has titled 'responsible government'.[20] The constitutional movement centred on the Irish Parliamentary Party (IPP) which was led by Isaac Butt, a Protestant barrister (1873–79) and Charles Stewart Parnell, a Protestant landlord (1880–91). It campaigned on issues such as education, housing and tenant rights but advocated principally for Home Rule: self-government for Ireland within the United Kingdom. Journalists, entrepreneurs and former Fenians made 'respectable' manned the benches for the early Irish Parliamentary Party in the House of Commons. In 1900 John Redmond became the new leader of the IPP. Paul Bew has commented of his Party: 'the overwhelming impression is that it was representative of the mass of the nationalist population and its sentiments'.[21]

IRISH PARLIAMENTARY PARTY. 1886

The Irish Parliamentary Party's 'representation' of early twentieth-century Irish nationalism has been the subject of considerable historiographical debate. Earlier portrayals of a Westminster-based Party isolated from local constituents have been contested while recent studies have profiled a generation of nationalists confidently awaiting Home Rule. Much of the disagreement has centred on Nationalist Ireland's endorsement of John Redmond's interpretation of the Home Rule project. 'Redmondism' would be later used to describe Redmond's advocacy of a nationalist politics which was socially conservative, imperially conscious and conciliatory towards unionism and British political imperatives. While 'Redmondism',

2.5
The Irish Parliamentary
Party in 1886.
HH:2013.35

2.6
Postcard of John
Redmond (leader of
the Irish Parliamentary
Party, 1900–1918).
HE:EW.2530

it has been argued convincingly,
was a 'minority taste',[22] Redmond
himself continued to enjoy popular
political support in Ireland up
to 1910. Indeed despite Alvin
Jackson's assertion that 'there
was never anything approaching
a personality cult' surrounding
Redmond, Dillon and Devlin,[23]
the wealth of material artefacts
bearing their imprint within the
Easter Week collection suggests an
underappreciated iconography.

2.7
John Dillon plate.
DC:1971.32

The Irish Parliamentary Party's strategic objective, achieving Home Rule for Ireland, required skilled manipulation and persuasion of British political opinion at Westminster. Its parliamentary tactics ranged from obstructionism to debating, lobbying and voting at Westminster. Irish self-government, ostensibly, was but one of many 'domestic' issues facing the Conservative and Liberal parties in the period of Union; significantly, however, Liberal Party leader William Gladstone became a 'convert' to the cause of Home Rule for Ireland. Under Parnell's leadership, the IPP formed a parliamentary alliance with Gladstone's Liberals, the 'Union of Hearts', which led to unsuccesful Home Rule bills in 1886 and 1893. The first was defeated in the House of Commons and the second in the House of Lords, the Unionist-dominated chamber which possessed a power of veto over Commons legislation. While it has recently been argued that the issue of Irish self-government 'fired the public imagination' of late nineteenth-century British politics,[24] the damaging split in the Liberal Party over Gladstone's first Home Rule Bill negated any impulse to present comparable legislation before parliament in the 'new' liberal era of Asquith, Lloyd George and Churchill. The IPP, who would face continued Fenian accusation of having 'turned native' for their perseverance at Westminster, neither had the seats nor the suasion to effect self-government in Redmond's first decade.

Sinn Féin existed as alternative nationalist politics to Home Rule establishment. In a 1904 treatise entitled *The Resurrection of Hungary*, Dublin publicist–polemicist Arthur Griffith presented a pseudo-Fenian

2.8
Michael Davitt tea cup.
DC:1971.49

2.9
William O'Brien saucer.
DC:1971.21

solution to Ireland's loss of self-government under the Union: abstention from Westminster and the formation of a national parliament in Dublin.[25] Unlike the IRB, Griffith's politics were premised on passive resistance and dual monarchy. His Sinn Féin philosophy also emphasised economic self-sufficiency.[26] Griffith's proto-banking venture, the Industrial Cooperative Society, encouraged saving Ireland as investment. Although he published a weekly newspaper and nominally led a Dublin-based pressure group of the same name, Griffith's Sinn Féin has been seen as a party of circumstance. The failure of the Irish Council Bill in 1907 coincided with what has been termed the 'first Sinn Féin uprising'. Disillusionment over the Liberal Party proposal for a partially elected eight-department Irish administration instead of Home Rule self-government, and the IPP's association with the scheme in the public mind, prompted debate on the limitations of parliamentarianism.[27] Three IPP MPs resigned their seats in 1908. Charles Dolan stood for re-election as a Sinn Féin abstentionist candidate in his North Leitrim constituency but polled only one third of the vote from his former electors.[28] Was this the defeat of Sinn Féin?

The Gaelic League provided an 'adjacent forum' for Sinn Féin ideas across a longer gestation. In a seminal paper delivered to the Irish National Literary Society on 25 November 1892, Douglas Hyde impressed those present on 'The Necessity for de-Anglicising Ireland': 'we must at once arrest the decay of the language'.[29] Seven months later the Gaelic League was established by Hyde and Eoin MacNeill. Its stated aims were the extension of Irish as a spoken language, the teaching of Irish history and the advancement of the Irish-Ireland cause. Learning off O'Growney and learning of O'Donovan

2.10
Arthur Griffith.
HE:EW.5757

2.11
A specially issued Sinn Féin money box.
HE:EW.3458

2.12
Underwood Gaelic League
typewriter – the first to
use Irish characters. It was
later used to type letters
in the Irish language in
correspondence between the
Irish republican government
and the British government
leading up to the 1921 Truce.
HE:EW.4495

2.13
Patrick Pearse was born on
Great Brunswick Street,
Dublin to an English father
and Irish mother on 10
November 1879. He was
educated at the Christian
Brothers' School on Westland
Row and later UCD. He
studied law at TCD and the
King's Inn, and was called to
the bar in 1901.
HE:EW.317

Rossa, it was argued, would inculcate a Gaelic identity among the Irish people. By 1908 it had an estimated 671 branches across Ireland.[30] The most authoritative analysis, by Timothy McMahon, however, has suggested a large turnover of membership and a more attentive interest in League socials and processions.[31] Nights out à la Irish-Ireland were a medley of language classes, lectures, dances and dramas. Although it was an explicitly 'non-political' organisation, many commentators have suggested the League to have created 'politicians by accident' on account of individual members' later involvement in the Rising.[32] The Gaelic League's Coiste Gnótha by 1903 included Hyde, MacNeill, Agnes O'Farrelly and Patrick Pearse.[33]

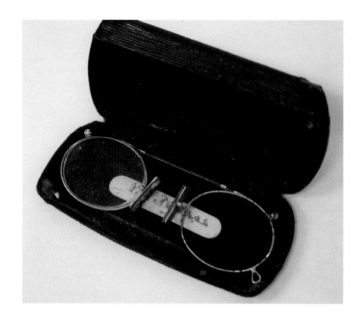

2.14
Patrick Pearse's spectacles.
HE:1996.10

A fluent obsessive, Patrick Pearse lived vicariously through the Gaelic League. Between 1898 and 1900, he missed only six meetings of the Coiste Gnotha, and those on League business.[34] From 1903 until 1909 he served as the editor of the organisation's bilingual journal *An Claidheamh Soluis*, and is widely credited for increasing its readership to 174,000.[35] His first editorial pithily presented his, and the Gaelic League's, foundational ideology: 'On the life or death of the language depends the life or death of the nation.'[36] Although the Gaelic revival has been traditionally viewed as a clerically reinforced siege against modernity,[37] more recent scholarship by Declan Kiberd and Philip O'Leary has delineated tensions between 'traditionalist' and 'modernist' outlooks within the movement.[38] Pearse, or rather the 'two Pearses' of which he self-identified,[39] personified these ideological tensions. Amid the ongoing controversy over 'authentically Irish' font,[40] Pearse used both Gaelic and Roman type on the League's bespoke

2.15
A Gaelic League organisational tour of the west of Ireland *c.*1911. Patrick Pearse is standing, second from right.
HE:EW.856

2.16
(Opposite page)
Seán Connolly and Countess Markievicz perform in Count Markievicz's play *The Memory of the Dead* at the Abbey Theatre.
HE:EWL.127

Irish language typewriter. Like many 'nativists' he exalted the rural west of Ireland as the locus of Irish identity but was also considered a 'progressive' Europhile, regularly attending the Pan-Celtic Congress and exploring cultural nationalist movements in Belgium, Denmark and France.[41] His establishment of a bi-lingual school for boys at St Enda's in 1908 evidenced an ambitious, if impractical, attempt to animate the Irish language through the arts and drama.[42] Here Thomas MacDonagh would become an earnest colleague and friend.

Staging the nation was more popularly the preserve of Anglo-Irish literary figures such as W.B. Yeats, Lady Gregory and Edward Martyn who, among others, founded the Irish Literary Theatre (1899), the Irish National Theatre Society (1903) and the Abbey Theatre (1904). Their 'rewriting' of Irish identity through the English language prompted bitter reproach from ardent Gaelic revivalists. Pearse infamously characterised Yeats as a 'mere English poet of the third or fourth rank', although he later softened his appraisal.[43] Less reconciliatory was D.P. Moran, editor of the canonical journal *The Leader*, who framed the simultaneous Irish-Ireland and Anglo-Irish revivals as 'The Battle of Two Civilisations'.[44] More recent scholarship has identified a deeper national support for the Anglo-Irish dramatic tradition and more creative collaboration with individual Leaguers than were contemporarily presented.[45] J.M. Synge's irreverent dramatisation of life in rural Ireland, *The Playboy of the Western World*, nonetheless, provoked the 'nativist' mind of the Gaelic League; rounds of rioting, not applause,

marked its premier performances in the Abbey. The Abbey's centrality to the Rising, meanwhile, has been presented by Fearghal McGarry less as a theatre of conflicting identities than a theatre of radical networks. Rebel actors such as Arthur Shields, Sean Connolly and Helena Molony would play their part in the coming drama.[46]

Ireland, much like the rest of the United Kingdom, was a deeply patriarchal society. Men defined the public sphere of politics, highlighted by their exclusive right to vote at national elections. Women, in Great Britain and Ireland, increasingly believed that as full citizens they could contribute unique qualities to public life: domesticity, morality, social responsibility. Activism under the umbrella of the National Union of Women's Suffrage Societies and the suffragist Women's Social and Political Union, thus, was a manifestation towards equal citizenship.[47] Women's participation in Irish political organisation, further, was a self-representation of national identity. This found clearest expression beyond the IPP. In 1900 Maud Gonne established Inghinidhe na hÉireann which advocated for Irish independence, Irish language rights and women's suffrage.

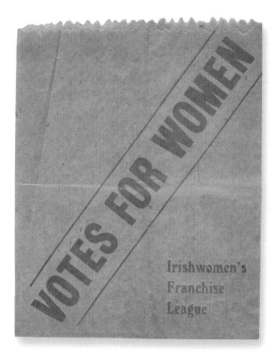

2.17
The Irish Women's Franchise League distributed material such as this imprinted bag at political meetings.
HH:1998.116

Organisers, including Helena Molony, Kathleen Lynn, Countess Markievicz and Alice Milligan, presented history lectures, staged plays and organised socials. 'Almost all members', Senia Pašeta has observed, 'prioritised nationalism over feminism'.[48] In 1908 Francis Sheehy-Skeffington, Hanna Sheehy-Skeffington and Margaret Cousins founded the Irish Women's Franchise League purposely in support of women's suffrage, publicising the issue at political rallies.[49]

Youth culture within Irish nationalism too was framed by the wider United Kingdom context but defined itself explicitly against it. Fears of national decadence and degeneracy, pervasive in Great Britain at the turn of the century, had intensified the imperative to preserve the 'manliness' of the next generation through vigorous

2.18
A band of Fianna
Éireann members
*c.*1909. Countess
Markievicz is seated
second from left.
HE:EW.1773.2

2.19
This Fianna Éireann
tunic and gun holster
belonged to John Kelly.
Kelly was only ten years
of age when he fought in
the Four Courts during
the 1916 Rising.
HE:EW.21.1; HE:EW.22

physical training and discipline, which would simultaneously build character and inner morality. The establishment of the Boy Scouts by Robert Baden Powell in 1908 gave organisational shape to this public thought. The formation of Na Fianna Éireann by Bulmer Hobson and Countess Markievicz in 1909 was initiated in direct response to Baden Powell's movement. This youth organisation similarly sought to counter physical and moral regression but with an Irish affectation. Members learned the Irish language and Irish history in addition to drill marching, first aid, map-reading and signalling. Membership was open to boys between the ages of eight and eighteen. Overtly republican, many of the recruits including Con Colbert, Seán Heuston and Liam Mellows would join the IRB, the Irish Volunteers and, subsequently, the 1916 Rising.[50]

2.20
James Connolly was born in
Cowgate, Edinburgh to Irish
parents on 5 June 1868. He was
initially educated at St Patrick's
Catholic primary school but was
forced to leave at the age of 11 to
find work in support of his family.
HE:EW.198.4

2.21
A sticker advertising a James
Connolly speaking tour. Connolly
was a well-known figure in
Dublin radical circles by 1900.
HE:EW.5298

Organised Irish labour operated within a United
Kingdom context. Unskilled workers had failed to co-
ordinate during the 'new unionism' wave of the 1890s and
looked to the British Trade Union Congress and emerging
British Labour party for leadership. The Liverpool-born
Dublin-based James Larkin attempted to change this
relationship of dependency. In 1908 he established the
Irish Trade and General Workers' Union (ITGWU) on a
syndicalist model i.e. organising workers into one collective
union with the aim of social reform and capitalist
overthrow through a general workers' strike. Implicit in the
formation of the ITGWU was a labour connection to Irish
nationalist identity.

Another figure to influence a determinedly Irish
labour movement was James Connolly. The Edinburgh-born
Connolly found international socialism during his poverty-
stricken upbringing, identifying with the grim realities depicted
in the writings of left-wing commentators elsewhere in Europe.
Despite leaving school at the age of eleven, he taught himself
enough French and German to read Marx and Engels.
Connolly was a relentless advocate of workers' rights through
political and industrial organisation. During his first residency
in Ireland, between 1896 and 1903, he established the Irish
Socialist Republican Party. His subsequent periods in the United
States saw him tour on behalf of the Socialist Labour Party,
addressing crowds in New York, Chicago and Los Angeles. One
contemporary observed: 'Larkin knew how to draw a crowd but
Connolly knew how to hold one.'[51] Returning to Dublin in 1910
Connolly published two seminal volumes on Ireland's particular
labour experience: *Labour, Nationality and Religion* and *Labour in
Irish History*.

The organisational initiatives and independence of thought
within Irish Labour also contributed to the currency of a 'new
nationalism' circulating in turn of the century Ireland. The
proliferation of self-reliant cultural, political and social ideas
was given most coherent expression within the welter of radical

journals populating the largely Dublin print circuit. A carousel of activists and ideologues composed their version of Irishness and vision of Irish independence within their pages: *Bean na hÉireann* (Countess Markievicz, Patrick Pearse, Thomas MacDonagh); *Irish Review* (Joseph Plunkett, Thomas MacDonagh, Patrick Pearse, Douglas Hyde); *The Republic* (Bulmer Hobson, Denis McCullough, P.S. O'Hegarty); *Irish Freedom* (Bulmer Hobson, P.S. O'Hegarty, Patrick Pearse). Thomas Clarke, who returned to Dublin in 1907, sold each of these titles from his tobacconist shop on, ironically, Great Britain Street. He would only contribute, however, to *Irish Freedom*, the IRB's journal.

2.22

Front pages of Dublin's radical press. *Sinn Féin* (HE:2007.1.432); *Irish Freedom* (HE:EW.1114); *Irish Citizen* (HE:EW.1982); *Bean na hÉireann* (HE:EW.908); *An Claidheamh Soluis* (HE:EW.4164)

2.23
Seán Mac Diarmada seated (bottom right). Mac Diarmada was born near Kiltyclogher, Co. Leitrim, to Irish parents on 27 January 1883. He was educated at the local Coracloona national school but also attended Tullynamoyle national school in Co. Cavan in search of Irish language tuition. He moved to Belfast in 1905.
HE:EW.3280

The manager of *Irish Freedom*, Seán MacDiarmada, was 'the classic hectic activist'.[52] Interested at first in the Ancient Order of Hibernians, he later joined the Gaelic League, Gaelic Athletic Association and Sinn Féin, for which he served as national organiser from 1907. However, it was his unrelenting commitment to the republican cause which marked him out as a young protégé to Thomas Clarke. Along with Bulmer Hobson and Dennis McCullough, he formed a 'neo-Fenian' nucleus of young separatists determined to sharpen the IRB's purpose. Fresh faced and charismatic, he travelled 'three thousand miles' around the country as IRB organiser between 1908 and 1916. His contraction of polio in 1911, which forced him to walk with a cane, did little to debilitate his republican standing. In the same year he was elected onto the IRB's Supreme Council. More significantly he would remain close in the counsel of Clarke. Together they would prepare a Fenian Rising.

2.24
Hurley stick made by Seán MacDiarmada.
HE:1996.4 (Allen)

This amalgam of advanced nationalists, isolated by or on the fringes of the Irish Parliamentary Party, was frequently identified by Dublin Castle detectives as a 'Sinn Fein' movement. They themselves identified with a range of ideological beliefs and campaigns which collectively sought to re-assert Irish nationality as the 'endemic condition' of life under the Union. The proliferation of these ideas through material culture – ceramics, textiles, wood carvings, metal work – evidences the extent to which nationalism had, for some, reached 'behind [their] counters and desks and into their lives and minds'.[53] R.F. Foster's magisterial work *Vivid Faces* has captured the zeitgeist of this nationalist counterculture. Exploring the radicalisation of young nationalists in turn of the century Ireland, Foster has directed scholarly attention to their cultural conditioning through shared experiences and activities: learning, playing, writing fighting. The 'enclosed, self-referencing, hectic world which the revolutionaries inhabited' forged a new generational mentality inimical to both the Home Rule movement and the British State. Theirs would become the 'generation of 1916'.[54]

This self-conscious sense of generation was beautifully captured in a single photograph taken outside Galway Town Hall on the occasion of the Gaelic League Ard-Fheis in the late summer of 1913. Staring through the lens of history we see an ensemble of familiar faces: the bearded MacNeill, a boyish-looking Hobson, Pearse at ease out of profile and the cross-armed glare of Seán Mac Diarmada. Others of later prominence were here too: the scholarly suited Éamon de Valera, the Director of the National Museum Count George Noble Plunkett with his resplendent wife Countess Josephine Plunkett, the properly seated Seán T. O'Kelly and The O'Rahilly with bristled moustache and squinted look. This was Irish nationalism's 'Edwardian summer'. Within months Ireland, and those pictured, would be in the grip of the Home Rule-Ulster crisis.

2.25
(Page 34)
Attendees at the Gaelic League Ard-Fheis, Galway (1913).

THE HOME RULE-ULSTER CRISIS

It is a truism that the Acts of Union defined unionism. That the Union defined Ulster unionism, however, can be called into question. The legislation brought into effect on 1 January 1801 created a framework whereby living with(in) the British State could be identified with communal ascendancy. British citizenship offered Irishmen (less obviously Irishwomen) opportunities for upward social mobility within the administration of Ireland and indeed the British Empire, access to global economic markets, and connections to the centre of parliamentary democracy. The extent to which one adhered to this legislative contract depended on political, religious and social disposition, and significantly the period of Union. The disenfranchisement of Catholics from politics in the early nineteenth century contrasted with the state's belated legislation on Catholic emancipation, disestablishment of the Church of Ireland and the eventual 'greening' of Dublin Castle. 'Constructive unionism' which had earlier strengthened the status of the Irish gentry later weakened their investment in the Union, as a consequence of recurrent late nineteenth-century legislation for the transfer of land ownership from landlord to tenant. Accepting the constitutional status quo, most benignly, identified Ireland as a nation of Union. Others, however, identified the United Kingdom emphatically as a consolidation of British State and nation.

'The Irish question was, of course, older than the Union,' A.T.Q. Stewart acknowledged.[55] Unionism, however, as a concentrated political movement was shaped in the late nineteenth century. The increasing separation of Church and state pressured Anglo-Irish gentry and Ulster Presbyterian entrepreneurs into a 'cross-class' unionist consensus. The Orange Order added a grassroots sectarian 'ingredient' to organised unionism. Opposition to Home Rule united over a perceived threat to British citizenship. This position was supported by different arguments. Southern unionists emphasised their loss of social status and political influence if policies were to be decided in a Dublin parliament. Unionists in Ulster stressed their economic and religious disadvantage in a rural 'Rome Rule' Ireland. Political lobby groups such as the Irish Unionist Alliance, of which Edward Carson was a member, presented these concerns coherently at Westminster.

2.26
(Opposite page)
Orange and purple collarette of the Loyal Orange Lodge 106.
HH:1979.38

LAID AT WESTMINSTER
·1912·
HOME RULE
-BUT-
WON'T HATCH IN ULSTER
(Copyright Reg⁴)

2.27
Living with the Home
Rule crisis. Egg-shaped
anti-Home Rule ceramic
salt dispenser.
HE:EW.5841

From the early twentieth century Irish unionism became increasingly defined by Ulster unionism. Political opposition to Home Rule was organised within the Ulster Unionist Council (UUC) (1904), while from 1911 Orangemen paraded with rifles before UUC leaders such as James Craig. The 'Ulsterisation' of unionism, Alvin Jackson has suggested, gained purchase from the 'drift' towards 'popular mobilisation' in British and Irish political culture.[56] Paul Bew, conversely, has underlined the popularity of W.F. Moneypenny's pamphlet 'The Two Nations' as the 'greatest evocation of the mood'.[57] Moneypenny's thesis that Ulster constituted a separate ethnic 'nation' from the rest of Ireland had been first propagated in 1896 but was gradually pushed to the fore of unionist debate from the turn of the century.[58] This was not the argument of unionist Ireland. Nonetheless, a 'two nations' mentality, it has been claimed, was well entrenched in the Ulster pysche.[59] The nationalist orthodoxy, conversely, dictated the denial of ethnic differences in Ireland, let alone Ulster exceptionalism.[60] 'The idea of two nations in Ireland', John Redmond would remark, 'is to us revolting and hateful'.[61]

Redmond was speaking from a position of power: the balance of political power at Westminster. Between 1909 and 1911, the United Kingdom was in the grip of a constitutional crisis over the principle of the House of Lords' legislative veto, the Liberal Party seeking to reduce the former's control of parliamentary legislation. In 1910 two general elections were fought on the issue, both resulting in a hung parliament. The well-oiled Irish Parliamentary Party, however, won over eighty seats in each campaign, empowering them to put a party

in government. In return for a new Home Rule Bill, the IPP supported
a Liberal government. In August 1911, meanwhile, the Parliament Act
was passed which removed the House of Lords' power of veto, only
now permitting the Unionist-heavy chamber the power to delay House
of Commons legislation for up to two years. On 11 April 1912, the
Third Home Rule Bill was introduced to the House of Commons by
Prime Minister Herbert Asquith.

The Government of Ireland legislation provided for a bicameral Irish
legislature: an Irish House of Commons, of 164 elected representatives,
and an Irish Senate of forty members, appointed for eight years. It
ostensibly had the 'power to make laws for the peace, order and good
government of Ireland' but this was heavily redacted with clauses
prohibiting legislation on the Crown, war and peace, the army and
navy, treaties, control of general taxation, land purchase, the collection
of taxes and the Royal Irish Constabulary (for a period of six years).
The Irish Parliament, further, would be subordinate to the Westminster
Parliament, although forty-two Irish MPs would still be entitled to sit in
the House of Commons.[62] While the bill itself generated an indifferent
response from Irish Parliamentary Party supporters, nationalists more
generally 'projected' and 'predicted' political life in a Home Rule
Ireland.[63] Jim Larkin, James Connolly and William O'Brien established

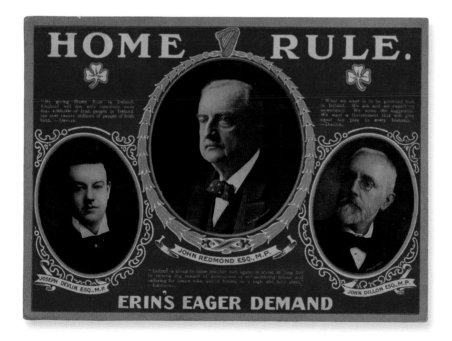

2.28
One in a series of
postcards acclaiming
the Irish Parliamentary
Party leadership. From
left to right: Joseph
Devlin, John Redmond,
John Dillon.
HE:EW.2599

the Irish Labour Party in readiness while Eoin MacNeill and Patrick Pearse shared a platform with John Redmond in Dublin to discuss the future of the Irish language. Speaking in Irish, Pearse declared: 'Let the English understand that if we are cheated once more there will be red war in Ireland.'[64]

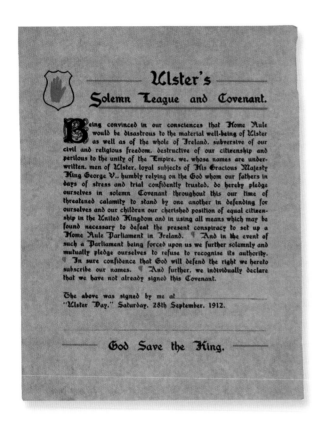

2.29
The Ulster Covenant.
HE:EW.Temp.396

The Ulster Covenant, however, was representative of contemporary (Ulster) unionist concerns. On 28 September 1912 Edward Carson and James Craig formally signed the Ulster Covenant in Belfast City Hall. Signing the Covenant was no blood sacrifice. In total 237,638 men signed the document. A further 234,046 women signed the supporting Ulster Declaration. Women had become increasingly visible within unionist political culture in the early twentieth century, notably forming the Ulster Women's Unionist Council in 1911.[65] The development of Ulster resistance, however, was to be more circumscribed. Up to 100,000 male signatories, the Ulster Unionist Council agreed, would form an Ulster Volunteer Force (UVF).

The establishment of the UVF, on 13 January 1913, marked the militarisation of the Home Rule crisis. The formation of this force three days before the Government of Ireland Bill passed the House of Commons has ascribed to Edward Carson the historiographical role of *agent provocateur*. The latter's militant rhetoric and publicised review of Volunteer regiments would suggest that he has not entirely been typecast. However, recent scholarship has questioned the extent to which the formation of the UVF 'began' this militarisation. Both Paul Bew and Alvin Jackson have argued that Carson's intervention was an attempt to bring a prevailing local militancy under the political control of the UUC.[66] Timothy Bowman's

PRAYER

To be said daily by each member of the Ulster Volunteer Force—Morning and Evening.

O HEAVENLY FATHER, hear we pray Thee, the prayer of Thy children who call upon Thee in their time of danger and difficulty. Forgive me, I pray Thee, for all my sins which I have so often committed against Thee in thought, word, and deed. Make me " ready to endure hardness, as a good soldier of Jesus Christ." Fill me with Thy Holy Spirit, that I may know Thee more clearly : love Thee more dearly : and follow Thee more nearly. Strengthen and uphold me in all difficulties and dangers, keep me faithful unto death, patient in suffering, calm in Thy service, and confident in the assurance that Thou Lord wilt direct all things to the glory of Thy name and the welfare of my church and country. Bless the King, whom we serve, and all the Royal Family. O Lord grant me Thy grace that no word or act of mine may be spoken or done rashly, hastily, or with anger towards those who differ from me. Bless all my comrades in the Ulster Volunteer Force ; and make me loving and gentle : obedient to my leaders, and faithful to my promises : and in Thine own good time bring peace to Ireland. All this I beg for Jesus Christ's sake. AMEN.

M'Watters, Armagh.

2.30
Prayer to be recited 'morning and evening' by members of the Ulster Volunteer Force.
HE:EW.5774

systematic analysis of 'Carson's Army' supports this argument and has further evidenced a tradition of local militancy dating from the earlier Home Rule debates of 1886 and 1893, and the continued primacy of local command over central direction from Belfast in 1913–14.[67] The ideology of volunteering in Ulster, buttressed by historical allusions to the late eighteenth-century Irish Volunteers, was perhaps less a mobilising factor than contemporary militarism.[68]

Extra-parliamentary activity was, above all, period drama. The threat of violence was ritual politics during the United Kingdom's 'Edwardian Crisis'. Andrew Bonar Law, the leader of the Conservative Party, had prefaced both the Ulster Covenant and the UVF when he declared in July 1913: 'I can imagine no length of resistance to which Ulster will go, in which I shall not be ready to support them.' Suffragist and trade unionist campaigns which alternated between street politics and street violence, meanwhile, increasingly took centre stage in Great Britain. This had seen an Irish variant from late 1913 during the Dublin lockout when 25,000 members of the ITGWU were locked out of their workplaces for refusing to disclaim membership of James Larkin's

2.31
A Dublin Metropolitan
Police baton used on
'Bloody Sunday' (31
August 1913).
HA:1995.143 (Allen)

2.32
Irish Citizen Army
recruitment handbill.
HE:EWL.325.1

REASONS WHY

YOU SHOULD JOIN

The Irish Citizen Army.

BECAUSE It pledges its members to work for, organise for, drill for and fight for **an Independent Ireland.**

BECAUSE It places its reliance upon the only class that never betrayed Ireland—the Irish Working Class.

BECAUSE Having a definite aim to work for there is no fear of it being paralysed in the moment of action by divisions in its Executive Body.

BECAUSE It teaches that "the sole right of ownership of Ireland is vested in the people of Ireland, and that that full right of ownership may, and ought to be, enforced by any and all means that God hath put within the power of man."

BECAUSE It works in harmony with the Labour and true National Movements and thus embraces all that makes for Social Welfare and National Dignity.

Companies Wanted in Every District.

RECRUITS WANTED EVERY HOUR.

Apply for further information, Secretary, Citizen Army, Liberty Hall, Dublin.

Irish Paper.]   City Printing Works, 12 Stafford Street, Dublin.

union. An attack on protesting workers by the Dublin Metropolitan Police on 31 August would kill two and injure 300. An Irish Citizen Army of labour volunteers was subsequently established by Larkin, James Connolly and Jack White on 25 November 1913.[69] Ideas around the creation of an Irish Volunteers, P.S. O'Hegarty affirmed, emerged during this 'psychological moment'.[70]

Eoin MacNeill's argument for volunteering in Ireland, 'The North Began', is often construed as accusative case. Such interpretations are grammatically incorrect. In a memorable article published in *An Claidheamh Soluis* on 1 November 1913, MacNeill extolled the formation of the UVF and suggested that National Volunteers would soon be in existence: 'it is manifest that all Irish people, Unionist as well as nationalist, are determined to have their own

way in Ireland. On that point, and it is the main point, Ireland is united'.[71] Three weeks later, on 25 November, the Irish Volunteers was publicly launched on the grounds of the Rotunda in Dublin. The meeting was attended by 7,000 people. Approximately half of this number signalled their intention to sign enrolment forms. MacNeill was joined on the platform by Patrick Pearse and Laurence Kettle, two members of a self-appointed twenty-five man Provisional Committee formed to oversee the direction of the Irish Volunteers. MacNeill's invocation to inclusivity resonated consciously with Maurice Moore and the Antrim-born Roger Casement, who insisted on the body adopting its particular title: 'IRISH Volunteers, not NATIONAL or NATIONALIST Volunteers (the latter wholly damnable)'.[72] While many of the other Provisional Committee delegates may have been minded by MacNeill's mobilisation of national unity, they were not taken in by his manifesto alone.

2.33
Handbill advertising the launch of the Irish Volunteers at the Rotunda.
HE:EW.561

2.34
At the launch of the Irish Volunteers (left to right): Eoin MacNeill, Thomas MacDonagh, Michael Davitt, Patrick Pearse and Laurence Kettle.
HE:EW.5638

2.35
Irish Volunteers enlistment form.
HE:EW.1046.1

The regenerated Irish Republican Brotherhood had viewed the creation of the UVF as a 'development of the first importance' to their underlying objective of arming Irish nationalism. In their designs on an Irish Volunteer militia, Bulmer Hobson was to the fore. Hobson, who had been advocating for a Volunteer movement within IRB circles from July, and had already begun training a nucleus of Fianna Volunteers to that effect, suggested its development to The O'Rahilly, as editor of *An Claidheamh Soluis* and confidant of MacNeill. The subsequent appearance of 'The North Began' provided Hobson and the IRB with sufficient public momentum to arrange a meeting of 'advanced nationalists' on 11 November. Of the twelve invited by Hobson, and The O'Rahilly, five were IRB men: Seán Mac Diarmada, Hobson himself (who did not attend so as not to overtly suggest the Organisation's guiding hand), Seamus Deakin, Piaras Béaslaí and Éamonn Ceannt.[73]

Ceannt's presence may have further alleviated concerns over the IRB's influence. As a member of the Gaelic League's Coiste Gnótha and the Sinn Féin Executive Committee, he was acquainted with MacNeill and The O'Rahilly. However, the Ulster Crisis would inculcate in Ceannt a subterranean radicalism. By early 1913 he had assembled a private firing range, was secretly contributing articles to *Irish Freedom* and had been sworn into the IRB.[74] In a later piece to its official journal he revealed his growing militancy, using the metaphor of an Irish giant for the Irish Volunteers: 'he looks the Hope and Hero of Ireland … will he fight?'[75] Ceannt was again present at a meeting on 14 November. When the meeting adjourned, however, Eoin MacNeill, had become chairman of a twenty-five man Provisional Committee, seventeen of whom were not Organisation men.

Beyond the assumed IRB clique, its members were just as uncertain as to the loyalties of those seated around the Committee. Indeed the non-Organisation members defied clearest categorisation. Surveying this large group, F.X. Martin discerned the presence of what he termed 'constitutional separatists': 'they aimed at an independent Ireland, but to be attained by constitutional means'.[76] Martin spotlighted

MacNeill, although Casement, Moore, The O'Rahilly, and Thomas and Laurence Kettle have each been identified by this term. More coherently their espousal of the Irish Volunteers as a 'citizen army', in the eighteenth century tradition, denoted a politics of precedence: mobilisation to ensure the legislative implementation of Irish self-government.[77] Eoin MacNeill indeed wrote to a wary John Redmond to assure him of the Volunteers' loyalty to the Home Rule project. The contemporary resonance of this position, however, is questionable. Although individual members of the Irish Parliamentary Party, Ancient Order of Hibernians and United Irish League had joined the committee, the IPP, as a body, was not formally included.[78] As Matthew Kelly has observed 'adherence to the Volunteers inescapably bespoke a critique of Redmond's strategy and constitutional nationalism more generally'.[79]

The volunteering of two former UIL Young Ireland members instanced this commentary. Thomas MacDonagh and Joseph Plunkett, befriended by their mutual interest in the Irish language, poetry and theatre, and later the Gifford sisters, joined the Irish Volunteers in support of the Home Rule project. It soon, however, came to define their nationalist identity. Enthralled by the new movement, MacDonagh and Plunkett converted their literary journal into the unofficial organ of the Irish Volunteers, to the marginalisation of their existing readership and personal interests. 'I am a different man since joining the Volunteers' Plunkett would later admit.[80] So too already was Patrick Pearse. MacNeill's 'The North Began' appears to have clarified Pearse's own mind as to the purpose of his 'mysterious development' since 1912.[81] In an article entitled 'The Coming Revolution' published in *An Claidheamh Soluis* one week later, Pearse laid bare his radical trajectory for Ireland: 'Let our generation not shirk its deed, which is to accomplish the revolution … the coming of Home Rule, if come it does, will make no material difference in the nature of the work that lies before us … the substantial task of achieving the Irish

2.38
(Bottom image)
Joseph Plunkett was born on Upper Fitzwilliam Street to Irish parents on 21 November 1887. He was educated consecutively at the Catholic University School on Leeson Street, a Marist School in Paris and Belvedere College, Dublin. He later studied philosophy at the Jesuits' Stonyhurst College in Lancashire. Though Plunkett suffered recurrent ill-health on account of tuberculosis, he travelled widely including to North Africa (as pictured here in Arabic clothing).
HE:EW.2407

nation … I am glad, then that the North has "begun". I am glad that the Orangemen have armed, for it is a goodly thing to see arms in Irish hands … We must accustom ourselves to the thought of arms, to the sight of arms, to the use of arms.'[82] Three weeks later he was inducted into the IRB. Pearse's conversion during the Home Rule crisis to what R.F. Foster has termed the 'cult of guns'[83] was given tangible expression with the purchase of a revolver. Thomas MacDonagh and Joseph Plunkett each acquired a German mauser pistol. The Volunteers organisationally, however, were poorly financed and armed.

2.39
Patrick Pearse's Mauser pistol.
HE:EW.1731.1

2.40
Joseph Plunkett's automatic pistol.
HE:EW.971

2.41
Countess Markievicz's automatic pistol.
HE:EW.1735

The short supply of arms was even more pronounced in provincial Ireland, where recruits were forced to parade with wooden rifles or without. However, the participation of Nationalist Ireland should not be overstated. By February 1914 Irish Volunteer companies had only been formed in seventeen counties.[84] The available county studies on this subject, moreover, suggest the early organising influence of the IRB.[85] Although the IRB issued directives to followers to exert control over local committees, and the IPP expressed quiet disdain of same, some members of the AOH and UIL did join other more 'advanced' nationalists in its ranks, lending the early Irish Volunteers an 'amorphousness' of purpose and political allegiance.[86]

Wary of the Hibernian 'Frankenstein',[87] particularly in view of increasing tensions in Ulster, MacNeill, Moore and Casement approached the IPP independently of the Provisional Committee with the view to securing the Party's endorsement of the Irish Volunteers.[88] These early discussions in March and April centred on the accommodation of IPP representatives on the Provisional Committee. Enlistment in the Volunteers was finally increasing. On 9 March Asquith introduced the second reading of the Home Rule Bill with a proposal for the temporary (six year) exclusion of any Ulster county as determined by local plebiscite; the IPP reluctantly agreed. Meanwhile, on 20 March, sixty British army officers at the Curragh, who were presented with the impression that they would be instructed to carry out military operations against the UVF, suggested that they would rather resign. News of the Curragh 'mutiny' alarmed Nationalist Ireland as to British leniency towards Ulster militancy; Irish Volunteer membership climbed to 10,489.[89]

Such outrage would only intensify following the Larne gun running. The successful purchase of 20,000 rifles and two million rounds of ammunition in Hamburg by the UVF's Director of Ordnance, Major Fred Crawford was followed by the smooth transfer of the weapons to waiting couriers at Larne, Donaghadee and Bangor on the night of 24–25 April. The episode was deliberately publicised in the unionist press as an audacious military coup.[90] This, however, was read differently within the nationalist press which, only weeks after the Curragh 'mutiny' and in the throes of the Ulster amending

2.42
The Larne gun-running.
HE:EW.1086

2.43
Members of the Dublin
Brigade, Irish Volunteer
Force.
HA:2010.2.18

bill, questioned the willingness of the British State to confront unionist defiance of Home Rule.[91] Irish Volunteer membership almost doubled to 19,206 in late April.[92]

The successful passage of the Home Rule Bill in the House of Commons on 25 May, though still awaiting amending legislation on Ulster, prompted the IPP to finally move on the Irish Volunteers. The increasingly bullish Redmond demanded that twenty-five IPP nominees sit on the Provisional Committee, publicly threatening to establish a rival Volunteer corps if refused. The constitutional separatists had been out-negotiated.[93] Although the Provisional Committee's IRB junta rejected the ultimatum, Hobson reluctantly agreed, calculating that splitting the movement at this juncture would be even more disastrous.

So began Hobson's estrangement from the IRB leadership. Clarke never forgave him, famously asking: 'What did the Castle pay you?'[94] The Irish Volunteers, however, skyrocketed under the Party's auspices to 181,732 by September.[95] The Ulster Volunteer Force, comparably, had upwards of 100,000 recruits. Charles Townshend's evaluation is apposite: 'This was a truly revolutionary situation. The limits of the possible had been broken.'[96]

This was also the view of the highest power in the land. On 21 July, King George V counselled: 'today the cry of civil war is on the lips of the most responsible of my people'.[97] He had delivered the speech at the opening of the Buckingham Palace Conference, intended to resolve the outstanding issue of the Home Rule Bill: partition. Attended by Asquith, Lloyd George, Bonar Law, Redmond, Dillon and Lord Lansdowne, a southern unionist representative, the delegates failed to secure agreement on its territorial- and time-limits. Carson's arguments for the exclusion of the entire Ulster province or its six 'plantation' counties was rejected during the three-day proceedings, although there is evidence that Redmond was coming around to the unionist view.[98] Two days later the Irish Volunteers successfully smuggled 1,500 mauser rifles and 49,000 rounds of ammunition into Howth and Kilcoole. Initiated by Volunteer leaders such as Casement and MacNeill, and wealthy Volunteer sympathisers such as Alice Stopford Greene and Erskine and Molly Childers, the arms were transported from Hamburg to Howth on Childers' yacht, the *Asgard*. The British Army's belated attempt to intervene was followed by an ugly scene at Bachelor's walk when frustrated troops opened fire on a Dublin crowd killing three and injuring thirty-eight.[99]

2.44
Members of the West Belfast Regiment, Ulster Volunteer Force.
HE:EW.2005

2.45
Irish Volunteers waiting
for rifles at Howth pier.
HE:EW.1548.14.2

2.46
Molly Childers and
Mary Spring Rice
aboard the *Asgard*.
HE:EW.1548.5.1

Was Ireland on the verge of civil war? The situation was most acute in Ulster where the UVF was better and more substantially armed than the Irish Volunteers.[100] The British Army, further, had received no policy lead from Asquith or the British government on how to deal with such a crisis.[101] Ireland's 'July crisis' ran parallel to escalating tensions between Europe's major powers following the assassination of the Austrian Archduke Franz Ferdinand in Sarajevo. Assessing the United Kingdom's potential involvement in the looming continental conflict, Asquith wryly observed '[it will be akin to] cutting off one's head to get rid of a headache'.[102]

2.47
The 1871 model Mauser
rifle smuggled in by
the Irish Volunteers at
Howth. This specific rifle
was given by Thomas
Clarke to John Daly in
Limerick.
HE:EW.158

2.48
The 1884 Brescia model
Vetterli rifle smuggled in
by the Ulster Volunteers
at Larne.
HE:1995.48 (Allen)

THE FIRST WORLD WAR

On 3 August 1914, Germany declared war on France and one day later was at war with Belgium. Bound to uphold Belgian neutrality and wary of German militarism, Prime Minister Asquith and his cabinet brought the United Kingdom, Ireland included, into the Allied War against the Central Powers on 4 August.

The Irish Parliamentary Party, as Home Rule government in waiting, was faced with two immediate political issues: ensuring the safe passage of the Government of Ireland Bill into law, and safeguarding 'essential unity' under that legislation; and Ireland's martial contribution to the war effort. Both decisions would be effected by John Redmond, Ireland's putative prime minister, without consultation with his Irish 'cabinet members' or constituents.[103] In the beginnings of what James McConnel has termed his 'independent war policy',[104] Redmond addressed the House of Commons before Asquith had formally announced for war:

2.49
John Redmond.
HE:EW.2707

> I say to the Government that they may withdraw every one of their troops from Ireland. I say that the coast of Ireland will be defended from foreign invasion by her armed sons, and for this purpose armed Nationalist Catholics in the South will be only too glad to join arms with the armed Protestant Ulstermen in the North.[105]

Neither Dillon nor Devlin had been briefed on this announcement and Redmond would remain in London for the next six weeks, removed from Irish opinion, with the objective of unilaterally negotiating the wartime security of Ireland's Home Rule parliament.[106] On 15 September, following intense lobbying by Redmond, Asquith announced his intention to enact the Home Rule Bill, alongside emergency legislation which would immediately suspend the implementation of Irish self-governance for a period of between twelve months and the end of the war. A further Amending Bill, providing for the potential

2.50
A postcard image of
Ireland under Home
Rule. It was popularly
imagined that an
armed Irish Volunteer
force would protect the
implementation of this
legislation.
HE:EW.4397

modification of the Home Rule legislation over the issue of partition, would be brought before Parliament ahead of the actualisation of Dublin's new bicameral legislature. The Government of Ireland and Suspensory Acts became law three days later.[107] A jubilant Redmond pre-empted these formalities, issuing a personal manifesto on 17 September which underlined the momentousness of the European conflict for engendering mutual understanding between the armed forces of Catholic Nationalist and Protestant Unionist Irishmen on the battlefield. These volunteers, Redmond added, imperiously, could fight together as an 'Irish Brigade'.[108]

Was this the politics of personality or the politics of war? It has been suggested that this individual political manoeuvring marked the paramountcy of 'Redmondism' over a more inclusive, but less conciliatory, nationalism inherent in the Irish Party's local structures.[109] The promise of becoming Ireland's premier may have encouraged this proto-statesmanship. However, it is difficult to extract Redmond's public diplomacy from the critical context of the War. Redmond shared the conviction of many contemporaries that the war would be short-lived.[110] From this perspective, the rhetoric of co-operation with Ulster unionists, much less the United Kingdom's war against 'Prussianism', was politically adept. Redmond's gestural loyalty had matched that of

Edward Carson, who had earlier offered the Ulster Volunteer Force for home defence, but was given much greater prominence within British opinion, which had been less expectant of an explicit Irish nationalist loyalty at the outbreak of war: Home Rule, home fronts.

On his return to Ireland three days later Redmond addressed a unit of the East Wicklow Volunteers at Woodenbridge:

> I have no intentions of making a speech … I know that you will make efficient soldiers, efficient soldiers for what … your duty is a twofold duty … at all costs, to defend the shores of Ireland against foreign invasion … that Irish valour proves itself, on the field of war it has always proved itself in the past … the interests of Ireland, of the whole of Ireland are at stake in this war … I say to you … account yourselves as men not only in Ireland itself but wherever the fighting line extends in defence of right, of freedom and religion in this war.[111]

Writing in 1968, F.S.L. Lyons characterised it as a speech 'apparently spontaneous and almost accidental, but serious in its consequences'.[112] Lyons' analysis would prove representative of almost half a century of comment. Redmond's remarks have been judged fatal to his political career in Ireland,[113] earning him the unenviable title: 'one of the great losers of Irish history'.[114] Sympathetic portrayals of Redmond have underlined the spontaneity of his speech, delivered while en route from Parliament to his family home at Aghavannagh. Criticism, it has been argued, should be tempered accordingly.[115] This portrayal has not withstood more careful scrutiny. Conor Mulvagh has pointed to the choreography of Redmond's arrival and performance at Woodenbridge.[116] Daithí Ó Corráin, meanwhile, has evidenced the growing pressure within the Irish Parliamentary Party to engineer the removal of advanced nationalist elements from the Irish Volunteer leadership, suggesting Redmond's speech to have been calculatedly provocative.[117] Other commentators have invested in Redmond's speech a determined, but less Machiavellian, wartime strategy. Alvin Jackson has presented the Woodenbridge speech as an 'opening gambit' in a very public bid to create a distinctive Irish army corps.[118] Paul Bew has argued, most strenuously, that Redmond's remarks were aimed at British political and public opinion with the view to securing a better negotiating position on 'Ulster' after the war.[119] Joseph Finnan, meanwhile, has suggested that Redmond's 'program' to encourage enlistment was premised on nationalists and unionists 'making common cause' in the trenches to the diminution of their differences.[120]

On 24 September the Irish Volunteers split. A statement signed by Eoin MacNeill, The O'Rahilly, Thomas MacDonagh, Joseph Plunkett, Patrick Pearse, Bulmer Hobson, Éamonn Ceannt, Seán Mac Diarmada and twelve others, removed IPP nominees from the provisional committee in opposition to Redmond's perceived recruitment of the Volunteers for the British armed forces. Over the next five weeks the weight of the Party machine was deployed across the country to hold Volunteers to the Redmondite position.[121] By early November between 10,000 and 13,000 had sided with Eoin MacNeill as the Irish Volunteers while approximately 120,000 men, it was claimed, adhered to Redmond's leadership, under the 'new' title, the National Volunteers.[122] It would prove to be a Pyrrhic victory. Michael Wheatley's study of 'middle Ireland' has evidenced a 'rapid local decline' in Nationalist activism in late 1914, pointing to the War's accentuation and acceleration of a pre-existing trend towards a downturn in both Volunteer and UIL activity.[123] Moreover, only 29,928 of the National Volunteers had joined the British Armed Forces by mid-March 1916.[124]

Was Redmond's policy representative of Nationalist Ireland by the end of 1914? John Dillon, though supportive of the Party's solidarity with the war effort, was concerned as to Redmond's re-orientation of the Home Rule movement in favour of active participation, and quietly distanced himself from the policy in its fullest form.[125] Many Irish Party MPs adopted a similarly 'qualified' approach to recruitment, borne out of personal disinclination or perhaps the views of their constituents. It has been suggested, that Party MPs' reticence to publicly advocate enlistment may have reflected their expectation of the imminent formation of Redmond's 'Irish

Brigade'.[126] However, when this decision was finally taken by the British authorities, it was underwhelming. On 16 October, Lieutenant General Parsons, commandant of the 16th Division, informed Redmond that this unit would serve as the much vaunted 'Irish Brigade'.[127]

Approximately 200,000 Irishmen fought in the British armed forces during the First World War. Some 58,000 existing regulars and reservists in August 1914 were joined by 44,000 voluntary recruits in late 1914 and a further 45,000 voluntary recruits in 1915.[128] Why Irishmen enlisted has, historically, been a question freighted by polemic. The Irish Parliamentary Party, and John Redmond, were traditionally presented within republican discourse as unscrupulous 'recruiting sergeants' for the 'killing fields' of the Western Front. Recruits, similarly, were assumed to have volunteered for the 'King's shilling'.[129] Recent scholarship has considered the 'logic' of enlistment more dispassionately. In an influential quantitative analysis, David Fitzpatrick has posited that the social influence of 'fraternities' – colleagues, family, friends – provided the most compelling 'logic' for enlistment in urban Ireland and, simultaneously, the underlying reluctance to join in agricultural Ireland.[130] Building on Fitzpatrick's work, Catriona Pennell has contributed qualitative studies of Ireland's recruitment experience, suggesting that stratified propaganda played an 'important persuasive role'.[131] 'Little Catholic Belgium', it has been argued, was a particular mobilising influence, the arrival of Belgian refugees from October 1914, offering tangible evidence to propagandist claims of German military excesses.[132]

In May 1915, however, John Redmond was offered historical reprieve. Between 18 and 25 May, he was invited by Asquith three times to become a member of the new British Cabinet. Crises on the war front (Gallipoli) and the home front (the Shell scandal) had forced the introduction of the first coalition government in British politics. To the existing thirteen Liberals were added nine Unionists, including Edward Carson. Redmond declined the opportunity to join them: 'the

2.51
An anti-recruitment cartoon parodying John Redmond's call for volunteers.
HE:EW.368

55

principles and history of the party I represent make the acceptance of your offer impossible'.[133] This decision has, in retrospect, been considered a 'missed opportunity'.[134] Was this the case in actuality? The rejection appeared to undermine Redmond's short-term strategy of reconciliation to British war imperatives and his ideological loyalty to the imperial project. His response to Asquith betrayed his sense of frustration, bitterly objecting to Carson's appointment and conceding that he was 'more sorry than words can express' to not be able to accept the offer.[135] Significantly, the decision was taken with Irish opinion in perspective. Unlike his solo run earlier in the war, Redmond consulted Dillon, placed the issue before the Irish Party and presented his argument to Nationalist Ireland in the *Freeman's Journal*.[136] Redmond's credibility and electability as Ireland's Prime Minister appeared to be at stake. Home Rule, moreover, was due to come into effect no later than September. To this end, Redmond and Dillon had been increasingly visiting Augustine Birrell and Matthew Nathan, the new under-secretary at Dublin Castle, in preparation for the transfer of power.[137] If the war was indeed to be over, and Home Rule become a reality before the leaves fell a second time, Redmond may have been looking to shore up his Irish constituency.

The myth of the 'short war', however, was becoming increasingly transparent to Nationalist Ireland. The conventional wisdom that censorship screened the cataclysm of the war from the civilian population has been conclusively challenged in recent scholarship.[138] Local newspapers in Ireland continued to document the ensuing stalemate, present images from the Fronts and publish lists of the dead. News of the calamity at Gallipoli, including 3,000 10th (Irish) Division deaths at Suvla Bay, reached Irish readers, albeit at months' delay. Conscription, meanwhile, was increasingly perceived as a looming reality. The Unionist presence in the Coalition government sustained fears that conscription would be forced on Ireland.[139] The prevailing anxiety reinvigorated advanced nationalists of all persuasions who, from the summer of 1915, became increasingly visible on a platform of opposition to conscription. Radical journals such as James Connolly's *Workers' Republic*, Arthur Griffith's *Nationality* and Eoin MacNeill's *Irish Volunteer* editorialised against compulsory

'What is called the Sinn Féin movement is simply a temporary cohesion of isolated cranks in various parts of the country ... they have no policy and no leader and do not amount to a row of pins as far as the future of Ireland is concerned.'

John Redmond, July 1915

NO CONSCRIPTION
NOW! or AFTER the Harvest.

No Economic Pressure!

Lá na mBan.

The **Woman's Day**,
SUNDAY, JUNE 9th.

FOR HOME & COUNTRY.

IRISHWOMEN,
STAND BY YOUR COUNTRYMEN
IN RESISTING CONSCRIPTION.

SIGN THIS PLEDGE AT THE CITY HALL ON
ST. COLMCILLE'S DAY.

" We will not fill the places of men deprived of their
work through refusing enforced military service."
" We will do all in our power to help the families of
men who suffer through refusing enforced military service."

REFUSE to fill Posts vacated by MEN because
of Compulsory Military Service.

All information from Secretary, 18 Kildare Street.

2.52
Anti-conscription
handbill c.1915.
Cumann na mBan was
a female paramilitary
organisation
established in April
1914.
HE:EW.3126

military service; Irish Volunteers protested at recruitment meetings; while Cumann na mBan and the Irish Citizen Army paraded militant opposition.[140] Activists in the anti-conscription front were decisively, if disingenuously, labelled 'Sinn Feiners' by the Dublin Castle authorities. However, there was nothing decisive about their response to that 'movement'. While some 'Sinn Fein' newspapers were suppressed and agitators interned under the Defence of the Realm Act, these were intermittent.[141] The overtly seditious funeral of Jeremiah O'Donovan Rossa at Glasnevin Cemetery in August was attended by tens of thousands and no arrests were made of the 'Sinn Fein' activists present. As Eunan O'Halpin has surmised: 'there was no pattern or coherence to this activity'.[142] Anti-conscription activity intensified, particularly after the Derby scheme was opened in October, implying the application of conscription across the United Kingdom. Dublin Castle's weakness in countering such activity derived primarily from its transitional status. John Dillon repeatedly counselled the apprehensive Birrell and Nathan against arresting, and therefore legitimising, the 'Sinn Feiners', ahead of the Home Rule takeover.[143] The threat of conscription would, eventually, strangle the Home Rule movement.

PLANNING THE RISING

The September 1914 split in the Irish Volunteers had, in some ways, been mutual. While early accounts of the period emphasised the depression of the MacNeillite Irish Volunteers in the wake of the Irish Party's 'vampirisation' of the movement,[144] more recent appraisals have discerned the quiet satisfaction of those who remained Irish Volunteers for having removed the 'parliamentary' influence.[145] Writing to Joseph McGarrity in Philadelphia, Patrick Pearse was cheered by their 'small, compact, perfectly-disciplined, determinedly *separatist* force'.[146] MacNeill himself had exclaimed the IPP to be 'altogether hopeless' after Joseph Devlin had rejected out of hand his proposal to establish a provisional Home Rule government at the outset of the war.[147] On 25 October, an Irish Volunteer Convention, organised by MacNeill and attended by 160 delegates, restored the pre-Redmond Central Executive, including Bulmer Hobson, Patrick Pearse and Éamonn Ceannt. The declarations of policy adopted included: 'to resist any attempt to force the men of Ireland into military service under any Government until a free National Government is empowered by the Irish people themselves to deal with it.' MacNeill and The O'Rahilly were later designated the responsibility of purchasing arms.[148]

In his famous formulation, inspired in part by T.M. Healy, F.X. Martin described the 1916 Rising as 'the revolt of "a minority of a minority of the minority"'.[149] The attendant extrapolation, the unrepresentative nature of the seven-man Military Council relative to

2.53
Irish Volunteers Defence of Ireland Fund collection box.
HE:EW.970

the Irish Republican Brotherhood and the Irish Volunteers, however, is germane only to the military action which did take place not the military actions which might have taken place. The First World War exposed the prevalence of preparations for rebellion, however provisional, within an Irish Volunteer movement once removed. As early as mid-August, the IRB Supreme Council had agreed, in principle, to stage a Rising before the end of the war.[150] In that same month members of Clan na Gael, and Roger Casement, approached German representatives in New York with the view to securing military support for a rebellion. Suitably encouraged, Casement sailed for Berlin in October.[151] Although opposed to proposals which contravened the IRB's 1873 constitution requiring 'the will of the people' to begin an insurrection, Bulmer Hobson followed Casement's mission with intent and prepared detailed plans for guerrilla warfare in Ireland, should the military capability of the Irish Volunteers be improved by German support or threatened by British intervention.[152] Eoin MacNeill, the arch-antagonist of the eventual rebellion to generations of history readers, meanwhile, was only amenable to the idea of a Rising if there was a 'reasonably calculated or estimated prospect of success … if they do not come to nullity, then let us see what they do come to.'[153] Others, it would seem, were fundamentally interested in preparing for a Rising. At a secretly convened meeting at the Gaelic League rooms in Dublin on 9 September, an array of advanced nationalists, including Thomas Clarke, Éamonn Ceannt, Arthur Griffith, Seán Mac Diarmada, John MacBride, Patrick Pearse, Seán T. O'Kelly, James Connolly, Joseph Plunkett, William O'Brien and Thomas MacDonagh, met to discuss the staging of a rebellion during the War.[154] It was from this meeting that an 'Advisory Committee' was first formed to draw up a provisional military plan. The committee was later described by senior IRB figure Diarmuid Lynch as comprising 'a considerable number of prominent Irish Volunteer officers'.[155]

On 6 December 1914 the Irish Volunteers had established a military headquarters staff to oversee organisation and training. Under Eoin MacNeill as Chief of Staff, five officers were appointed to individual portfolios: The O'Rahilly (Director of Arms), Thomas MacDonagh (Director of Training), Patrick Pearse (Director of Military Organisation),

Joseph Plunkett (Director of Military Operations), Bulmer Hobson (Quartermaster).[156] It has been something of a commonplace to suggest the nefarious influence of the IRB within the Irish Volunteer leadership at this point. However, only two of the above, Pearse and Plunkett, were both officially sworn into the IRB and the wider advanced nationalist plan for rebellion. Lynch, meanwhile, advised Thomas Clarke to let the 'unwieldy' Advisory Committee fall away in favour of a more clandestine Fenian operation. In late May 1915, Clarke and Lynch, the controllers of the IRB Executive Council, established a Military Committee unbeknownst to the rest of the IRB Supreme Council: Patrick Pearse, Joseph Plunkett, Éamonn Ceannt.[157] Three months later Ceannt was appointed Irish Volunteer Director of Communications.[158] The Military Council, under the spiritual guidance of Clarke and Seán Mac Diarmada, then in prison, was in reality grounded in the pre-existing militancy of its three members.

The First World War distilled Patrick Pearse's beliefs into 'blood sacrifice' singular. Historians have debated the point when Pearse became consumed by what Yeats termed the 'vertigo of self-sacrifice',[159] but most are agreed that he had 'turned his face' to rebellion by early 1915.[160] His increasingly reclusive reading of Tone, Davis, Lalor and Mitchel gave rise to a prodigious volume of writing on the existential threat to Irish nationality during the calendar year, bookmarked by the completion of *The Singer*, an allegorical play in which the protagonist exclaimed: 'One man can free a people as one Man redeemed the world. I will take no pike. I will go into the battle with bare hands. I will stand up before the Gall as Christ hung naked before men on the tree.'[161] However, it was his commentary on the European war, also in December 1915, which became his abiding character reference: 'It is good for the world that such things should be done. The old heart of the earth needed to be warmed with the red wine of the battlefields.'[162] Scrutinising Pearse's statements during this period, Ruth Dudley Edwards concluded that 'the wine had gone to Pearse's head'.[163] However, a more recent portrait by Joost Augusteijn has presented his

2.54
Patrick Pearse *c.*1914.
HE:EW.3559

rhetoric as representative of a wider European discourse on the 'cult of sacrifice', embodied by the participation of millions in the First World War.[164] Indeed, as Augusteijn points out, Pearse's impassioned eulogy of the war was tempered only a few lines later: 'War is a terrible thing, and this is the most terrible of wars. But this war is not more terrible than the evils which it will end or help to end.'[165]

In a further counterpoint to the view of 'blood sacrifice' as Pearsean irrationality, Fearghal McGarry has drawn attention to the motivation of the wider Military Council to act.[166] Éamonn Ceannt is pertinent to this, more balanced, assessment. The war appears to have fortified Ceannt's 'neo-Fenian' frame of mind, perhaps more immediately than Pearse. William O'Brien's memoir notes that Ceannt was the enthusiastic organiser of the early meeting at the Gaelic League rooms to prepare for the Rising while several associates recalled his sense of urgency in staging a rebellion before the war was over.[167] Writing in the *Irish Volunteer* journal weeks later, he expressed his conviction that: '[Britain had never] redressed an Irish grievance before the Irish people had made clear their determination to take the law into their own hands.'[168] Ceannt would volunteer his home at Dolphin's Barn for the early meetings of the military committee.

2.55
Joseph Plunkett working on wireless equipment *c.*1914.
HE:EW.2405

The plans for the Rising, detailed at these meetings, were presented by Joseph Plunkett. The latter's professional investment in the Irish Volunteers and personal interest in military strategy inspired his theoretical designs on a potential rebellion. His attendance at the advanced nationalist meeting of 9 September hardened the reality of his military application. The Advisory Committee was instructed to devise a tactical plan for 'fighting in Dublin'.[169] Plunkett, who may have already discussed ideas along these lines with Pearse,[170] was almost certainly the key strategist behind this proposal, first presented to Clarke and Mac Diarmada in early 1915, to which the former expressed satisfaction, but felt required further elaboration.[171]

Was this the tactically defensive Dublin-only Rising which largely transpired in 1916? And if so, was 'blood sacrifice' its strategic objective? The available evidence points to an initial advocacy of, and concentration on, a Dublin-centred rebellion much as it became. The original proposal, like the eventual plans, has not survived. Extant sources, consisting of personal reminiscences and contemporary ephemera, thus, can present only circumstantial evidence of the early thinking of the military committee. According to P.S. O'Hegarty, fellow Fenian Seán Mac Diarmada was both clear and confident in their rationale for a Rising, as early as May 1915: 'they contemplated a Dublin

insurrection only, an insurrection which would make its protest […] "We'll hold Dublin for a week, but we'll save Ireland."'[172] Both O'Hegarty and Piaras Béaslaí, stated retrospectively that they had been apprised of plans for the occupation of buildings identical to those taken during Easter Week, in the opening months of 1915.[173] Meanwhile in March, Pearse ascertained from Edward Daly, Thomas MacDonagh, Éamonn Ceannt and Éamon de Valera, the newly appointed commandants of Dublin's four Irish Volunteer battalions, their preparedness to take part in a city rebellion.[174] Plunkett, Pearse and Mac Diarmada were awed by the resonance of Robert Emmet's insurrection of 1803 and spoke widely of their desire to emulate his failed rebellion.[175] 'The minds of the little committee' Charles Townshend has surmised 'were plainly mesmerized by the physical and symbolic weight of the city'.[176]

(Clockwise from top left)
2.56
Edward Daly, Commandant
1st Battalion Irish Volunteers.
HE:EW.198.9

2.57
Thomas MacDonagh,
Commandant 2nd Battalion
Irish Volunteers.
HE:EW.198.3

2.58
Éamon de Valera,
Commandant 3rd Battalion
Irish Volunteers.
HE:EW.2904

2.59
Éamonn Ceannt,
Commandant 4th Battalion
Irish Volunteers.
HE:EW.390

Writing of these early motions towards a rebellion, Michael Tierney has charged: 'it is surely more likely that plans to resist conscription were later attributed, as plans for a rising, to the men who actually brought one about … more substance than they deserve has been accorded to these vague and shifting schemes.'[177] Though speculative in its suggestion, this critique interjects a healthy scepticism to readings of the inevitability of the Rising as it eventually happened. The formative plans of the Advisory and Military committees for a Dublin rebellion were indeed neither necessarily ideological nor final. The initial emphasis on action in the capital may well have been grounded in the practical limitations of the Volunteer movement in early 1915. The post-split Irish Volunteers was heavily centred on Dublin. Moreover, it has been argued that the adoption of defensive tactics was not synonymous with a strategy of 'propaganda of the deed'. Advocates of city fighting within the Irish Volunteers, although amateurish, argued for the tactical advantage of defensive positions and street fighting.[178] This view was most consistently put forward in 1915 by James Connolly in a series of articles in the *Workers' Republic* entitled 'Insurrection and Warfare'. Using the Belgian Revolution (1830), the June Days uprising in Paris (1848) and the Moscow Insurrection (1905), as examples, he emphasised the tactical superiority of defensive warfare if reinforced by cleverly positioned barricades, thereby exposing state forces to lateral lines of fire from insurgents.[179] Connolly's arguments were widely discussed within the Volunteers to whom he was invited to lecture.[180] Others, notably the militarily resourceful Bulmer Hobson, Eimar O'Duffy and J.J. O'Connell, were trenchant in their belief that guerrilla warfare, first introduced to Irish Volunteer training in November 1914, was the ideal tactical approach in view of their resources, although its strategic value was not apparent without a stronger Volunteer presence in the provinces.[181] Only 9,603 Irish Volunteers existed in Ireland outside Co. Dublin in late 1914; local companies, moreover, were prone to fading out of existence.[182] On Pearse's directive, six organisers were appointed and a general council established in early 1915 to maintain contact with provincial units.[183] While strongly favoured by the military committee, plans for a Dublin-dependant rebellion may have been imposed thus, not by symbolic defeatism, but by the early organisational weakness of the Volunteer movement beyond the capital. Indeed their best laid plans, documentarily, suggest that their proposals were evolving in 1915 towards an aspirant national Rising which was more hopeful of military victory. These were contained in the Ireland Report.

In March of that year Joseph Plunkett set out for Germany under the auspices of the advisory committee. Travelling the circuitous route of Paris–San Sebastian–Barcelona–Genoa–Florence–Lausanne, to avoid detection, he eventually arrived in Berlin on 20 April. Here he had arranged to

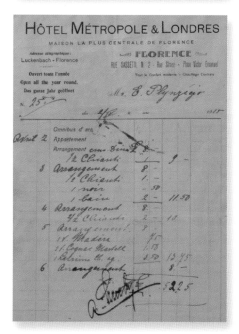

2.64
Joseph Plunkett in
Berlin (April 1915).
HE:EW.3080

2.65
Roger Casement and
John Devoy in New
York (1914).
HE:EW.2101

meet Roger Casement. Casement's original mission, under the support of John Devoy, was to secure a declaration of German support for Irish independence, mobilise an 'Irish Brigade' from among Irish prisoners of war and secure arms for military action in Ireland.[184] It was on this third, vital point of arms, that Casement's aims most obviously matched Plunkett's. Together they prepared a thirty-two page document, entitled the 'Ireland Report', which presented the strategic case for German military intervention in Ireland. Arguing that a joint German–Irish armed force would severely drain British military resources in the ongoing war, they requested German assistance in the form of 12,000 troops and 40,000 rifles. These were to be landed along the river Shannon, simultaneous to the beginning of rebellion in Dublin. Beginning in Limerick, the report continued, Volunteers from the west of Ireland and German expeditionary forces could launch a campaign of guerrilla warfare to overcome British resistance, and sweep towards the capital. Casement and Plunkett presented the report to the German General Staff and the latter returned to Ireland in June, without confirmation of German support.[185]

Brian Barton and Michael Foy, who first published the contents of the Ireland Report, have confidently asserted: 'Plunkett's memorandum provides a unique insight into the attitudes, intentions and aspirations of the Military Council.'[186] Charles Townshend has provided the most rigorous critique of this argument, pointing out that while the ambition for a national Rising may well have been genuine, many of the document's assertions were not, particularly those relating to the Volunteers' strength in provincial Ireland and the extent of their training in guerrilla warfare:

'it is hard to avoid the conclusion that it contained a fair amount of window dressing'.[187] It is impossible to establish, with any certainty, the collective thinking of the nascent military committee on the Ireland Report at this juncture. Plunkett's communication with Ireland during his time in Germany was limited, while he appears to have been given considerable latitude to formulate the earlier Advisory Committee plan. Retrospective accounts from those closest to the military committee suggest that the acquirement of arms from Germany was central to their original plans for a Dublin Rising but these plans appear to have been changing by the late summer. The absence of early response from Germany precluded a suggested September 1915 rebellion.[188] Moreover, the expansion of the Irish Volunteers in provincial Ireland, as a consequence of Pearse's organisation and the threat of conscription respectively, may have made a national Rising more viable as the year progressed, with or without a German expeditionary force. The activities of its members appear to support this reorientation of potential military strategy. In August, Plunkett was sent to New York to update Clan na Gael on the committee's progress. In that same month, Thomas Clarke sent Limerick Volunteer Robert Monteith to Limburg to assist the increasingly beleaguered Casement in his enlistment of an 'Irish Brigade'.[189] During this period, meanwhile, Pearse directed Diarmuid Lynch to ascertain suitable landing points for an arms shipment in Co. Kerry and began to brief Volunteer leaders in Co. Limerick on possible military action, discussions apparently overheard by Eoin MacNeill.[190]

2.66
Robert Monteith's 'Irish Brigade' cap.
HE:EWL.229.4

2.67
Robert Monteith in full 'Irish Brigade' uniform.
HE:EW.3440

2.68
A printed edition
of Patrick Pearse's
O'Donovan Rossa
funeral eulogy.
HE:EW.1662

Pearse, Joe Lee has noted, was a 'suitable front man' for the military committee.[191] The funeral of O'Donovan Rossa on 1 August 1915 illustrated this point. Behind Pearse's dramatic performance at Glasnevin Cemetery, Thomas MacDonagh was auditioning for his place on the military committee. MacDonagh, who had been part of the initial Advisory Committee, and was promoted to Commandant of the Irish Volunteers Dublin Brigade by Pearse in early 1915, was sworn into the IRB in April of that year.[192] Clarke, who had asked John Devoy to allow him to make the arrangements for Rossa's body, tasked MacDonagh with orchestrating the funeral procession. While history has remembered Pearse's vociferous speech of that day, public opinion at the time was more widely impressed by the solemnity and scale of the funeral ceremonies.[193] MacDonagh arranged a three day lying-in-state at City Hall where thousands of citizens filed past Rossa's remains while the funeral cortège through the city centre was to include representatives of the Irish Volunteers, Irish Citizen Army, Fianna, Cumann na mBan and the National Volunteers. Newspaper reports commented effusively on the funeral's 'spectacle'.[194] Clarke had given MacDonagh's close friend and IRB senior Patrick Pearse the role of orator: 'make it as hot as hell, throw discretion to the winds'.[195] Pearse's carefully scripted panegyric was ominous:

> We know only one definition of freedom: it is Tone's definition, it is Mitchel's definition, it is Rossa's definition … life springs from death; and from the graves of patriot dead and from the graves of patriot men and women spring living nations. The defenders of this Realm … think that they have pacified Ireland. They think that they have purchased half of us and intimidated the other half. They think that they have foreseen everything, think that they have provided against everything; but the fools, the fools, the fools! They have left us our Fenian dead, and while Ireland holds these graves, Ireland unfree shall never be at peace.[196]

The speech was followed with Irish Volunteer rifle fire over the grave. Noticeably absent was Eoin MacNeill. The IRB's public manipulation of the O'Donovan Rossa funeral on 1 August, allied with their infiltration of the Gaelic League's Coiste Gnótha six days earlier, however, was bound to call his attention to clandestine manoeuvring.[197] Huddled around the graveside were many of those who had last met together at the Gaelic League rooms in September 1914 and were now contributors to the many O'Donovan Rossa funeral sub-committees: Arthur Griffith, John MacBride, William O'Brien, Seán T. O'Kelly and James Connolly.

2.69
The O'Donovan Rossa funeral committee, August 1915.
HE:EWT.20

Connolly's biographer, Ruth Dudley Edwards, has chaptered his final twenty months 'desperation'.[198] It is a laconic title. Throughout this period Connolly betrayed a restlessness with the world around him, a restlessness which hurried him to violent insurrection. It is impossible to overestimate the psychological impact of the First World War on Connolly. He witnessed millions of working-class men abandon the Red Flag, and 'rush' to their respective colours; decades of exhaustive campaigning, speaking and writing on the socialist revolution had been shattered: 'We are helpless!!! What then becomes of all our resolutions, all our protests of fraternisation … all our carefully-built machinery of internationalism, all our hopes for the future? Were they all as sound and fury, signifying nothing?'[199] This was his Macbethian moment. Connolly's later attendance at the Gaelic League Hall meeting on 9 September marked his regression from depression to anger. Addressing a public meeting in the city he exclaimed: 'revolutions do not start with rifles; start first and get your rifles after. Make up your mind to strike before your opportunity goes'.[200] One month later Connolly took on the role of Commandant of the Irish Citizen Army, leading recruitment; intensifying training and carrying out reconnaissance of capital buildings. The ICA, numbering just three hundred and sixty-three, was primed for insurrection, independent of IRB–Irish Volunteer initiative.[201]

2.70
Irish Citizen Army members drilling at Croydon Park, *c.*1915.
HE:EW.214

Was this blood sacrifice? Pearse's ode to the First World War had met a terse response from Connolly: 'blithering idiot'.[202] Nonetheless, the latter's determination to rise up against British authority, even with such a small military force, had a Pearsean quality. First-blood sacrifice may be a more fitting description. Connolly advanced the idea that an ICA rebellion would provoke the people of Ireland into supportive action. He had also hoped that taking it would lead socialists across Europe to follow suit: 'Ireland may yet set the torch to a European conflagration that will not burn out until the last throne and the last capitalist bone and debenture will be shrivelled on the funeral pyre of the last warlord.'[203]

By mid-January, the date for at least one 1916 Rising had been set. The Military Council, which now included both Thomas Clarke and Seán Mac Diarmada, had decided upon Easter Sunday 23 April. This information was relayed to John Devoy, reaching New York on 5 February, who in turn transmitted the message to his German contacts:

> Unless entirely new circumstances arise we must have your arms and munitions in Limerick between Good Friday and Easter Saturday. We expect German help immediately after beginning action. We might be compelled to begin earlier.[204]

Allowances for an earlier date may have been driven in part by Connolly's increasingly transparent declarations of an imminent Irish Citizen Army Rising: 'the time for Ireland's battle is NOW the place for Ireland's battle is HERE'.[205] Connolly confirmed his designs to the apparent mutual concern of MacNeill and Pearse at Irish Volunteer HQ on 16 January. Pearse offered to dissuade Connolly from his lone mission.[206] Five days later he had become the sixth member of the Military Council. The myth of Connolly's enforced captivity between 19 and 21 January has been widely debunked.[207] The Military Council in fact spent three days with Connolly at Dolphin's Barn in an attempt to convince him of the seriousness of their plans for a Rising. In Joseph Plunkett in particular he encountered a kindred spirit. Though informed of the anticipated national Rising, and German military support, Connolly locked himself in discussion with Plunkett over the latter's tactical plan for a defensive operation in Dublin, later acclaiming him a 'brilliant military man'.[208]

Connolly's designation as Commandant-General of the Dublin Brigade and Pearse as Commander in Chief of the Irish Republican Forces during Easter week may have stemmed from this meeting, to imbalanced military effect. The decision already taken to use Volunteer manoeuvres on Easter Sunday as a secret mechanism of mobilisation appeared opportune. The military exercises on St Patrick's Day brought out 1,400 Volunteers in Dublin and a further 4,500 in the provinces.[209] One week earlier the Military Council had received confirmation that the Germans would send 20,000 rifles and ten machine guns to Fenit, Co. Kerry on 20 April. Preparations for this landing were likely dependant on Pearse. His position as Irish Volunteer Director of Military Organisation afforded him access to provincial units in the spring of 1916 and he had more connections to local officers than others on the Military Council. However Pearse, who 'did not excel in practical organisation work',[210] communicated few tactical plans to provincial commandants after the strategic instructions passed to IRB leaders in January 1916, in keeping with the outlines of the 'Ireland Report': Cork Volunteers were to hold the south of the county with a contingent meeting the Kerry brigade to the west; Limerick Volunteers were to hold the line of the Shannon in tandem with Clare and Galway Volunteers. The latter, it was suggested to Dennis McCullough and Patrick McCartan in March, would include the Belfast and Tyrone Volunteers who were to march westwards coming under the command of Liam Mellows.[211] Though some provincial Volunteers anticipated standard manoeuvres for Easter Sunday, others expected military action.[212]

Ordinary Volunteers in Dublin, however, became increasingly aware from March that mobilisation would mean rebellion. The foreshadowing of military action was suggested in lectures, training exercises and through the capital's compact network of activists.[213] Connolly's repeated supervision of manoeuvres in the city, meanwhile, prepared activists, wittingly or otherwise, for the impending conflict.[214] Another potential indicator that a rebellion was in train was the arrival of Volunteers from British cities. Between late January and early April 1916, eighty-seven

Irish men and women associated with Cumann na mBan, the
Irish Volunteers and the Irish Republican Brotherhood travelled
from London, Liverpool, Manchester and Glasgow to Dublin.[215]
Ostensibly escaping the application of conscription, the arrival
of these 'refugees' beyond January, however, was bound to raise
suspicions; many of these activists were aware that a Rising was
imminent. The new arrivals were billeted on Joseph Plunkett's
Larkfield estate where they began producing bullets, grenades and
pikes for forthcoming military action. They would become known
as the 'Kimmage garrison'.[216] Among those who arrived from
London was Michael Collins who, on account of his administrative
ability and Fenian connections, was in closer contact with members
of the Military Council, becoming Plunkett's aide-de-camp.[217]
The Dublin commandants of the Irish Volunteers and Irish
Citizen Army, meanwhile, were informed of the impending Rising
within two weeks of Easter Sunday. It was during this period,
according to Diarmaid Lynch, that Thomas MacDonagh became
the seventh member of the Military Council.[218] Though never
satisfactorily explained, MacDonagh's belated admission into the
Military Council proper it seems was connected to Eoin MacNeill's
willingness to join the signatories.[219]

2.71
Bullet mould used
at Larkfield Camp,
Kimmage.
HE:1998.47a

2.72
Eoin MacNeill (centre)
reviewing Irish
Volunteers at Killarney.
HE:EW.1696

MacNeill was implicitly aware of the Military Council's arguments for a Rising by Holy Week and almost certainly aware of conspiratorial planning to that effect. Hobson had been hinting as much to him since February and very publicly denounced the impending military action at a Volunteer meeting on 16 April.[220] MacNeill would need to be convinced, not that a Rising was going to take place but that it could succeed and/or was necessary. In a lengthy statement to the military staff of the Irish Volunteers in mid-February, MacNeill had vigorously opposed the many arguments which he had heard to justify a Rising: 'it is essential that Ireland should take action during the present war'; 'Ireland has always struck her blow too late … we should take the initiative'. He was, however, less dismissive of the position that 'lives must be sacrificed, in order to produce an ultimate effect on the national mind', on the clear proviso that 'if the destruction of our nationality was in sight, and if we came to the conclusion that at least the vital principle of nationality was to be saved by laying down our lives, then we should make that sacrifice without hesitation'.[221] On Wednesday of Holy Week MacNeill and other Dublin nationalists were presented with an apparent fait accompli in the form of the 'Castle Document' which purported to signal the imminent arrest of leading figures from the Irish 'Sinn Fein' Volunteers, Sinn Féin and the Gaelic League and the seizure of nationalist offices and residences in Dublin. MacNeill's reaction was telling: 'The Lord has delivered them into our hands!' Although its contents were based on a real document, they had been 'sexed up' by Joseph Plunkett and Rory O'Connor to appear as imminent Dublin Castle action. Unaware of this deception, MacNeill urgently issued a general defensive order to all Irish Volunteers across the country. Within twenty-four hours, however, he was positively informed by Hobson, J.J. O'Connell and Eimar O'Duffy that a Rising was secretly being prepared for Easter Sunday. In a tense meeting at midnight on Thursday 20 April, the allegations were confirmed by Pearse, who revealed the existence of an IRB Military Council within the Volunteers. Affronted by Pearse's covert manipulation of the Irish Volunteers and apparently unaware of the Military Council's actual plans for the Rising, MacNeill vowed to do everything he could to prevent their rebellion without advising Dublin Castle. Orders cancelling any directive from Pearse were issued to the Volunteers. The protagonists barely had time to sleep on the night's debate. At 8.00 a.m. the following morning, Friday 21 April, MacNeill was met at his home by Pearse, MacDiarmada and MacDonagh, who informed him that German arms were presently en route as part of careful preparations for the Rising. This, it would seem, was enough to convince MacNeill of the justification for a Rising: 'if that is the state of the case I'm with you.' The Military Council, however, remained uncertain of MacNeill's commitment to their Rising and in a pre-emptive move they placed Hobson, their chief detractor, under house arrest.

Secret Orders issued to Military Officers.

The cipher from which this document is copied does not indicate punctuation or capitals.

" The following precautionary measures have been sanctioned by the Irish Office on the recommendation of the General Officer Commanding the Forces in Ireland. All preparations will be made to put these measures in force immediately on receipt of an Order issued from the Chief Secretary's Office, Dublin Castle, and signed by the Under Secretary and the General Officer Commanding the Forces in Ireland. First, the following persons to be placed under arrest :— All members of the Sinn Fein National Council, the Central Executive Irish Sinn Fein Volunteers, General Council Irish Sinn Fein Volunteers, County Board Irish Sinn Fein Volunteers, Executive Committee National Volunteers, Coisde Gnota Committee Gaelic League. See list A 3 and 4 and supplementary list A 2.   .   .   .   .   . Dublin Metropolitan Police and Royal Irish Constabulary Forces in Dublin City will be confined to barracks under the direction of the Competent Military Authority. An order will be issued to inhabitants of city to remain in their houses until such time as the Competent Military Authority may otherwise direct or permit. Pickets chosen from units of Territorial Force will be placed at all points marked on Maps 3 and 4. Accompanying mounted patrols will continuously visit all points and report every hour. The following premises will be occupied by adequate forces, and all necessary measures used without need of reference to Headquarters. First, premises known as Liberty Hall, Beresford Place ; No. 6 Harcourt Street, Sinn Fein building ; No. 2 Dawson Street, Headquarters Volunteers ; No. 12 D'Olier Street, 'Nationality' Office ; No. 25 Rutland Square, Gaelic League Office ; No. 41 Rutland Square, Foresters' Hall ; Sinn Fein Volunteer premises in city ; all National Volunteer premises in city ; Trades Council premises, Capel Street ; Surrey House, Leinster Road, Rathmines. THE FOLLOWING PREMISES WILL BE ISOLATED, AND ALL COMMUNICATION TO OR FROM PREVENTED :— PREMISES KNOWN AS ARCHBISHOP'S HOUSE, DRUMCONDRA ; MANSION HOUSE, DAWSON STREET ; No. 40 Herbert Park ; Larkfield, Kimmage Road ; Woodtown Park, Ballyboden ; Saint Enda's College, Hermitage, Rathfarnham ; and in addition premises in list 5 D, see Maps 3 and 4."

2.73
'The Castle Document'.
HE:1998.44 (Allen)

75

2.74
The Irish frieze
overcoat worn by Roger
Casement on landing at
Banna Strand.
HE:EW.61

The calamities in Co. Kerry between 20 and 21 April would, ultimately, confirm MacNeill's judgement that the rebellion had no chance of success. The continued neglect of the organisational system for a national Rising by Pearse resulted in its inevitable breakdown. The failure to land the German arms was but its final symptom. On 12 April, Austin Stack, the pre-arranged contact in Tralee for the reception and distribution of German arms, sent a subordinate to discuss the arrangements with Pearse. Two days later Philomena Plunkett, Joseph Plunkett's sister, met John Devoy in New York with an urgent despatch from the Military Council for the German authorities: 'Arms must not be landed before midnight of Sunday, 23rd. This is vital. Smuggling impossible. Let us know if submarine will come to Dublin Bay.' Though the impetus for this message is unclear it seems certain that Stack, accordingly, now expected the German arms to arrive with military efficiency on 23 April. This belated change of dates was compounded by inadequate preparation for contingency. The Germans, the Military Council and Stack (presumably) knew, had sent a cargo boat, the '*Aud*', under the command of Karl Spindler, to deliver the arms on 10 April. Five days later, Roger Casement and Robert Monteith, who had proven unsuccessful in their attempt to form a sufficient 'Irish Brigade', were also on their way to Kerry, aboard the U19 submarine. Casement, it has been claimed, was intent

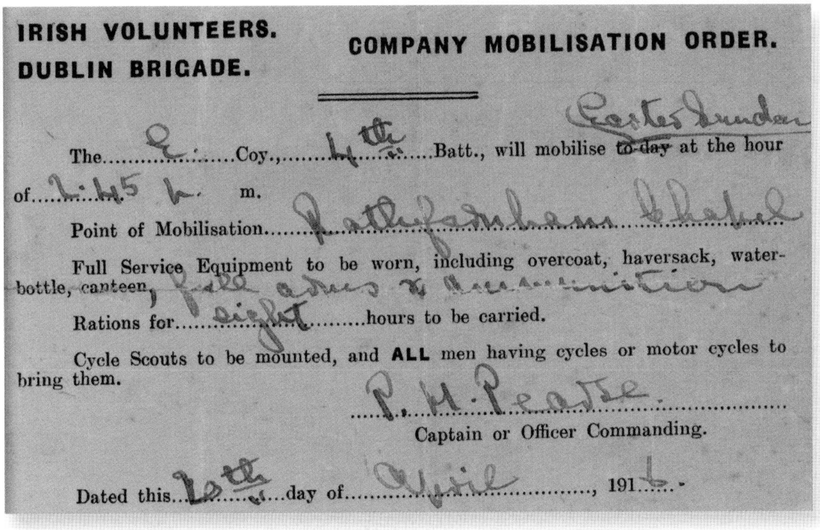

IRISH VOLUNTEERS.
DUBLIN BRIGADE.

COMPANY MOBILISATION ORDER.

The...........E.........Coy.,............4th........Batt., will mobilise to-day at the hour of.....1.45....... m. *Easter Sunday*

Point of Mobilisation........*Rathfarnham Chapel*

Full Service Equipment to be worn, including overcoat, haversack, water-bottle, canteen, *full arms & ammunition*

Rations for...........*eight*...........hours to be carried.

Cycle Scouts to be mounted, and **ALL** men having cycles or motor cycles to bring them.

P. H. Pearse.
Captain or Officer Commanding.

Dated this...*12th*......day of...........*April*..........., 191*6*. -

2.75
Easter Sunday mobilisation order issued to E Company 4th Battalion Irish Volunteers, signed by Patrick Pearse.
HE:EW.2698

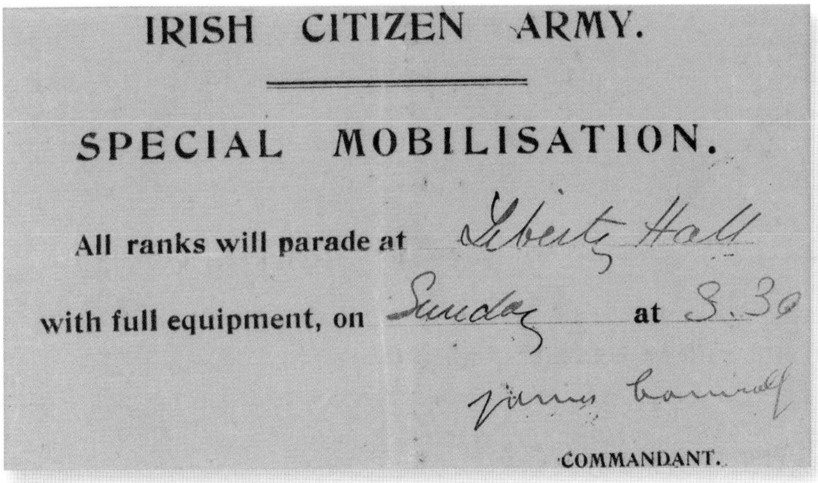

IRISH CITIZEN ARMY.

SPECIAL MOBILISATION.

All ranks will parade at *Liberty Hall*

with full equipment, on *Sunday* at *3.30*

James Connolly
COMMANDANT.

2.76
Easter Sunday mobilisation order issued to the Irish Citizen Army, signed by James Connolly.
HE:EW.162

on preventing the Rising taking place. Crucially, neither vessel could maintain radio contact with the mainland. Spindler's arrival in Tralee Bay on 20 April, on time according to his original instructions, thus, met no Volunteer response. Later that night, meanwhile, Casement and Monteith came ashore at Banna Strand. Casement was arrested by local RIC constables early on the morning of Friday 21, as Monteith was raising the alarm among the local Volunteers, Stack included. The increasingly disconcerted Spindler, meanwhile, sailed the 'Aud' aimlessly

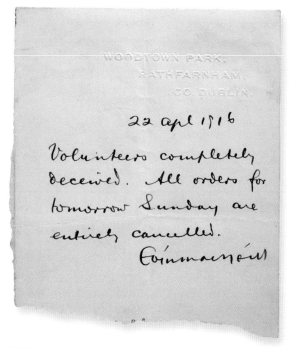

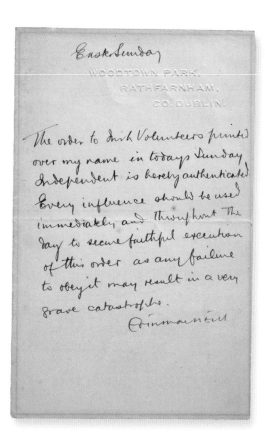

2.77
The countermanding
order issued by Eoin
MacNeill on 22 April
1916.
HE:EW.1127.3

2.78
A letter issued by Eoin
MacNeill on 23 April
1916 authenticating the
countermanding order
published in the *Sunday
Independent.*
HE:EW.372

along the Kerry coastline, intercepted eventually by British naval trawlers
who conveyed the boat to Queenstown. Here, Spindler scuttled the vessel
rather than have it commandeered by British forces. The famed German
arms consignment, 20,000 rifles and ten machine guns, went down with
the ship.

News of these events reached Dublin in their fullest form that
afternoon, Saturday 22 April. By then MacNeill had also learned of
the 'Castle document' forgery and Hobson's arrest. Combined, they
convinced the already pessimistic MacNeill that the Rising must not go
ahead: 'the enterprise was madness [and] would mean a slaughter of
unarmed men'. That evening he despatched The O'Rahilly and others
to circulate new countermanding orders to the provincial Volunteers, in
an attempt to prevent their mobilisation on Easter Sunday. Later still he
presented himself at the offices of the *Sunday Independent* with the imperative
of publishing a countermanding order in the following day's newspaper.

It was Eoin MacNeill's countermanding orders, in the minds of the Military Council, which most undermined the possibility of a successful Rising. The arrest of Casement had registered dismay and the loss of the German arms had, more gravely, instilled serious doubts about the scope for military action in provincial Ireland. However, it was MacNeill's countermanding orders which were the central point of discussion at an emergency meeting in Liberty Hall at 9.00 a.m. on Easter Sunday morning. The circulation of orders to provincial organisers, it was argued, was now unreliable, as MacNeill had influence over official channels. The printed countermanding order had been clear and authoritative. Its appearance in the *Sunday Independent*, moreover, created the very real possibility, for those inclined to believe the premise of the 'Castle Document', that the authorities would indeed attempt to suppress their movement. This possibility was heightened by the plausibility that Volunteers would begin attacks independently on Easter Sunday without waiting for further orders. After a heated discussion, the seven-man Military Council agreed, with only Thomas Clarke dissenting, to postpone military action until midday the following afternoon: Easter Monday, 24 April 1916.[222]

2.79
The trestle top table in Liberty Hall around which the leaders sat on Easter Monday morning and may have gathered around for their emergency meeting on Easter Sunday afternoon.
HE:EWL.132

3

EASTER WEEK

At 10.00 a.m. on Monday 24 April 1916, members of the Irish Volunteers, Irish Citizen Army and Fianna Éireann began to assemble at Beresford Place, Dublin, to take part in a Rising in the city. The 1916 Rising, and the Irish Republic which was proclaimed, would last for six days. Civilians and combatants experienced the conflict in real time: scene by scene, person by person, day by day. The following is a recreation of the world of Easter Week as it was lived by those who experienced it, exploring the tangible effects of life and death during the Rising.

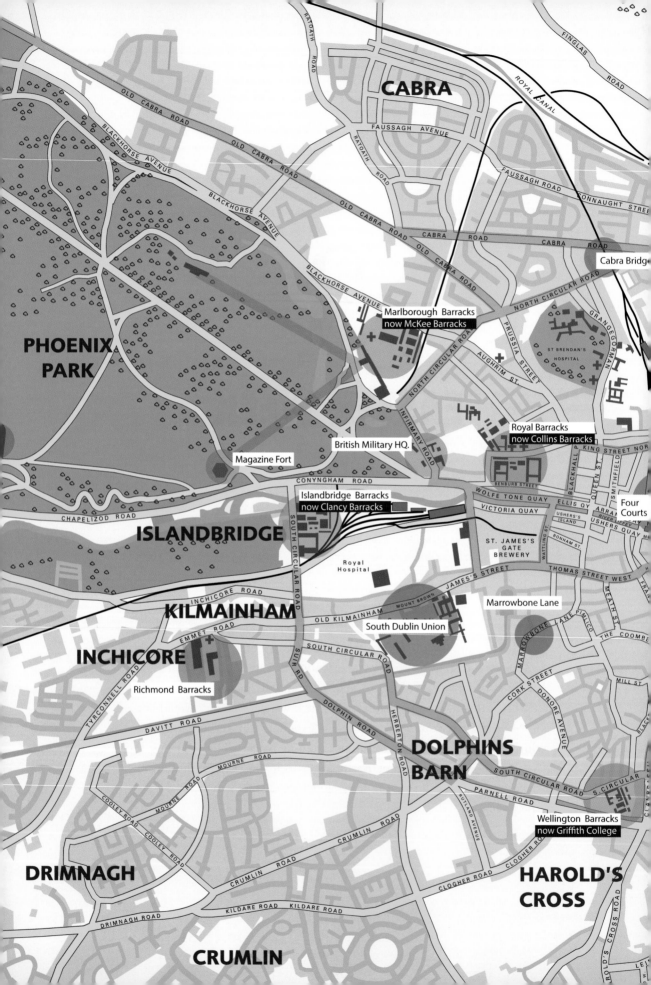

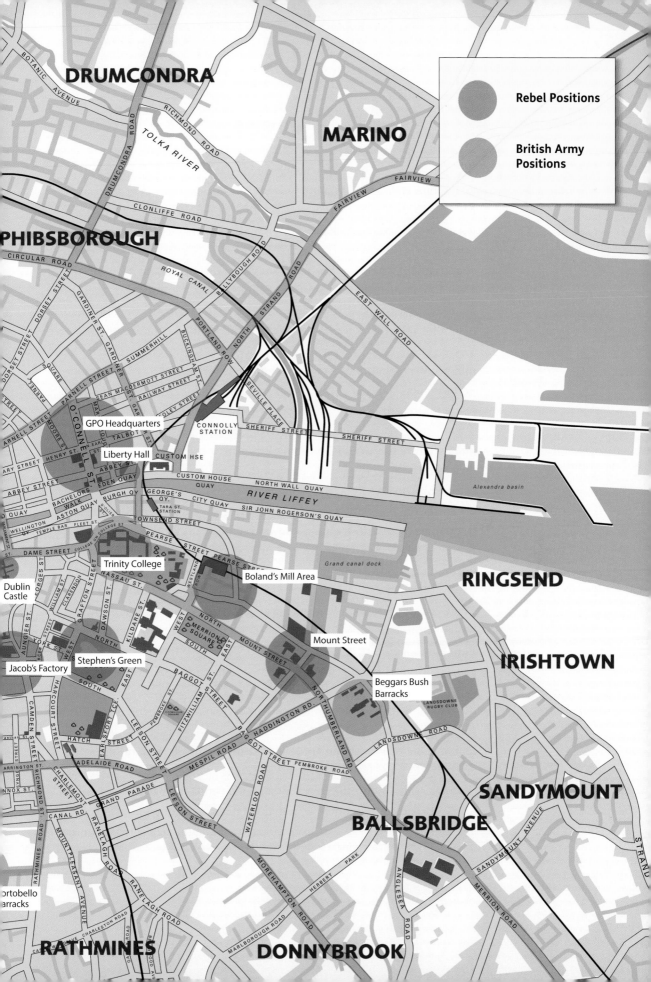

DRUMCONDRA

MARINO

PHIBSBOROUGH

Rebel Positions

British Army
Positions

BOTANIC AVENUE

DRUMCONDRA ROAD

RICHMOND ROAD

TOLKA RIVER

CLONLIFFE ROAD

FAIRVIEW

FAIRVIEW

CIRCULAR ROAD

ROYAL CANAL

DORSET STREET

DORSET STREET

GARDINER STREET

GARDINER ST

SUMMERHILL

BALLYBOUGH ROAD

STRAND ROAD

EAST WALL ROAD

PORTLAND ROW

NORTH

PARNELL STREET

PARNELL ST

SQUARE

MOORE'S ST

O'CONNELL ST

SEAN MACDERMOTT STREET

RAILWAY STREET

FOLEY STREET

BUCKINGHAM ST

SEVILLE PLACE

O'CONNELL ST

GPO Headquarters

TALBOT ST

CONNOLLY
STATION

HENRY STREET

ABBEY ST

Liberty Hall

CUSTOM HSE

SHERIFF STREET

SHERIFF STREET

MARY STREET

ABBEY STREET

EDEN QUAY

BACHELORS

WALK

BURGH QY

CUSTOM HOUSE

QUAY

NORTH WALL QUAY

ASTON QUAY

GEORGE'S

QY.

CITY QUAY

Alexandra basin

QUAY

WELLINGTON

QY

TEMPLE BAR

FLEET ST

COLLEGE

ST

TARA ST

STATION

SIR JOHN ROGERSON'S QUAY

RIVER LIFFEY

TOWNSEND STREET

DAME STREET

COLLEGE GN COLLEGE ST

PEARSE

STREET

PEARSE STREET

Grand canal dock

RINGSEND

GEORGES ST

Trinity College

NASSAU ST.

WESTLAND

Dublin
Castle

CLARENDON

GRAFTON STREET

KILDARE ST.

DAWSON ST.

NORTH

MERRION

SQUARE

Boland's Mill Area

AUNGIER ST

WILLIAM ST

NORTH

WEST

SOUTH

EAST

MOUNT STREET

YORK ST.

Mount Street

IRISHTOWN

Jacob's Factory

Stephen's Green

SOUTH

EAST

BAGGOT STREET

NORTHUMBERLAND RD.

Beggars Bush
Barracks

LANDSDOWNE
RUGBY CLUB

CAMDEN STREET

HARCOURT STREET

EARLSFORT TCE.

LEESON STREET

PEMBROKE ST

FITZWILLIAM

FITZWILLIAM SQUARE

LANDSDOWNE ROAD

HATCH

ADELAIDE ROAD

MESPIL ROAD

HADDINGTON RD.

BAGGOT STREET PEMBROKE ROAD

SANDYMOUNT

CHARLEMONT

STREET

GRAND PARADE

LEESON STREET

WATERLOO ROAD

PARK

HERBERT

SANDYMOUNT AVENUE

MERRION ROAD

STRAND

CANAL RD

RANELAGH ROAD

MOREHAMPTON ROAD

ANGLESEA ROAD

MOUNTPLEASANT AVENUE

ortobello
arracks

BALLSBRIDGE

RATHMINES

DONNYBROOK

MONDAY

3.0
(Page 80)
The Birth of
the Republic by
Walter Paget.
HE:EWP.23

3.1
(Pages 82 & 83)
Map of Dublin city
showing rebel and
British Army positions
during Easter Week.

'Bill we are going out to be slaughtered', James Connolly confessed to his labour colleague William O'Brien outside Liberty Hall on Easter Monday morning. 'Is there no chance of success?' O'Brien asked. 'None whatever'.[1] Connolly's depressed view of the military situation facing the rebels following the failure of the German arms venture and the countermanding order, has contributed to the prevailing view of the 1916 Rising as a 'blood sacrifice' military action. Earlier thoughts (or fantasies) of a symbolic revolt had almost certainly become the hardened reality for members of the Military Council by the beginning of Easter Week. The attendant corollary, advanced by some scholars, that the military strategy implemented by the rebels formed part of a dramatic performance staged on the streets of the capital,[2] however, has been revised in recent works. 'The rebels who went out to do battle', Charles Townshend has surmised, 'shared one expectation: that the British military response would be rapid and hard. This may have influenced their choice of positions and procedures in ways that cannot be exactly clarified.'[3] Dublin's four Irish Volunteer battalions, it has been suggested, occupied buildings which seemed to indicate an attempt to block British troop movement into the city. The 1st Battalion under the command of Edward Daly occupied the Four Courts building and a series of outposts northwards along Church Street with the view seemingly to cutting off British troops at Athlone arriving via Broadstone station. Thomas MacDonagh's 2nd battalion took over Jacob's Biscuit Factory on Bishop Street with the intention, it has been posited, to hinder troop movement from Portobello barracks. The 3rd battalion led by Éamon de Valera, principally garrisoned at Boland's Mill, was intended to cover the southeast reaches of the city with the view to preventing the movement into the city of British Army reinforcements arriving at Kingstown harbour. Meanwhile, Éamonn Ceannt's 4th battalion, who occupied the South Dublin Union, was stated to have had the remit of preventing troops entering the city from Richmond barracks. These strategic positions, however, were undermined by fundamental problems. Daly's men failed to take Broadstone station and remained detached from Thomas Ashe's 5th battalion to the north. MacDonagh's garrison neglected to seize sufficient outposts to block troop movement in the area. Meanwhile de Valera and Ceannt were both overextended in terms of the areas they had to cover. All the garrisons, furthermore, went into the conflict with less manpower than expected.[4] However, if the Four Courts, Jacob's Factory, Boland's Mill and South Dublin Union could be ascribed a loose strategic rationale, other positions had less obvious military value.

At 11.50 a.m. James Connolly, Patrick Pearse and Joseph Plunkett led approximately 150 men from Liberty Hall to Sackville Street whereupon the order was given: 'Left Wheel!-The GPO!-Charge!' Clarke and Mac Diarmada, who had arrived by motor car in advance of the party, watched the rebels rush the GPO and evacuate the building of employees and customers (a number of British soldiers were held as prisoners). Connolly's gunshot warning 'everybody out!' cleared the remaining stragglers. Connolly served as Commandant-General of the Dublin Brigade, and thus became the rebel's de facto military leader during Easter Week, although Pearse held the title of 'Commander in Chief of the Irish Republican Forces'. All rebels under their command henceforth collectively formed the 'Army of the Irish Republic'. The other members of the Military Council based at the GPO assumed less central military roles during the fighting. Work began immediately to construct defensive barricades around smashed-out window frames in the GPO. W.J. Brennan-Whitmore recalled

the scene: 'every kind of material had to be hastily pressed into doing duty – books, ledgers, pads of money orders, telegram pads, files of correspondence, tables, loose desks'.[5] Later that afternoon Brennan-Whitmore and others were tasked with the construction of street barricades using assorted material from establishments along Sackville

3.2
Despite believing the Rising to have no chance of success, The O'Rahilly arrived at Liberty Hall on Easter Monday morning: 'I've helped to wind up the clock – I might as well hear it strike.' He wound up his De Dion-Bouton motor car with this starting handle and drove to the GPO, parking on Prince's Street.
HE:EWL.173

3.3
The burnt-out remains of The O'Rahilly's motor car on Prince's Street.
HE:EWP.30

Street. Outposts were also taken at Kelly's gunpowder store ('Kelly's Fort') and the Hopkins & Hopkins jewellery store, both on the corners of lower Sackville Street. The fortification of the Sackville Street area corresponded with Connolly's earlier advocacy of city-based defensive warfare. This seemed to be borne out at approximately 1.15 pm when four lancers, sent out from Marlborough barracks to establish what was taking place, were fired upon by the rebels in the GPO. Three of the British soldiers were killed and another later died of his wounds. Charles Townshend has argued that the GPO was 'unquestionably' a strong position in the sense that the 'British forces never even considered trying to assault it directly'.[6] Fearghal McGarry, however, has inclined to the view that the action around the GPO was 'ultimate street-theatre, orchestrated by a Military Council dominated by dramatists'.[7] It was the latter which was most in evidence on the afternoon of Easter Monday.

Just after 3 p.m. the ever-reliable Seán T. O'Kelly was despatched by James Connolly to Liberty Hall to retrieve two flags, accidentally left behind during the earlier mobilisation. Soon after, on his return, the flags were hoisted simultaneously above the GPO.[8] The Irish Republic flag was raised above the Prince's St corner of the Post Office building.[9] According to Harry Walpole the flag had been made at Fry's Poplin Factory on Cork Street. The gloriously named Theobald Wolfe Tone Fitzgerald painted the letters 'Irish Republic' onto the banner at the home of Countess Markievicz where it hung on the wall of her top bedroom for a week before the Rising.[10] The second flag, a tricolour of green, white and orange, was flown over the Henry Street corner of the GPO.[11] While debates among veterans over the positions and personnel involved continued well after the Rising, there was little doubt about the distinction of the flags flying above the city centre at the time. Writing on the significance of flags in conflict, Iver Neumann has commented: 'the basic function it had on the battlefield, [was] namely separating "us" from "them"'.[12] Several rebels recall the flying of the Irish Republic and Irish tricolor flags, as opposed to the reading of the Proclamation, as the legitimate moment of the Rising. 'What caught my attention, however, and fairly astonished me because, despite having already been in action, I had not wakened fully to the reality of the business,' Charles Saurin confirmed 'was the sight of the green flag and the Tricolour flying over the GPO.'[13] Patrick Caldwell made a similar observation: 'the fact that the Irish Flag was flying on this particular building was the first

clear indication I had that a Rising was in progress'.[14] However, flags also traditionally served 'as rallying points – emblems or images around which allies could gather on the battlefield or at times of crisis'.[15] This was also later attested to by rebels. The Louth-based Seán MacEntee, who had walked to Dublin that afternoon after earlier taking two RIC constables prisoner at Castlebellingham, remembered his relief on finally locating the rebel garrison: 'Never have I beheld so brave a flag, such rich, bright green, such deep, living orange.'[16] Many others belatedly arrived at the GPO having not received mobilisation orders in time, or were moved by a sense of loyalty to the cause or to those involved. It was only after repeated representations were made that members of Cumann na mBan were officially allowed into the GPO that evening. Here they joined Elizabeth O'Farrell, Julia Grenan and Winifred Carney (James Connolly's secretary), already stationed at the GPO. Éamon de Valera was notable, among the other garrison commandants, for refusing to allow women to serve as part of the Boland's Mill garrison.[17] Women, however, did mobilise on Easter Monday within units of the Irish Citizen Army.

3.4
The 'Irish Republic' flag flown over the Prince's Street corner of the GPO during Easter Week.
HE:EW.3224

As James Connolly led his group to the GPO on Monday, a smaller detachment, comprising thirty members of the Irish Citizen Army, were marched by Seán Connolly towards Dublin Castle. Dublin Metropolitan Police Constable James O'Brien was on duty at the Castle Gate when Connolly's group approached, just before midday. As O'Brien tried to prevent their entry, Connolly drew his revolver and shot him from point-blank range. Within Dublin Castle, the Under Secretary Matthew Nathan was in conference with Sir Arthur Hamilton Norway (Manager of the General Post Office) and Ivor Price (British Intelligence Officer for Ireland). 'They have commenced', Norway exclaimed on hearing the firing. His later assessment of the parlous situation facing the Dublin Castle authorities is striking: 'They [the rebels] could have done it as easily as possible [seized the Castle]. Twenty-five determined men could have done it. I think there was only a corporal's guard there at the time.'[18] Price emerged into the Castle Yard firing at the rebels with his revolver. Although they had overcome six soldiers in the adjacent guardroom, Connolly's armed force unexpectedly retreated. Instead they took command of a number of buildings around Parliament and Dame Street, including City Hall and the offices of the *Dublin Express* newspaper. Connolly's decision not to press on with the assault on Dublin Castle has confounded explanation. Some veterans later claimed that the scale of the Castle grounds would have made it indefensible for Connolly's small party.[19] However, Fearghal McGarry has provided a persuasive argument for the merits of even occupying the building: 'Not only would its seizure have represented a tremendous propaganda coup, it would have netted leading members of the Irish administration and provided the rebels with a strategically important stronghold … the Military Council must have considered the possibility at some length.'[20] It took another two hours for British reinforcements to arrive at the Castle.

At 11.40 a.m., meanwhile, Commandant Michael Mallin had led a force of approximately forty rebels from Liberty Hall to St Stephen's Green via Westmoreland and Grafton Street. The predominant Irish Citizen Army force was supplemented by members of the Irish Volunteers, Cumann na mBan and Fianna Éireann. Originally a despatch carrier, Countess Markievicz was appointed Mallin's second-in-command following her later arrival. Their objective ostensibly was to secure and defend the Green. The strategic significance of this location remains open to interpretation. Charles Townshend has referred to the area as a 'transport hub' to the city centre while Paul O'Brien has described it as a connector between the Jacob's and Boland's Mill garrisons.[21] On Mallin's orders the rebels cleared St Stephen's Green of civilians, closed its gates and dug defensive trenches near its entrances. Barricades were constructed in the surrounding streets using commandeered motor vehicles, carts and furniture. By Monday afternoon, armed rebels were positioned along the railings and shrubbery on the north side of the Green, facing the Shelbourne Hotel. The tactics employed at the St Stephen's Green garrison have never been satisfactorily explained. Michael Mallin, a highly-respected commandant with military experience, declined to take the Shelbourne Hotel, the dominant building overlooking the rebels' positions. Frank Robbins attributed Mallin's inaction to the garrison's depleted numbers.[22] Others have judged it a damaging tactical oversight.[23] Still more perplexing was the decision to dig trenches at the entrances to St Stephen's Green. It is unclear if this was part of the original Military Council plan, or was Mallin's own initiative; he had experienced trench warfare during British Army service in India.[24] F.X. Martin would later describe it as 'the high point of futility'.[25] Without cover from the Shelbourne Hotel, the rebels were fatally exposed.

3.5
Michael Mallin,
Commandant of the
St Stephen's Green
garrison.
HE:EW.2754

The St Stephen's Green area was notable for its violence on the first day of the Rising. On 24 April, twelve police and civilians were shot by rebel forces, resulting in three fatalities.[26] One of those killed was Michael Cavanagh, a guest in the Shelbourne, whose lorry of theatrical props had been commandeered by members of the garrison to form part of their makeshift barricades. At approximately 5.00 p.m. he attempted to retrieve his vehicle but was shot in the head by at least one of the rebels. His killing in broad daylight on a busy Dublin street was reported on by different witnesses. The differentiation in these accounts offers an insight into how incidents during the Rising were represented (and misrepresented) from different perspectives. James Stephens (local resident): 'He [Cavanagh] walked directly to the barricade. He stopped

3.7
(Opposite page)
Countess Markievicz's
bandolier with pouches for
ammunition.
HE:EWL.222.2

3.8
(Opposite page)
The fedora hat worn by
James Connolly during
Easter Week. A bullet hole
can be seen in the rim.
HE:EW.251

3.9
(Opposite page)
The Irish Volunteers
military uniform worn by
some during the Rising.
HE:1917.109

3.6
The wristwatch worn
by Countess Markievicz
during Easter Week.
HE:EWL.5

and gripped the shafts of a lorry … armed men appeared at the railings "put down that lorry. Let out and get away"… he [Cavanagh] did not attend to them … the man slowly drew his cart down by the footpath. Then three shots rang out in succession. At the distance he could not be missed, and it was obvious they were trying to frighten him … he walked over to the Volunteers … ten guns were pointing at him, and a voice repeated many times: "Go and put back that lorry or you are a dead man. Go before I count four. One, two, three, four …" A rifle spat at him, and in two undulating movements the man sank on himself and sagged to the ground.'[27] Alfred Fannin (local resident): 'Mrs. Travers Smith told Nan yesterday that she saw a driver of a lorry shot dead near the Shelbourne because he refused to give up his lorry, it was three times demanded and then they shot him.'[28] An *Irish Times* reporter: 'He [Cavanagh] was coming up to the Shelbourne Hotel to submit some theatrical scenery to actors who are staying in the hotel, when he was stopped and ordered to get down off the vehicle on which he was seated. His response to the order was apparently not quick enough to satisfy the rebels and he was shot dead.'[29]

Inconsistencies of account surround another fatal incident at St Stephen's Green. Countess Markievicz has long been associated with the killing of D.M.P. Constable Michael Lahiff in narratives of the Rising. Constable Lahiff was found in a pool of blood near Fusiliers' Arch just after midday on Easter Monday. One eyewitness placed Markievicz at the scene, running through the Green exuberantly shouting 'I got him.'[30] This evidence has been generally accepted by authors such as Max Caulfield who has reprinted this single oral testimony in his account of the Rising. However, no substantiating evidence has been brought to bear on this claim. Indeed later research has suggested that Markievicz was actually at City Hall at the alleged time of the incident.[31]

Constance Markievicz was one of the most provocative figures of Easter Week. Several civilian accounts refer to her military bearing as she paced around St Stephen's Green, suggesting in passing that she was in fact the commandant of the garrison.[32] Such inferences may have derived in part from the military materials which she was wearing. During Easter Week Markievicz donned dark-green-coloured breeches and an Irish Citizen Army tunic, topped with a feathered lady's hat. A bandolier filled with ammunition was draped across her body. A number of rebels recalled seeing Markievicz during Easter Week; more specifically their recollection was of Markievicz in uniform: 'I remember Madame was prominent in her uniform and revolver'; 'saw the Countess in her uniform'; 'she was in a uniform with a feather in her hat. She looked defiant'.[33] Markievicz's aura of authority was self-made. Helena Molony described Markievicz's careful assembly of her garments for the Rising ('she always liked militarism') while Nancy Wyse-Power recalled Markievicz's 'childish delight' when parading her uniform.[34] Others self-consciously bore the trappings of what has been termed the 'citizen soldier'. Both Thomas Clarke and Seán Mac Diarmada wore civilian suits while James Connolly sported a fedora hat during Easter Week. The rebels' civilian apparel would be commented upon by a number of eye witnesses concerned over the British Army's inability to read the difference between civilian and combatant.[35]

The civilian appearance of the conflict was further manifest with the killing of members of the Dublin Volunteer Training Corps by members of the Boland's Mill Garrison. Although Éamon de Valera's battalion had mustered less than 130 men, they occupied a wide area near Boland's Mill, including outposts at Westland Row Station and Mount Street. The latter was under the command of Michael Malone who placed fourteen rebels in buildings along Lower Mount Street. Just after 3.00 p.m., a group of Dublin's Volunteer Training Corps passed through the area. This was an unarmed home guard

3.10
Armlet with the letter
GR worn by the
Georgius Rex.
HE:EW.1078.1

of civilians above military age. Wearing civilian clothes with a 'GR' armlet ['Georgius Rex'], they had come to be known humorously as the 'Gorgeous Wrecks' by the citizens of Dublin. Returning to Beggars Bush barracks following training in the Wicklow Mountains, they were fired upon by the rebels. Four were killed and a further three were wounded.[36]

Transport around the city was less dangerous for rebels than their opponents. Only four hundred Irish-based British Army troops were in the city's garrisons as the rebellion broke out while later that afternoon the Dublin Metropolitan Police recalled constables from uniformed duty in the capital. In the absence of train and tram services, cut off in parts by the rebels themselves, the bicycle became a key mode of movement from one garrison to the next. Michael Walker, who had represented Great Britain as a cyclist at the 1912 Olympic Games in Stockholm, was mobilised to Jacob's Factory on Easter Monday. His main role was to courier despatches between garrison posts. On the same

3.11
Terence Simpson joined
the Rising on Easter
Monday, arriving at
Jacob's Biscuit Factory
from Drumcondra on
this bicycle.
HE:EW.1088

day, meanwhile, James Connolly's daughters, Nora and Ina, travelled to Coalisland, Co. Tyrone, from Liberty Hall with fresh orders for mobilisation in Ulster. On Holy Saturday Patrick McCartan and Dennis McCullough had sent several couriers to Dublin seeking confirmation of Pearse and Connolly's January orders. By then, over one hundred Belfast Volunteers were mobilised in Co. Tyrone. Casement's arrest and Eoin MacNeill's countermanding order, however, convinced McCartan against carrying out the original plan. Frustrated by the inaction of the Tyrone leadership and the incoherence of news from Dublin, McCullough ordered his men back to Belfast on Easter Sunday. Nora and Ina Connolly's despatch instructed the rebels in Ulster to carry out attacks on railway bridges and police barracks in order to delay troop movement towards Dublin. Confused, the Tyrone leadership decided not to re-mobilise the Volunteers. McCullough would be later arrested in Belfast on Friday of Easter week, while McCartan went on the run.[37] Others, however, took advantage of the relative ease of movement between the capital and the country. Having learned that the Rising had begun, on Monday afternoon, fifteen Volunteers, including Domhnall O'Buachalla, walked from Maynooth to Dublin city centre, arriving at the GPO well after midnight.[38]

The suspension of public transport was frequently cited within civilian accounts as the first inclination that something was afoot in Dublin. Those travelling from the suburbs were particularly dependant on tram and train services: 'things must be really serious, no trams running'.[39] Arrival in the city centre brought further confusion. Witnesses noted the general absence of motor cars in the streets while significant venues were unexpectedly closed. The playwright Joseph Holloway was disconcerted to find both the Empire and Abbey theatres unavailable.[40] The antagonistic

3.12
On Easter Monday afternoon the National Museum was closed because of its proximity to the fighting at Kildare Street. Assistant Keeper Liam Gógan placed this sign on the front door.
DA-820-A-1916

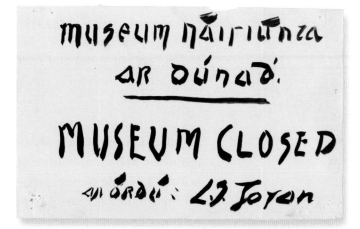

reaction of Dublin civilians to the Rising has been well documented. Rebels at the Four Courts, Jacob's Biscuit Factory and South Dublin Union remembered the opposition of locals on Easter Monday, particularly that of women.[41] Criticism of the rebels in the St Stephen's Green area has also been reinforced by numerous civilian accounts.[42] That this reaction was prevalent near garrisons themselves is hardly surprising. The rebels' actions of seizing public buildings or public space, commandeering vehicles, household items and personal effects for the creation of barricades and the general disruption and danger caused by their presence in those areas inevitably prompted hostility. James Stephens' survey of public opinion at St Stephen's Green, following the killing of Michael Cavanagh, was timely: 'at that moment the Volunteers were hated'.[43] The response of wider Dublin opinion is less perceptible. A number of civilians wandering the city expressed less explicit views of the rebels. One priest who had made his way to St Stephen's Green that afternoon recorded: 'They [the rebels] didn't hinder us passing and were very civil and respectful.'[44] Joseph Holloway recounted a rebel conversing with him at George's Street corner: 'Firing is going on in many places but you are safe where you are.'[45] Seventeen-year-old Michael Taafe, residing in Donnybrook, wrote presciently of Dublin's civilians needing 'time to sort out their feelings regarding the unexpected and catastrophic phenomenon of the Rebellion'.[46]

Many of the contemporary accounts of Easter Monday are primarily descriptive. Beyond the immediacy of the city's garrisons, it would seem, it took civilians time to offer an informed opinion of events. Walking through the city, Ernie O'Malley soaked up the atmosphere 'rumours circulated and recirculated, changing as they passed on … all through the evening rumour passed on rumour'.[47] Some suggested that 16,000 Germans had landed at Bantry Bay, others that rebels had come out in Cork, Limerick and Belfast simultaneously; others still that Dublin Castle had indeed been taken.[48] More wildly, some heard that a whale had escaped from Dublin zoo and was swimming down the River Liffey devouring civilians![49] The majority of those living in the capital returned to their homes without answers to the day's questions. Reflecting on the tumultuous events of 24 April, one civilian concluded succinctly 'At the moment the city is no longer under British rule; this night at least, the Republican flag floats over its centre.'[50]

TUESDAY

Tuesday morning brought little relief to Dublin's civilians. Many who lived near the GPO, Boland's Mill and St Stephen's Green garrisons remembered a sleepless night, the sound of bullets close by keeping residents awake.[51] Across the city, meanwhile, people woke up to a disorientating news shortage. Neither the *Freeman's Journal* nor the *Irish Independent* went to press on 25 April on account of their proximity to the disturbances at Prince's Street and Sackville Street respectively. Of the Dublin dailies, only the *Irish Times* was published on the second day of the Rising. In its limited coverage of 'the outbreak' it outlined the failed attempt to take Dublin Castle, the seizure of City Hall, Harcourt Street Station, Westland Row Station and the St Stephen's Green area. Fighting, it reported, continued at the South Dublin Union while incidents around the GPO were reported.[52] This issue appears to have had little impact on the public beyond the north city. Diarists in Merrion Square, Ballsbridge and Blackrock wrote frustratingly on the absence of information in their areas: 'there were no newspapers to be got, no post, no trams, no trains running, no telegraphs or telephones, but an air of suspense and uncertainty, over everyone'.[53] The desire for news drew people across the river. Many spoke of the irresistible allure of the city centre: 'people were sucked as it were by a whirl-pool into places of extreme danger by an indomitable spirit of curiosity and excitement'.[54] Some were determined to see action. William Cant, residing in the North Circular Road, brought his friend Molly into the city as the latter 'wanted to see some excitement, and by jingo she got it'. The two took in Henry Street and Sackville Street (including a chance encounter with James Connolly) and adjourned to the Gresham for lunch, before observing the fighting at City Hall, clamouring over barricades at Phibsboro before completing their day at 6.00 p.m.: 'we reached home tired out'.[55] In the absence of mainstream news the anecdotes of rebellion tourists, conflated and contorted by local rumour, formed an unreliable social media within the capital.

The rebel leaders in the GPO attempted to fill this vacuum. On Tuesday an improvised propaganda news-sheet entitled *Irish War News* was issued in the capital. This had been written by Pearse early on

IRISH WAR NEWS

THE IRISH REPUBLIC.

Vol. I. No. 1   DUBLIN, TUESDAY, APRIL 25, 1916.   One Penny

"IF THE GERMANS CONQUERED ENGLAND."

In the London "New Statesman" for *April 1st*, an article is published—"If the Germans Conquered England," which has the appearance of a very clever piece of satire written by an Irishman. The writer draws a picture of England under German rule, almost every detail of which exactly fits the case of Ireland at the present day. Some of the sentences are so exquisitely appropriate that it is impossible to believe that the writer had not Ireland in his mind when he wrote them. For instance :—

"England would be constantly irritated by the lofty moral utterances of German statesmen who would assert—quite sincerely, no doubt—that England was free, freer indeed than she had ever been before. Prussian freedom, they would explain, was the only real freedom, and therefore England was free. They would point to the flourishing railways and farms and colleges. They would possibly point to the contingent of M.P's, which was permitted, in spite of its deplorable disorderliness, to sit in a permanent minority in the Reich-

stag. And not only would the Englishman have to listen to a constant flow of speeches of this sort ; he would find a respectable official Press secret bought over by the Government to say the same kind of things over and over, every day of the week. He would find, too, that his children were coming home from school with new ideas of history. They would ask him if it was true that until the Germans came England had been an unruly country, constantly engaged in civil war. . . . The object of every schoolbook would be to make the English child grow up in the notion that the history of his country was a thing to forget, and that the one bright spot in it was the fact that it had been conquered by cultured Germany."

"If there was a revolt, German statesmen would deliver grave speeches about "disloyalty," "ingratitude," "reckless agitators who would ruin their country's prosperity. . . . Prussian soldiers would be encamped in every barracks—the English conscripts having been sent out of the country to be trained in Germany, or to fight the Chinese—in order to come to the aid of German morality, should English sedition come to blows with it."

"England would be exhorted to abandon her own genius in order to imitate the genius of her conquerors, to forget her own history for a larger history, to give up her own language for a "universal" language—in other words, to destroy her household gods one by one, and put in their place

The first issue of the *Irish War News* dated 25 April 1916.
HE:2007.1.3

Tuesday morning, with possible input from Connolly, and printed in nearby Halston Street by Joseph Stanley and a team of compositors and printers.[56] A 'stop press' bulletin, it included news of the declaration of the Irish Republic, the names of those constituting the Provisional Government and a round-up of rebel military successes in the city. The people of Dublin, it stated further, were 'plainly with the Republic'.[57] It was an audacious if auspicious project. Pearse was later criticised by some contemporaries for his pre-occupation with writing 'memoranda couched in poetic phrases' during Easter Week but keeping up morale is an important aspect of military leadership, a characteristic acknowledged by others.[58] Moreover, rumours of military successes circulated widely in the GPO on Tuesday: 'stories of the progress of events in other centres came up to us from below of the most varied and sometimes fantastic nature – some said the Germans had landed here, there and everywhere – a German submarine was coming up the Liffey – the Volunteers were marching up from the country, the whole of the country was up in arms and so on'.[59] In reality the Rising was stillborn in many parts of the country, notably in Munster. In Cork, over one thousand Volunteers had assembled on Easter Sunday under the command of Tomás MacCurtain. However, having received nine confusing or contradictory despatches from Dublin, the Cork leadership decided against fighting during Easter Week. Despatches to Dublin, along with correspondence from the equally inactive Cork and Kerry units, also heightened the paralysis of the Limerick Volunteers. The failure of the arms landing during Holy Week appears to have been a significant factor in the Munster leaders' respective decisions. Without them, the fighting in Dublin could appear sacrificial.[60]

This was already becoming apparent at certain Dublin garrisons. At 4.00 a.m. on Tuesday morning, British machine-gunners, who had slipped into the Shelbourne Hotel unnoticed, opened fire on the St Stephen's Green garrison from the fourth-floor windows. By 8.00 a.m., Mallin had ordered the garrison to evacuate, the rebels escaping to the nearby Royal College of Surgeons, previously taken by the Citizen Army. Later, tunnels were dug through adjoining buildings in the direction of Grafton Street, in an attempt to tackle British machine-gunners. However, the garrison remained under intense fire, as did the Royal College of Surgeons, for the rest of Easter Week. By Thursday it would lose all communication with the GPO. The City Hall garrison was experiencing a similar fate. British Army reinforcements to Dublin Castle on Easter Monday had seen fierce fighting with the rebels. The 10th Battalion Royal Dublin Fusiliers from the Royal barracks, and other troops coming in from the Curragh, surrounded City Hall; the battle intensified and within hours Seán Connolly had been killed. Despite the arrival of reinforcements and the continuation of fighting at the Exchange Hotel on Parliament Street, the garrison was forced to surrender late on Tuesday morning.

3.14
The barricaded doorway of the Royal College of Surgeons.
HE:EW.1606.2

Not all of the rebel positions suffered early defeat or even heavy fighting. The garrison at Jacob's Biscuit Factory was at a physical remove from much of the conflict during Easter Week. Led by Thomas MacDonagh, and his second in command John MacBride, an approximate 150-strong band of Irish Volunteers, Irish Citizen Army, Fianna Éireann and Cumann na mBan, had taken the Factory on Bishop Street just after midday on Monday. While shots were fired at a passing convoy of British troops within an hour of their occupation, most of the rebels saw no action during Easter Week, an experience frustratingly documented in later accounts. 'The only inconvenience to us', Michael Molloy recorded, 'was that the lights were turned off from the Power Station and we had to use candles which we got from Jacob's.'[61] Alleviating the monotony of checking defensive positions and weaponry became an essential feature of everyday life at the garrison. An old piano was discovered in an upper floor and played to offset the noise

3.15
A chess board found in
Jacob's Biscuit Factory
after the surrender.
HE:EW.2429

3.16
A toffee axe thrown at
a civilian during the
looting on Sackville
Street.
HE:EW.5699

of fighting elsewhere in the city, a makeshift library was established within the building while a miniature ceilidh was held on one occasion.[62] The rebels were also relatively well off for supplies. When the novelty of the Factory's ready-made supply of confectionary, cakes and tea wore off, meat, milk and vegetables were commandeered from local shops and civilians in the area.[63]

The act of seizing property was more problematic in the surrounds of the GPO garrison. The removal of the Dublin Metropolitan Police from the streets had opened the floodgates for civilians to descend on the north side's commercial thoroughfares. Looting of shops and outlets began late on Monday night but became most visible during Tuesday. It was widely recorded in fellow civilian testimony: 'The motley loot that came hurtling and splintering through the crowds waiting ravenously below – picture-frames, ornamental knick-knacks, books, toilet outfits, royalty on postcards, Teddy Bears, hand-cameras. It rained fountain pens.'; 'The looters took everything … clothing, boots and shoes from True Form … one old woman … was heard to exclaim angrily "The bloody robbers. They've only left odd ones!"'; 'awful looting of Lawrence's toy shop, about 2,000 women and children and some men fighting like fiends for possession of the various articles … it was a sight to see the arms full of pictures and toys carried away by the crowd'.[64] The propensity of references to women and children looters seems to have been fairly representative of the scenes, although as Fearghal McGarry has noted, class differences may have coloured the criticism of diarists.[65] The social deprivation of residents has been presented as a mobilising factor behind the looting of Sackville Street and adjoining areas.[66] However, the actions of the rebels themselves may also have offered a perverse rationale for looting. Seizing public buildings,

3.17
A cricket bat from the window of Elvery's sport shop on Sackville Street, with a bullet lodged in the spine.
HE:EW.5142

commandeering vehicles and assembling barricades from civilian property set a dangerous precedent for others to follow. Indeed many of the early newspaper reports described the first day of the rebellion as a 'riot'.[67] In this context the response of the rebels to the looters may have further shaped civilian attitudes to the Rising. The leadership in the GPO was frustrated with the outbreak of looting. In the 'Manifesto to the Citizens of Dublin', read out on Sackville Street that evening, Pearse alluded directly to the scenes: 'such looting as has already occurred has been done by hangers-on of the British Army. Ireland must keep her new honour unsmirched'.[68] Meanwhile, both Connolly and Mac Diarmada were reported to have remonstrated with the looters.[69] Other rebels shot above looting civilians in an attempt to discourage their behaviour.[70] Rumours that the rebels were shooting at civilian looters had formed a strong part of public opinion towards the Rising on Tuesday evening. Across the river in the St Stephen's Green area, James Stephens recorded, 'it was current that the Volunteers had shot twenty of the looters'.[71] At Portobello Bridge it was said that 'civilians including women and children were also being deliberately shot'.[72] News of the shooting of the unarmed Georgius Rex, meanwhile, reached some for the first time.[73] While other commentators discharged the rebels from accusations of deliberately targeting civilians, they were nonetheless frequently blamed for what was termed 'desultory shootings' in the city.[74] Several diarists recorded cases of friends, family and neighbours having been killed or injured by flying bullets or shrapnel: 'every day we heard of the death of some of our friends'.[75] Many civilians, moreover, were

3.18
The Irish Women's
Franchise League badge
worn by Francis Sheehy-
Skeffington on the day
of his arrest.
HE:EWL.336.2

traumatised by the death and destruction instigated by the Rising's occurrence: 'some limp victim to hospital, face and clothes running blood', 'sickening sight of corpses littering the streets', 'dead horses, dead Sinn Feiners'.[76]

Others attempted to police the increasingly reckless civilian looters. Armed with wooden batons provided by Pearse, Jeremiah O'Leary and a group of volunteers had attempted to disperse the crowds along Sackville Street and Earl Street on Monday night but gave up after a few hours.[77] Others were more persistent. Francis Sheehy-Skeffington, who had been in Dublin city raising a civilian force to prevent looting, was arrested on Tuesday and brought to Portobello barracks. That evening, Captain John Bowen-Colthurst led forty soldiers from Portobello barracks into the city centre, carrying Sheehy-Skeffington as hostage. On Rathmines Road, Bowen-Colthurst shot and killed 19-year-old James Coade and Volunteer Richard O'Carroll. The troops also entered the tobacconist shop of Alderman James Kelly and arrested journalists Thomas Dickson and Patrick McIntyre. The next morning, Bowen-Colthurst ordered Sheehy-Skeffington, Dickson and McIntyre to be brought to the yard in Portobello barracks, where they were shot by firing squad. Their bodies were hastily buried in the barracks grounds.

3.19
A bullet fired during the
execution of Francis
Sheehy-Skeffington
lodged in a brick behind
him along Portobello
barracks wall.
HE:EW.683

WEDNESDAY

The Rising transitioned sharply from civil conflict to military conflict on Wednesday of Easter Week. Brigadier General William Lowe had arrived early on Tuesday to take command of the military situation. By Wednesday morning, the existing three thousand troops were being reinforced by arrivals from Britain. Meanwhile, Lord Lieutenant Wimborne's declaration of Martial Law the previous evening was widely circulated on Wednesday morning. Civilians in Dublin woke to a noticeably different atmosphere. Early risers caught the announcement of martial law (but no other news of the Rising) in that morning's *Irish Times* while the declaration was plastered along railings in the St Stephen's Green area.[78] What most transformed perceptions of the Rising that morning, however, was the astonishing sound of artillery fire. Mary Louisa Norway recorded the startling wake-up call: 'While we were dressing a terrific bombardment with field guns began – the first we had heard – and gave me cold shivers.'[79]

At 8.00 a.m. the armed steam yacht, the HMS *Helga*, had sailed up the River Liffey and begun firing shells at Liberty Hall, which British military officials believed was a key garrison of the rebels. Although the building was empty of rebels, the damage inflicted was almost total. Stationed at 'Kelly's Fort', an outpost on the corner of Sackville Street, Joe Good remarked: 'it was reduced to a husk'.[80] For Good and the other rebels stationed near the GPO the *Helga* was less of an immediate threat than artillery and machine-gun fire from British stations across the river. British machine gunners on the roofs of Tara Street Station and Trinity College spewed bullets onto Sackville Street, largely clearing the area of civilians and combatants. Those rebels who were chosen to carry messages between buildings ran the gauntlet. Although

3.20
A shell fired by HMS *Helga*.
HE:EW.134a

sniper fire was returned from the roof of the GPO, the rebels were less well armed than the British forces in the area. In the frontline of these attacks, Good was forced to try and take out machine-gunners armed with only a shotgun.[81] By late morning, however, the rebels at the GPO's outposts faced the more ominous threat of artillery shells from two eighteen pounder field guns stationed at Trinity College. The effect was seismic: 'I [Good] was coming down the banisterless stairs when the first shell shook our building … it shook the old house and plaster fell all over the place. With the explosion I was nearly pitched forward on to my head.'[82] At 2.30 p.m. Good and the 'Kelly's Fort' garrison were evacuated to the GPO by Connolly. Meanwhile, news reached him that the Mendicity Institution Garrison had surrendered.

3.21
The Mendicity
Institution garrison flag.
HE:EWL.413

Formerly the residence of Lord Edward Fitzgerald, the Mendicity Institution had become a home for the destitute of Dublin. For the first two days of the Rising it was occupied by Seán Heuston and members of 1st Battalion D Company. Though nominally under the command of Edward Daly, Heuston in fact took orders directly from James Connolly who directed 'Captain Houston [sic] to seize the Mendicity at all costs'.[83] Approximately twenty-five men evacuated its inhabitants and established it as a military outpost.

Strategically, the Garrison formed a key position. Located on Usher's Island on the south side of the River Liffey, it served as a defensive base for the obstruction of troop movement into the city from both Kingsbridge Station and the Royal barracks. A party of Royal Dublin Fusiliers had been repulsed on Monday as they proceeded along the North Quays. Connolly, who anticipated much stronger troop reinforcements to arrive via the Mendicity Garrison as the week progressed, sent twelve members of the Fingal Battalion as reinforcements on Tuesday. This, it has been pointed out, marked the most substantial redeployment effort of republican forces during Easter Week.[84] An expected British Army force had surrounded the building by early on Wednesday morning. Heuston estimated the number to have been four hundred. Armed with Lee Enfield rifles the rebels continued to stave off an attack. However, by late morning they were running dangerously short of ammunition while British Army personnel were able to fire grenades from as close as twenty feet. Seán McLoughlin, who served as a courier for the garrison, observed the scene nearby: 'The firing seemed to reach a very high pitch; loud explosions as if bombs were being thrown and then suddenly it was all over.'[85] At midday Heuston was forced to surrender the Mendicity Institution Garrison. 'His short stand', Charles Townshend has judged, 'became one of the scattered mini-epics of Easter week.'[86]

3.22
Seán Heuston,
Commandant of the
Mendicity Institution
garrison.
HE:EW.198.12

The events at Mount Street Bridge contributed a longer saga. Almost simultaneous to the end of the fighting at the Mendicity Institution, British troops south of the Liffey were descending on the city centre along the Northumberland Road. These were the 2/7th and 2/8th Battalions of the Sherwood Forresters. Two infantry brigades of inexperienced British servicemen had embarked from Kingstown port that morning. The battalions, which marched via Blackrock and Donnybrook, encountered little resistance. The 2,000 troops who proceeded towards Lower Mount Street, however, walked into a 'lethal killing zone'.[87] Michael Malone's men at 25 Northumberland Road, Clanwilliam House and the parochial hall created a triangulation of fire to which the Sherwood Forresters would be exposed. Their commander Brigadier-General Maconchy had been briefed on the rebels' positions but proceeded with a frontal assault past the twelve-man garrison. The results were disastrous. Between midday and approximately 8.00 p.m., British troops were caught in a deadly field of fire. Aiming from the parochial hall, William Christian relived the scene: 'As the British troops drew nearer, the bullets fell on the roof of the school opposite like a shower of hail. Excitement gripped us and we braced ourselves for the encounter … we opened fire and men fell like ninnypins.'[88] Column after column was cut down. Dismayed by the growing casualties, Brigadier

3.23
Mauser bullets used by
the republican forces
during the Battle of
Mount Street bridge.
HE:EW.898c

3.24
Civilians queue for
passes at Store Street
Dublin Metropolitan
Police station.
HE:EW.4451.31

Maconchy made contact with General Lowe to establish if another route could be taken. Lowe ordered the defeat of the Mount Street Bridge garrison at all costs. The protracted fighting was a disconcerting experience for local civilians, twenty of whom were killed in the crossfire. Several accounts recall the torturous battle scenes in terms of time. The staccato diary entries of Lady Eileen Chance, who awaited news of the British soldiers from her home at 90 Merrion Square, evinces the ongoing tension throughout Wednesday. 1 p.m.: 'Still no soldiers – where are they?' 3 p.m.: 'Awful firing somewhere near – Mount Street or Grattan Street I think … it seems so near … still firing at Mount Street Bridge, machine guns and volley firing, they do make a row.' 5 p.m.: 'Less firing down Mount Street way, though lots everywhere else. There is a big fire near Mount Street.' 7.30 p.m.: 'Play Bridge but very hard to keep our minds on the game with all the shots round us … there are said to be snipers all over the place … no use trying to get away. Early bed after a very trying day. All our tempers getting short.'[89] By the end of the battle the British troops had overrun the rebel positions. The 220 military casualties incurred by the Sherwood Forresters at Mount Street Bridge, however, counted almost half of the entire British casualty list for Easter Week.

The constraints of martial law required that all civilians be indoors after 7.30 p.m. A number of diarists and memoirists noted that they and others flouted this regulation with the view to getting a glimpse of the destructive spectacle caused by the British military bombardment: 'It looks as if the whole city is ablaze and reminds us of the picture "The Burning of Rome".'[90]

The British counter-offensive was the dominant subject among those who recorded their experiences. Several commentators expressed relief that British soldiers were arriving: 'the doctor tells me that a whole division consisting of more than 15,000 have come to help us, thank God'.[91] There is no reason to assume that this feeling was not widespread, if only with thoughts of the fighting being brought to an end. Other writers, however, alluded to a growing sympathy (not quite support) for the rebels by mid-Easter Week. Much has been made of James Stephens' chronicle of public opinion in the St Stephen's Green area: 'There is almost a feeling of gratitude towards the Volunteers … for had they been beaten the first or second day the City would have been humiliated to the soul.'[92] However, Stephens' account on Wednesday was less focused on the length of the rebels' fight as their survival against disproportionate military power. Watching the artillery bombardment of Kelly's Fort, Stephens confided: 'one's heart melted at the idea that human beings were crouching inside that volcano of death'.[93] Ernie O'Malley evoked a similar theme on that day: 'In the city Irishmen were fighting British troops against long odds. I was going to help them in some way.'[94] Writing from Ballsbridge, Margaret Mitchell again referred to the disparity: 'the Sinn Fein rifles are feeble

3.25
A live photograph of the fires on Sackville Street.
HE:EW.1372.3

in sound compared with the military's rifles which are generally fired in a volley, whereas the enemy's rifles are single shots'.[95] The application of asymmetric warfare may have softened public anger towards the rebels from the middle of Easter Week.

According to the Military Council's early strategy, the aim of Galway's Rising was to hold the line of the River Shannon using weapons from Germany. Royal Irish Constabulary barracks were also to be raided for arms. However, the destruction of the *Aud* undermined this plan. On Easter Sunday and Monday, the Volunteers were mobilised and demobilised by orders and counter-orders, but eventually went 'out' under the local authority of Liam Mellows. On the morning of Tuesday 25 April, seventy-five Volunteers attacked Clarinbridge RIC station, injuring one RIC officer. That afternoon, three Volunteer companies attacked Oranmore RIC barracks, later retreating to the Athenry Agricultural Station. In the early hours of Wednesday morning, Castlegar and Claregalway Volunteers, en route to Athenry, were confronted by the RIC at Carnmore Cross. One RIC officer was killed in the ensuing firefight. By Wednesday, approximately 700 Volunteers were assembled at the Agricultural Station. In the absence of instructions from Dublin and arms from Kerry, Mellows simply attempted to maintain Volunteer mobilisation. An RIC scouting party had been fired on that morning, with the Volunteers afterwards camping at Moyode Castle before marching twenty kilometres to Limepark on Friday. Following news of surrender in Dublin, the Galway Volunteers slowly disbanded. Mellows and others went on the run.

3.26
The nun's veil used by Liam Mellows to escape arrest by the RIC.
HE:EW.1108

THURSDAY

Between 2.00 a.m. and 8.00 a.m. on Thursday morning, the town of Enniscorthy was occupied by Wexford rebels. Eoin MacNeill's countermanding order had caused enough uncertainty to forestall military action in the county for the first twenty-four hours. However, thereafter the failure to take up arms appears to have been less about communication problems as command problems. News of the Rising had reached towns in Wexford by Monday night through civilians and travelling couriers.[96] However, local Volunteer impulses to seize Enniscorthy lacked the conviction and co-ordination of an authoritative command. Volunteers at Ferns, Gorey and Wexford Town recall being mobilised and then stood down several times early in Easter Week.[97] It was only on late Wednesday evening that a singular command was followed. Arriving in Enniscorthy, having cycled from the GPO early on Tuesday morning, Wexford Commandant Paul Galligan informed fellow Volunteers of James Connolly's order to cut the railway line from Rosslare Harbour to Dublin in order to stem the arrival of British reinforcements. Ammunition was not to be wasted on attacks of RIC barracks.[98] Early on Thursday morning, approximately one hundred Enniscorthy Volunteers occupied the town.[99] They met little resistance from police, although they also did little damage to the railway. The Rising in Enniscorthy proved a highly symbolic event. The rebels' headquarters, marked by a tricolour, was the Athenaeum Club on Castle Street. Here armed Volunteers arrived from other parts of the county. A significant number were willing to exchange their guns for more symbolically loaded pikes.[100] Fifty members of Cumann na mBan, meanwhile, provided food for the men.[101] The rebels enforced the closure of shops and banks, issued food tickets and policed the town.[102] Seán Etchingham's diary attests to the precedence of their actions: 'We had

3.27
A bullet ladle used to create ammunition by the garrison at Enniscorthy.
HE:EW.1091.14

at least one day of blissful freedom. We have had Enniscorthy under the laws of the Irish Republic for at least one day.'[103] Their ambitions did not seem to extend beyond this symbolic action and the later attempt on Friday to attack the RIC barracks at Ferns and 'march on Dublin' reads as something of an afterthought.

General Lowe's attempt to tighten the inner cordon around the GPO and Four Courts in the capital required artillery bombardment in advance of any troop movement. Just after midday the British counter-offensive recommenced with artillery shelling of the rebels' outposts along Sackville Street. Sniper fire perforated the area. To the consternation of other rebels, however, James Connolly continued to traverse this terrain examining barricades. On one afternoon sortie into Prince's Street, Connolly took a stray bullet to the arm. He quietly had his wound dressed in the GPO before returning to Middle Abbey Street. Within minutes, however, he was injured again, this time seriously, a bullet having shattered his left ankle. Incapacitated and in acute pain, Connolly survived his final days in the GPO on a makeshift mattress. Most rebels' recollection of Connolly is of an authoritative military leader still despatching orders.[104] Later that afternoon the heavy shelling precipitated a sprawling fire which severely damaged the eastern side of Sackville Street, burning a line of buildings from Hopkins Bread Factory to the Imperial Hotel. Oscar Traynor watched the inferno spread from across the street at the Metropole Hotel: 'I had the extraordinary experience of seeing the huge plate-glass windows of Clery's stores run molten into the channel from the terrific heat.'[105] Later that night the fires extended to the Metropole itself.

3.28
The bloodstained vest of James Connolly, showing the location of his first wound.
HE:EWL.292.2

Elsewhere in the city close quarter fighting had erupted. Éamonn Ceannt's 4th battalion had successfully maintained control of the South Dublin Union for much of Easter Week. His principal contingent of approximately sixty-five rebels was tasked with defending the fifty-acre site (the country's biggest poorhouse), replete with hospitals, stores and dormitories. As Fearghal McGarry has commented, 'it remains difficult to understand why it was considered acceptable to locate a garrison [there]'.[106] The 3,000 inmates and staff were not evacuated. Its buildings were the scene of running battles with the Royal Irish Regiment during Monday. However, on Thursday 100 members of the Sherwood Forresters regiment entered the complex more determinedly. Under cover of machine gun fire from army headquarters at the Royal Hospital, they entered the building adjacent to the Nurses' Home (Ceannt's headquarters) at 3.00 p.m. Breaching the Nurses' Home wall they were repelled by intensive rifle fire. However, in the bitter exchanges Cathal Brugha was severely injured with twenty-five different wounds in his body. At 8.00 p.m. the assault on South Dublin Union was called off. Meanwhile at the nearby Jameson Distillery, 145 rebels of the Marrowbone Lane Garrison (including a collection of Con Colbert's Watkins' Brewery detachment), remained surrounded.[107]

3.29
The key to the
South Dublin Union
poorhouse.
HE:EW.5398

3.30
Cathal Brugha's Smith
and Wesson revolver
used during the fighting
at the Four Courts.
HE:EWL.442

3.31
A blood-stained bandage found
at Fr Mathew Hall.
HE:1998.26 (Allen)

3.32
The first-aid kit used by Christina
Hayes at Fr Mathew Hall.
HE:EWL.120

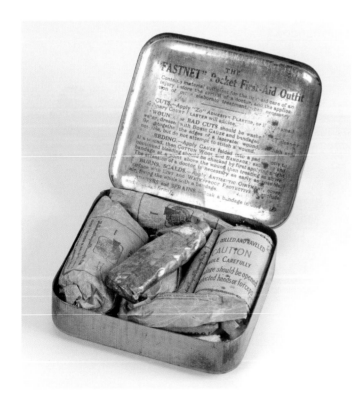

By Thursday evening Edward Daly's
1st Battalion was also under siege. His
garrison (numbering approximately 150)
had seized Bridewell and Linenhall barracks
and had set the latter alight. However, on
Thursday the British counter-offensive
targeted the Capel Street area, connecting
the Four Courts and GPO forces, in an
attempt to isolate the respective garrisons.
Units of the Sherwood Forresters fought
off sniper fire from Daly's men and had, by
midnight, established military posts in an
arc from upper Abbey Street to Capel Street to Parnell Street.
Daly, seeking to strengthen his defensive position, returned to
his command centre on Church Street: Fr Mathew Hall.[108] Fr
Mathew Hall had also become the centre of operations for
Cumann na mBan in the area. Here, they provided meals and
first aid to the Volunteers. On
Monday, Christina Hayes was
put in charge of the Fr Mathew
Hall First Aid Station. The
women had received intense
training in first aid. Eilís Uí
Chonaill served at the Hall, but
also delivered messages around
the city and transported food
to the various outposts around
Sackville Street. Before the
surrender she would transport
the wounded to Richmond
Hospital.[109] Some thirty-two
men received medical aid at this
station.

Although the *Irish Times* went to print again on Thursday (for the last time that week) it could offer readers no information on the Rising beyond the necessity to adhere to the provisions of martial law. Readers were encouraged to spend their housebound hours studying Shakespeare.[110] While a number of civilian commentators again described the effects of the fighting on the city, an increasing concern for provisions became discernible. The continued closure of shops and discontinuation of milk and bread delivery services was noted. Food carts, it was stated, were less frequently seen. Eileen Chance noted one particular scene: 'See a crowd round a baker's cart near Kildare Street … find it surrounded by poor women and people like ourselves from Fitzwilliam and Merrion Squares out for bread. Are lucky in getting a fair supply of fancy bread, as the women will only take plain loaves.'[111] Rumours about the Rising, meanwhile, continued to circulate among those willing to discuss it; some began to hear of Sheehy-Skeffington's killing for the first time.[112]

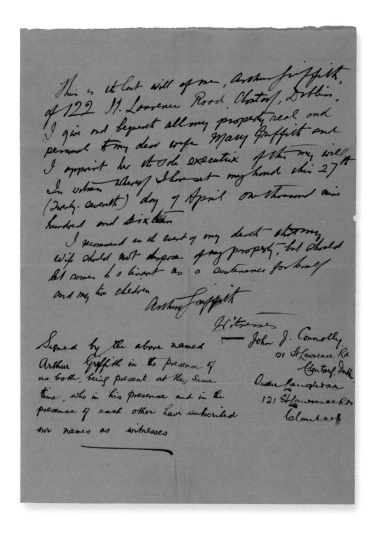

3.33
The will written and signed by Arthur Griffith on 27 April 1916.
HE:EWL.207

FRIDAY

In the early hours of Friday morning Major General Sir John Maxwell arrived in the capital, following his appointment by the Prime Minister Herbert Asquith as commander-in-chief of the British forces. At this stage, troop numbers had increased to 20,000.[113] Briefed by Lowe, who would continue with operational command in the city, Maxwell later described the fighting at the Four Courts as 'by far the worst that occurred in the whole of Dublin'.[114] A battalion of Sherwood Forresters began the assault on the Four Courts garrison at approximately 6.30 a.m. The British troops struggled to overcome rebel resistance over a 150 yard stretch of North King Street leading into Church Street. The morning and afternoon saw intensive house-to-house fighting,

3.34
The Four Courts
garrison flag.
HE:EW.794

particularly at 'Reilly's Fort', where reinforcements arrived from the Four Courts building itself. Fr Mathew Hall, meanwhile, became crowded with wounded. The close quarter fighting would continue for the rest of the day.[115]

Unbeknownst to the combatants in the besieged Four Courts area, a more open conflict was being waged further north by the Dublin Brigade's 5th (Fingal) Battalion at Ashbourne. Almost 120 of Thomas Ashe's Brigade had mobilised for manoeuvres on Easter Sunday but only half of those re-assembled the following day. Ashe, who was in daily communication with the GPO through his courier Mollie Adrien, lost a further twenty men to the fighting in Dublin on Connolly's orders. Richard Mulcahy was one of the few additions to the unit, leaving Ashe with forty men. In these small numbers, Charles Townshend has opined, 'may have lain their salvation […] he had happened upon what would be an ideal guerrilla "flying column" size'.[116] Ashe restructured the battalion into four compact units on bicycles creating a highly mobile force. On Wednesday and Thursday his Volunteers captured post offices and Royal Irish Constabulary barracks at Swords, Donabate and Garristown in north Co. Dublin. On Friday morning they received fresh orders from the GPO to cut the railway line at Batterstown (to prevent further troop movement into the city) and to take Ashbourne RIC barracks along the way. At approximately 11.30 a.m. Ashe's forces attacked the barracks with rifle fire and grenades, leading to the surprising surrender of its occupants. However, this short victory proved illusory, as a motorised column of seventeen RIC cars arrived. Despite being outnumbered and potentially outgunned, the resourceful Richard Mulcahy skilfully redeployed the Irish Volunteers. While six to seven men drew the fire of the RIC, Mulcahy manoeuvred the larger Volunteer force into hedges and banks around the police column outflanking them over the course of a number of hours. The RIC constables were unaware of the small scale of the battalion, and confusion ensued when their commanders were among the first casualties. After a dramatic charge led by Mulcahy, in which eight RIC, two Volunteers and two civilians died, the RIC surrendered to Ashe at 5 p.m. While this, as Fearghal McGarry has pointed out, was not the prototype for guerrilla warfare in the later War for Independence,[117] the Battle of Ashbourne was an elemental if belated victory for Bulmer Hobson's earlier 'hedge fighting' tactic.

3.35
Field glasses used by Thomas Ashe during the Battle of Ashbourne.
HE:EWL.273.1

By the culmination of victory at Ashbourne, the GPO was on the verge of collapse. This had merely been in abeyance since the early morning. Surveying the garrison, Seán McLoughlin remembered: 'everybody was gloomy and there was a sense of foreboding that the end was near'.[118] From his makeshift bed Connolly issued a rousing manifesto to the garrison, read aloud by The O'Rahilly, which glossed the perilous and/or powerless positions of the Dublin garrisons while claiming that provincial Ireland was well in the field: 'Courage boys, we are winning.'[119] The precariousness of their own position, however, clouded minds. At midday, as British machine gun fire raked the walls of the GPO, the women of the garrison were evacuated to Henry Street. Winifred Carney insisted on staying with Connolly. Artillery fire, which had rained down on Sackville Street from 6.00 a.m., found its range that afternoon. From 3.00 p.m., incendiary shells repeatedly struck the roof of the GPO, breaking the upper floor into flames. Rebels scrambled with hoses in an attempt to quench the fire but could not apply sufficient water. Thomas Devine recalled looking up at the scene: 'Daylight was visible in many places, twisted girders hung at queer angles, walls, floors and staircases were in a chaotic state.'[120] A sniper began firing on the fire fighters from the roof of the Imperial Hotel. At 6.00 p.m. the wounded rebels were evacuated via Henry Street and the British Army prisoners followed soon after. By this point the fire had engulfed the entire roof.

3.36
Fragments from the GPO and buildings on nearby streets damaged by the fires. (*Clockwide from left*) Glass from the roof of the GPO; a stone fragment from the pediment of the GPO; a burned watch from Hopkins & Hopkins jewellers; a portion of the roof of the GPO; barbed wire from the rebels' barricade on Sackville Street.
HE:EW.648;
HE:EW.1668;
HE:EW.657b;
HE:EW.657a;
HE:EW.657c

Seán MacEntee recalled that: 'We could hear the glass plates crack above our head and see the hungry flames leap through the broken spaces.'[121] Attempts to suppress the fire were abandoned and the remaining rebels gathered in the GPO Main Hall as fears mounted that the roof could cave in.

The intensity of the shelling on Sackville Street was remarked on by a number of civilian diarists. Some indeed continued to express admiration for the rebels' resolve against the perceived military superiority of British forces (the British Army was widely believed to have 60,000 troops in the city to the rebels' 10,000).[122] However, the majority of those taking notes on the Friday of Easter Week had ceased to be invested in the daily round of fighting. Scouring the conversations along St Stephen's Green, James Stephens recorded: 'I received the impression that numbers of them did not care a rap what way it went; and that others had ceased to be mental creatures and were merely machines for registering the sensations of the time'.[123] Many more accounts register the reclusive existence of civilians. In their confined context, any outward pre-occupations dwelt on the welfare of loved ones: 'our nearest and dearest friends might be buried without our knowledge'.[124] Psychological exhaustion with conditions in the city was exacerbated by dwindling rations of food. Writing from the relative salubrity of the Kilworth House Hotel, Robert Le Cren confided to his daughters 'at lunch and dinner today we had rations of two biscuits each in lieu of bread and Mrs. S [the proprietor] says she cannot feed us after Sunday'.[125] Working-class families in the city were undoubtedly worse off. Tired, starving and increasingly isolated, many Dublin civilians dragged through Friday, out of sight, out of mind. Stephens relived the eventual close of day: 'each night we have got to bed at last murmuring, "I wonder will it be all over tomorrow", and this night the like question accompanied us'.[126]

3.37
A sign from the front of the burnt-out GPO.
HE:EWL.7

4

SURRENDER

THE EVACUATION OF THE GPO

Entrenched in the Post Office under intense artillery fire, the leaders of the garrison ordered a break out towards Williams and Woods' Jam Factory on Great Britain Street at 7.30 p.m., with the view to retreating towards the Four Courts garrison thereafter. British machine-gunners massed along the intersection of Great Britain and Moore streets.[1] The latter became a veritable no man's land.

4.0
(Page 116)
Civilians emerge after
the Rising to survey the
damage on Moore and
Henry streets.
HE:EW.4451.21

4.1
The O'Rahilly.
HE:EW.2899

The O'Rahilly, sword in holder, gun in holster, had enthusiastically volunteered to lead an advance party of forty to break the British lines: 'Fancy missing this and then catching cold running for a tram.'[2] Many of the volunteers, however, did not have the bayonets required.[3] Under The O'Rahilly's command, they formed fours and rounded the corner at Henry Street–Moore Street: 'charge, for the glory of God and the honour of Ireland'.[4] Within thirty yards of their advance they met a barrage of machine gunfire. The 'whine' of fizzing bullets and 'thud' of falling bodies was vividly remembered. One group of men swerved to the left of the open street and attempted to edge towards the barricade, hugging shop fronts and houses, but were forced into Sampson's Lane under the intensity of fire. The O'Rahilly, meanwhile, darted ahead 'deer like' along the right, finally manoeuvring himself into a Sackville Lane doorway, just thirty yards from the British position. The follow-up party, however, only made it halfway up Moore Street before coming under heavy fire. Dennis Daly numbingly recalled the scene: 'everyone in front of me was shot down'.[5] Realising their perilous situation, The O'Rahilly double-backed towards his men but was immediately struck by flying bullets. His sword clattered to the ground. Breathing heavily, he dragged his body tortuously along the street into the adjacent Sackville Lane. Here, alone, he struggled to write his last words to his wife and son. The letter and The O'Rahilly, dead, were found one day later. Speaking candidly to Ernie O'Malley twenty years later, Dennis Daly attributed the heavy casualties on Moore Street to 'very bad scouting on our side'.[6] Similar misgivings were expressed by other veterans: 'I don't suppose a cat could have crossed Moore Street unscathed'; 'the wonder is our small force wasn't wiped out there and then'; 'would it not have been better, and fair to us all, to wait until it was dark?'[7]

After thirty minutes without reply from either The O'Rahilly or his advance party, it was decided that the evacuation of the remaining GPO garrison must proceed. The building, it was feared, could collapse at any minute. Led by Clarke, Plunkett and MacDiarmada, and followed by Pearse, some 250 rebels emerged onto Henry Street through the

side door of the Post Office. Connolly was stretchered along by four
Volunteers. Winifred Carney was by his side, followed by Elizabeth
O'Farrell and Julia Grenan. Under fire from Mary Street, the rebels
shot across into Henry Place. Confusion reigned. Echoes from machine
gun-fire in the middle of Moore Lane just ahead convinced some that
British forces were upon them. Rebels rushed for cover in doorways
and entries. One Volunteer accidentally shot himself trying to force
open a handle to safety.[8] 'Nobody seemed to be in charge once we left',

Eamon Bulfin relived, 'it
was every man for himself'.[9]
Under the supervision of
Clarke and Plunkett, the
rebels scurried past Moore
Lane and began tunnelling
through the adjacent
buildings in the direction
of Great Britain Street.
Starving, exhausted and,
in some cases, wounded,
they crawled through walls,
eventually stopping at No.
16 Moore Street. Here the
members of the Military
Council present deliberated

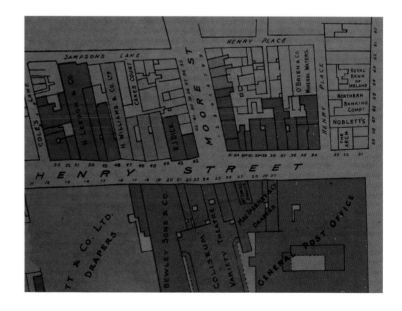

4.4

Sean McLoughlin, Commandant-General of the republican forces (28–9 April 1916).

4.5

On the morning of 29 April Thomas Clarke inscribed the wall of 16 Moore Street for posterity: 'Thos J Clarke 6th day I. R [Irish Republic]'.

HE:EWL.368

overnight. The enterprising Sean McLoughlin, appointed commandant general by Connolly himself only hours before, proposed a 'death or glory' attack on the British barricades, comparable to that of The O'Rahilly, and assembled men for the mission the next morning. Any such attempt, Pearse now adjudged, however, would only provide a pyrrhic victory; just after midday on 28 April the decision was made to surrender.[10]

DECISION TO SURRENDER

The decision to surrender, agreed by all the Military Council members eventually, was determined by Patrick Pearse. Those rebels who passed through No. 16 Moore Street at various points that morning recalled the emotional distress experienced as the leaders countenanced defeat. Julia Grennan remembered a teary-eyed Connolly: 'how terribly affected he was by the thought of surrender'.[11] Sean McGarry saw Thomas Clarke become 'very quiet, McDermott on the verge of tears'.[12] Joseph Plunkett remarked pithily: 'The doctors tell me I have only six months to live.'[13] Pearse however, Desmond Ryan remembered, was 'as firm as a rock'.[14] The fate of Dublin's civilians, it would appear, had influenced the final decision. Earlier that morning, Pearse had looked out the window of No. 16 with horror to the sight of three dead civilians on Moore Street. It 'angered and moved him deeply' Ryan recollected.[15] By midday his convictions and emotions had hardened.

The safety of Dublin's citizens was a topic Pearse would stress when later explaining the decision to surrender, most pointedly in the notes which he dictated, handwrote and signed.[16] It was also a theme which ordinary rebels on Moore Street returned to in retrospective accounts. Their emergence from the GPO on Friday evening of Easter Week exposed them, finally, to the cataclysm experienced by civilians in the surrounding area. It was a baptism of fear. Sean MacEntee, who had been part of The O'Rahilly's sortie, recalled the disturbing image of the 'pale, horrified face of a frightened woman' in a nearby window.[17] Rebels attempting to escape the chokehold of Henry Place were confronted with equally stark realities. Desperately trying to get through a house to safety, a volunteer opened fire on the lock of a door, accidentally killing a young girl and injuring her father in the process.[18] Burrowing through a house on Moore Street, meanwhile, Oscar Traynor came across a harrowing sight: 'a little family, an old man, a young woman and her children, cowering into the corner of a room, apparently terrified'.[19] Much of the energy of the rebels on late Friday and early Saturday morning was directed towards evacuating civilians from Moore Street and the adjoining lanes. A significant number, according to later accounts, espoused support for the rebels.[20] These claims are fairly convincing. Some of the local people knew the rebel leaders at first hand.[21] Meanwhile, as Fearghal McGarry has remarked of the North King Street area: 'many of the civilians, who had failed to evacuate … appear to have been sympathetic to the rebels'.[22] Not all of the civilians, however, escaped the fighting alive. A number of residents were found dead on Moore Street the next morning, some with white banners in their hands. Desmond Ryan looked upon the scene disbelievingly: 'Moore Street was strewn with debris, with waxen bodies in green and in khaki uniforms, with huddled and ragged forms of civilians with red gashes in their foreheads, and the same waxen look.'[23]

Seán Mac Diarmada took the responsibility of announcing the surrender to the rebels in Moore Street: 'We surrendered not to save you but to save the city and the people of this city from destruction.'[24]

Significant numbers of rebels, nonetheless, were incredulous on hearing of the surrender. 'We could hardly believe such a thing was possible,' Thomas Leahy explained, 'after working so hard to strengthen our new positions.'[25] Charles Saurin noted a mixed reaction when the rebels were advised that they would be allowed to return home: 'some cheered this announcement, others were bewildered at it and others again were frankly disgusted, for there were determined men in the crowd, as I could see, who did not understand the meaning of the word "surrender".'[26] Among these were the 'Kimmage garrison' who anticipated conscription into the British Army. Mac Diarmada attempted to quell potential 'mutiny' in their ranks with promises of a further republican round. More compellingly, he invited them to observe the devastation around them: 'the civilians nearest us were all very poor and would be butchered with us … this beautiful city would be razed'.[27]

4.6
The visible impact of British machine-gun fire on houses along Moore Street.
HE:EW.4451.12

'I never broke down until I saw
Tom Clarke with his face to the wall
and burst into tears. I went over to
him and begged him not to cry and
broke down myself.
Everyone's eyes I think were red
with tears – shed and unshed.
Tom Clarke as you know with
O'Donovan Rossa were the only
two, I think, who survived fifteen
years in Dartmoor. No wonder he
wept at surrendering himself to his
English jailors again.
Any feelings were of very great rage
because we had never before given
in to the authorities.'

Winifred Carney, letter to Ernest Carney

THE NORTH KING STREET 'MASSACRE'

In the boxed confines of 16 Moore Street, the Military Council were unaware of developments elsewhere in the city. In this context, the decision to surrender to further prevent civilian casualties was prescient. On that same morning, less than one kilometre away, the potential totality of any continuing conflict revealed itself along North King Street. Between 6.00 p.m. on 28 April and 10.00 a.m. on 29 April, fifteen civilians were killed in buildings just 150 yards apart. The men, aged between sixteen and fifty-three, were residents of the area. Some bodies had gunshot wounds, others indicated death by bayonet. Two, Patrick Bealen and James Healy, were discovered days later, buried in a shallow grave under a basement. Active along North King Street had been the 2/6th South Staffordshire Regiment, who had lost fourteen men in the process of marshalling the local area. Their actions during this period, however, proved highly contentious. Local citizens accused the soldiers of forcefully entering premises and killing indiscriminately, after local fighting had ceased. Their commanding officer countered that the men in question were suspected of being rebels. A military enquiry held weeks later adjudged individual soldiers innocent of the crimes for which they were accused, citing the lack of witnesses as a mitigating circumstance. Its confidential assessment, however, attributed many of the deaths to 'orders not to take any prisoners, which they took to mean that they were to shoot anyone whom they believed to be an active rebel'.[28]

Charles Townshend has surmised that the deaths on North King Street were 'perhaps inevitable in fighting of such claustrophobic intensity'.[29] Fearghal McGarry has concurred, noting that the Staffordshire Regiment had been hardened by the sight of their comrades' deaths on Mount Street Bridge and the sense that North King Street residents remained in sympathy with the rebels.[30] Most pertinently, perhaps, in respect of the decision to surrender, civilians in the vicinity of other garrisons would escape such sustained, saturated violence. An eventual deterioration of the Rising into close quarter combat elsewhere had the potential to expose Dublin's citizens, more widely, to the totality of this conflict. The surrender saved innocent lives.

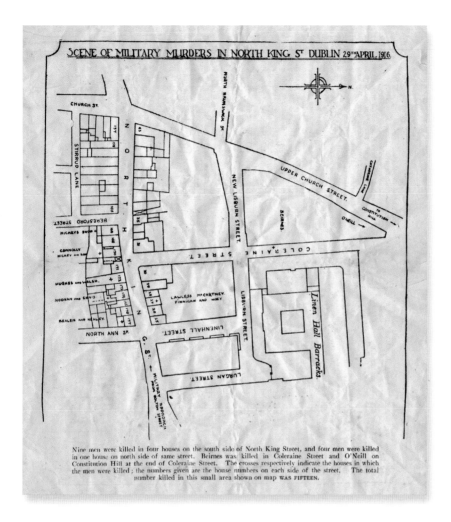

4.7
Map showing the locations
of the killings in the North
King Street area.
HE:EW.4945

However, for hundreds of civilians it was too late. The most recent estimate has placed the civilian death toll at 318. The youngest victims, Christina Caffrey and James Francis Foster, were just two years old. At least sixty of those killed, from civilians and combatants on both sides, were nineteen years of age or younger. In addition, some thirty-two unidentified bodies were buried in Deans Grange and Glasnevin Cemeteries respectively. Apart from the 16 executed leaders, 66 rebels were killed in action, along with 23 police and 128 British Army soldiers, 40 of whom were Irishmen. The death toll for the 1916 Rising, ultimately, reached 551.[31]

'I am prepared to receive you in Britain St at the north end of Moore St provided that you surrender unconditionally.

You will proceed up Moore St accompanied only by the woman who brings you this note under a white flag.'

W.M. Lowe

THE PROCESS OF SURRENDER

4.8
Elizabeth O'Farrell.

Elizabeth O'Farrell was tasked with establishing contact with the British forces on behalf of the rebel leaders. Flagged by a white flannel, she cautiously made her way to the barricade at Great Britain Street at 12.45 p.m. O'Farrell relayed Pearse's request to discuss terms with General Lowe. The latter detained her for questioning at Thomas Clarke's tobacconist shop nearby before allowing her return to Moore Street with a demand for unconditional surrender. Between 2.25 p.m. and 3.30 p.m. the 'Sinn Fein nurse' shuttled between the rebel leaders and General Lowe as they arbitrated over the conditions of surrender. At approximately 3.30 p.m. Patrick Pearse, accompanied by O'Farrell, surrendered unconditionally to General Lowe at the corner of Great Britain and Moore streets. O'Farrell agreed, further, to carry notice of the surrender to the other garrisons in the city.

4.9
The surrender of Patrick
Pearse, with Elizabeth
O'Farrell, to General Lowe
and his son Lieutenant
John Lowe. O'Farrell's
shoes and skirt can be
discerned behind Pearse.
The first publication of the
photograph in the *Daily
Sketch* on 10 May 1916 did
not include O'Farrell in
the image.
HE:EW.1740

In order to prevent the further slaughter of Dublin
citizens, and in the hope of saving the lives of our
followers now surrounded and hopelessly outnumbered, the
members of the Provisional Government present at Head-
Quarters have agreed to an unconditional surrender, and the
Commandants of the various districts in the City and Country
will order their commands to lay down arms.

P. H. Pearse
29th April 1916
3.45 p.m.

I agree to these conditions for the men only
under my own Command in the Moore
Street District and for the men in
the Stephen's Green Command.

James Connolly
April 29/16

On consultation with Commandant Ceannt
and other officers I have decided to
agree to unconditional surrender also.

Thomas MacDonagh

Pearse was then taken away by British military personnel in a motor car down Sackville Street for interrogation by General Maxwell. O'Farrell, who had again been stationed in Clarke's premises, received Pearse's typed surrender note, timed 3.45 p.m., approximately thirty minutes after it was signed. Connolly, who had been removed to Dublin Castle upon the surrender, had countersigned the document, issuing orders, however, only for his men in the Moore Street and St Stephen's Green areas. O'Farrell delivered the surrender notice to the rebels stranded in Moore Street, who were ordered to march to O'Connell Street and hand over their weapons. They would spend the night under armed guard on the green outside the Rotunda Hospital.[32]

Ensuring compliance with the surrender order at other garrisons was not straightforward. Nurse O'Farrell proceeded to the Four Courts that afternoon where she presented the signed surrender order to Edward Daly: 'he was very much cut up about it but accepted his orders as a soldier should'. Some of his garrison, however, decided to go on the run rather than be imprisoned while others destroyed their weapons.[33] Daly, teary-eyed, told his men that he would prefer to fight on but that he must obey the order to surrender. The Four Courts Garrison joined the remains of the GPO rebels outside the Rotunda. The following morning, Captain De Courcy-Wheeler drove O'Farrell to the other garrisons in the southern part of the city. At St Stephen's Green Countess Markievicz received her and was 'very much surprised' at the notice. Mallin described the surrender as 'painful'. A number of rebels wanted to fight on.[34] On subsequent arrival at Boland's Mill, she was interviewed by de Valera who at first thought the surrender issue was 'a hoax' and then insisted that he would not take any orders unless from Thomas MacDonagh, his immediate superior officer. At Jacob's Biscuit Factory, MacDonagh was even

4.10
(Opposite page)
Patrick Pearse's typed order for the unconditional surrender of the republican forces. The document was dictated and signed by Pearse. The note is timed 3.45 p.m.
HE:EW.992.24

4.11
Harry de Courcy-Wheeler was the Administrator of the Curragh military camp during the First World War. He became General Lowe's staff officer during the 1916 Rising.
HE:EW.1743

4.12
Éamon de Valera, marked
by an X, marches the
surrendered Boland's Mill
garrison to Richmond
barracks under the
supervision of British
military officers.
HE:EWT.59

more suspicious. Having been apprised of the situation by O'Farrell, he declared that he would not take orders from a prisoner and, as the next in command of the republican forces, he would only confirm the surrender on treating with Brigadier-General Lowe, a meeting which took place outside St Patrick's Park that Sunday afternoon. On final consultation with Éamonn Ceannt at Marrowbone Lane, MacDonagh and Ceannt surrendered their respective garrisons at approximately 6.00 p.m. MacDonagh countersigned Pearse's order. However, at that stage the other rebel positions in Dublin had already been surrendered. In O'Farrell's absence Éamon de Valera had approached the British position on Mount Street with the view to surrendering. This was taken moments later on Grattan Street.

Meanwhile, de Courcy-Wheeler was on hand to receive the surrender of the St Stephen's Green garrison outside the Royal College of Surgeons. Michael Mallin and Countess Markievicz both saluted him, but it was Markievicz who left the lasting impression: 'I requested her to disarm, which she did, and when handing over her arms she kissed her small revolver reverently.'[35]

4.13
Michael Mallin and Countess Markievicz pictured outside the Royal College of Surgeons after the surrender of the St Stephen's Green garrison.
HE:EW.78b

4.14
Countess Markievicz's repeating pistol. De Courcy-Wheeler stated positively that Markievicz had kissed her pistol, not her revolver, in his field message book, compiled only days after the Rising.
HE:EW.1734

4.15
Patrick Pearse's surrender
note, issued on 30 May,
for communication to
Enniscorthy's republican
forces.
HE:EWL.133

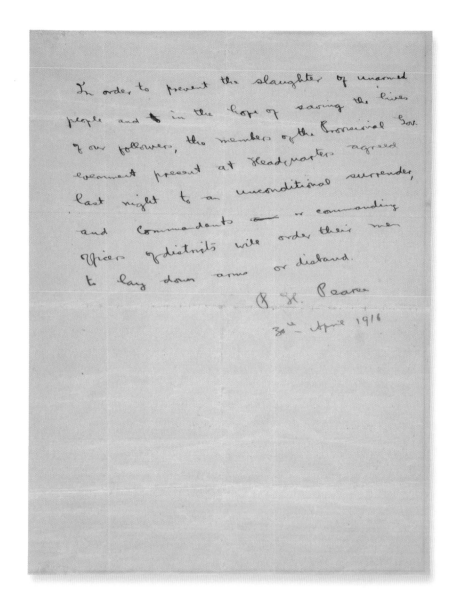

Word of the surrender, meanwhile, gradually filtered through
to rebels elsewhere in Ireland. At Ashbourne, the high morale of the
previous two days was shattered on Sunday morning with the arrival
of two local RIC men and news of the Dublin surrender. Disbelieving,
Thomas Ashe designated Richard Mulcahy to confirm the order
with Pearse in person. On Mulcahy's return that afternoon, the fifth

battalion was marched to Swords and then transferred to Richmond barracks.[36] The men at Enniscorthy were similarly incredulous when they received rumour of surrender in Dublin from community leaders. Seeking clarity, Seamus Doyle and Sean Etchingham were given safe passage, by the British authorities, to interview Pearse at Arbour Hill. The latter confirmed the surrender in writing and the Enniscorthy men handed over their arms to the RIC on the following day, 1 May. Within a week the rebels had also been transferred to Richmond barracks.[37] In the provinces of Connacht, Ulster and Munster, mention of surrender in the capital passed informally between activists late that weekend, but no official action was demanded of them by Pearse. In Cork city the local Volunteers handed over an arsenal of weapons to the mayor as an act of good faith.[38] The surrender of the Irish republican forces had been effected. What now for rebels and leaders?

4.16
The British Army's Royal Irish Regiment pose for a photograph with the captured Irish Republic flag at the Parnell Monument on Sackville Street on the day of the surrender.
HE:EW.3533

Irish Rebellion ~ May 1916.
A group of Officers with the captured rebel flag.

5

EXECUTIONS

THE SURRENDER AND PUBLIC OPINION

Gauging the reaction of the Dublin public at the end of the 1916 Rising is immensely difficult. The long-established meta-narrative of rebels under attack from 'separation women' as the former were being led through the streets of the capital[1] has been revised in more recent analyses. The democratisation of primary material, through the release of Bureau of Military History witness statements and digitisation of sources more broadly, has allowed for a more capacious Dublin opinion. Seeds of support for the rebels there undoubtedly were. Class, politics and geographical location have been variously suggested as contributing factors.[2] How prevalent was this sympathy? It is unlikely that a consensus will emerge on the subject. The very proliferation of primary sources means that public opinion can be seen from variant individual perspectives, not always recorded or remembered with historical accuracy in mind. Dublin's myriad reactions, while potentially representative of a city in flux, thus, may also evidence the subjectivity of first-person sources.

5.0
(Page 134)
A white cross marks the place of execution of the Rising's leaders in the Stonebreakers' Yard, Kilmainham jail, Dublin.

The majority of the Dublin rebels were marched from surrender points to Richmond barracks on Sunday 29 April. The hostility of the crowds weighed heavily on the recollections of those from the GPO and Four Courts garrisons after the relative silence of the still charring Sackville Street. Charles Saurin, whose party trudged over O'Connell Bridge, through College Green, Dame Street and Francis Street, noted shock on passing the latter: 'a mass of howling, shrieking women from the back streets who called us filthy names and hurled curses at us. The sentry on duty kept pushing them back with the butt of his rifle. They kept up their screeching till our column had passed them by'.[3] Michael O'Reilly's distinctive memory was of Thomas Street: 'particularly by reason of the barrage of abuse we got from the female residents'.[4] Thomas Devine recalled somewhat differently: 'An unpleasant memory of that morning is the hostile attitude towards us of certain Dubliners – mostly soldiers' dependants from the Coombe and adjacent districts.'[5] Others, it would seem, did not think the passage to Richmond barracks in any way remarkable.[6] Others still noted sympathetic reactions. Seán MacEntee remarked pointedly of his journey: 'Here and there, at some windows, were a few onlookers, most of them, so far as one could judge, sympathetic.'[7]

The surrender of the St Stephen's Green garrison is of particular interest. A disproportionate number of the available civilian accounts emanate from this part of the city. Their testimonies contrast with those of the rebels themselves, with regard to public opinion. James Stephens, Marie Louise Norway and Robert Cecil Le Cren witnessed the surrender, the latter less than empathetic: 'I saw them being marched off to prison … a scratch-looking lot.'[8] However, their statements do not identify any discernible mood among those present. It is reasonable to

5.1
Dublin citizens continue
to wait for the re-opening
of the Dublin Savings
Bank, Lower Abbey
Street.
HE:EW.3802

assume that Le Cren in particular would have recorded any manifest opposition, reflecting his own views. In contrast, the rebels seemed to search the public mood. Frank Robbins presented a somewhat confused scene outside the College of Surgeons: 'Hundreds of people from around the vicinity were standing about, some out of curiosity, a small number sympathetic towards us, but the vast majority openly hostile.'[9] Thomas O'Donoghue remembered a particular experience: 'some of the onlookers cheered. This gave us some heart.'[10] Others identified friends among the descending crowd.[11] More menacingly, William Oman remarked of their passage through Grafton Street: 'The mob attempted to attack us.'[12] The St Stephen's Green witness statements present snapshots of public opinion as seen through the eyes of involved participants. They may not be the full picture.

More representative of Dublin public opinion, perhaps, was a sense of relief. Although sniper fire was heard from the rooftops of outlying posts, Sunday afternoon and evening were, described by many citizens as, comparatively 'quiet'. While the city centre remained off-limits to wandering civilians, many took the opportunity to sample the mundane delights of civilian life in their neighbouring streets, before the curfew set in again at 6.00 p.m: 'we go down to Worthington's and purchase

5.2
The burnt-out remains of
the GPO after the Rising.
HE:EW.3804

5.3
(Opposite page, top)
Dublin civilians
contemplate the scale
of the destruction on
Sackville Street.
HE:EW.2340

5.4
(Opposite page, bottom)
The destruction on
Sackville Street.
HE:EW.391d

a Solomon … fresh from the tank, "and very nice too"'; 'managed to get to Mass and back without excitement'; 'the bakeries are opening this evening … it is quite strange to hear children playing again in the street outside.'[13] Localised and lacking accurate information, civilians evidenced a naïveté as to the devastation elsewhere in the city. For some it was enough to know one had lived through it. The writer Katharine Tynan captured this exhausted catharsis: 'With infinite relief and some incredulity, came the tidings of surrender … the end of good, impractical men's hearts' desire, the end of that Irish Republic … it is over now with its stresses and piteousnesses, its hopes, its prides, and devotions – over for ever, except its enduring memory.'[14]

The citizens of Dublin woke up on Monday 1 May to a city they did not know. Restrictions on movement within the city centre were lifted, allowing thousands of men, women and children their first opportunity to visit Rising sites north of College Green. It was a

CORNER OF SACKVILLE ST. & EDEN QUAY, DUBLIN.   CHANCELLOR, DUBLIN.

traumatic experience. Many were lost for words, even in later diary entries: 'it is absolutely impossible to describe the appalling devastation made by the fires ... I had no idea it was on such a huge scale ... truly an awful price to pay.'[15] Clambering around the rubble, civilians were periodically alerted to the discovery of dead bodies while a smouldering stench permeated the streets. Many lingered on Sackville Street discussing the scenes with other bystanders; comparisons were made with Ypres and Louvain.[16] Others looked on in quiet disbelief: 'Well loved places on the upper part of Eden Quay had vanished. The Seamens' Institute where I played violin solos for Seamens' Concerts and been rewarded with plenty of tea and cake afterwards; Smiths the ironmongers where you could buy a good magnet for a penny; Hopkins the jewellers where unbelievable watches ticked in the windows and a chronometer in the centre window set the time for DUBLIN.'[17] Thoughts also turned to the suffering that must have been endured by fellow civilians in the vicinity: 'hundreds of innocent people burned to death or shot. Imagine the raging inferno and no assistance for the helpless people trapped.'[18] Thousands more living outside the perimeter of the North and South Circular Roads had to present Dublin Metropolitan Police passes at examination posts to gain access to the heart of the city.[19] 'You will cry when you see Sackville Street' was a common warning.[20] It is impossible to overestimate the impact of the destruction in Dublin on public opinion. It preoccupied civilians in diaries, correspondence and newspaper reports for days. Physical and commercial reconstruction of Dublin's main thoroughfare, meanwhile, became protracted and politicised.[21] On the effect of the executions on Irish public opinion, Michael Laffan has commented: 'people responded with warm emotions'.[22] The impact of the devastation, however, may well have initially numbed Dublin opinion towards the immediate repercussions for the rebels.

TRIAL AND RETRIBUTION?

Repercussions for the rebels constituted internment, imprisonment or execution. The eventual punishment handed out to each rebel was, in effect, decided the day after the surrenders, 1 May. Billeted at Richmond barracks, they were paraded across the barracks square under the watchful gaze of Dublin Metropolitan Police Special Branch detectives, who carefully scanned the personal details which the prisoners had given to the British soldiers in attendance. Through this process, the majority were, over a number of days, marched to Dublin port, from where they were deported to internment camps and prisons in Great Britain.[23] The minority, 187 men and women, were segregated from this group and removed to large holding cells within the barracks where they were to await court-martial.[24]

The decision to try the rebels under field general court martial (FGCM) is mired in controversy. Under the military justice system, field general court martial offered a particular variant of legal procedure. Unlike general court martial, which could also impose the death penalty, field general court martial did not enshrine the statutory right of the defendant to prior notice of the charge, legal assistance before the case or indeed counsel during the hearing. Decisions on these matters were at the discretion of local officers 'having due regard to public service'.[25] Charles Townshend has observed more widely of British approaches to treatment of the surrendered rebels: 'The beautiful simplicity of the military mind began to run into the tangle of the law.'[26] The legality of the proceedings has drawn both bitter criticism and careful vindication. The trials took place under section 1(7) of the Defence of the Realm Act (DORA) invoked on 26 April, which suspended the civilian right to civil trial. David Foxton has argued that this amendment was originally prescribed for periods of 'emergency', which did not apply to the military position in Ireland in early May: 'had it been desired, civil trial – or at the very least, trial by general court martial – would certainly have been possible'.[27] Seán Enright has advised that although, under DORA, the trials may have been 'defensible, lawful and could not be impeached by public opinion', the 'dominant purpose of trial by FGCM was not to administer justice but to maintain army discipline on the field [of war]'.[28] Seán McConville, meanwhile, has presented the view that the 'courts martial proceedings in 1916 were brisk but did adhere to rough standards

5.5
Joseph and John Plunkett awaiting interrogation at Richmond barracks.
HE:EWT.36

5.6

Éamon de Valera under military supervision at Richmond barracks.
HE:EWT.63

5.7

A group of rebels detained at Richmond barracks after the Rising.
HE:2007.1.162

of elementary justice'.[29] The clinical procedure with field general court martial, notwithstanding, the decision to hold the trials *in camera* had no basis in law.[30]

Field general court martial was a First World War extremity. The executions, correspondingly, should be viewed in this immediate international context. The physical and psychological pressures of the First World War provided the only context within which British public opinion could interpret the 1916 Rising. Locked in a war of survival against Germany and the Central Powers, the Rising in Dublin was widely reported in the British press as a German invasion of the United Kingdom, a reality reinforced by a wave of Zeppelin raids over British cities during the rebellion and in the the weeks which followed.[31] Editorial opinion in the national press was belligerent towards Irish nationalists without qualification. The normally restrained *The Times* charged:

> At present it is the duty of us all to insist that firm measures shall be taken to overawe sedition and to suppress the organisation, so many of whose members have dropped the mask and appeared as declared rebels in collusion with our enemies. In all measures of that kind the Government can rely upon the unanimous and hearty support of the King's loyal subjects.[32]

More bellicose rhetoric still was expressed in the British provincial press. The *Liverpool Daily Post* editorialised: 'the whole future of Ireland in its relation to the Empire depends upon the resolute stamping out of both active and passive rebellion … a clean sweep of the disloyal element which has been a canker at the heart of the community.'[33] The *Manchester Evening News* was similarly hostile: 'there can be no doubt that the period of leniency; of half measures, of toleration, has passed; that the period of blood and iron, so far as the traitors are concerned, has arrived.'[34] The *Birmingham Daily Gazette* captured public opinion in the Midlands: 'there will be general support for the action of the Government in taking the extremist measures to put a final end to this "made in Germany" rising.'[35] Public opinion in Scotland was outraged according to the *Edinburgh Evening News*: 'the effect of the rebellion on the public mind has not been so alarming as exasperating. The revolt is a mad business, but the people abominate the treachery of the affair.'[36] The *Cambria Daily Leader* recorded the feeling in Wales: 'deep is the sense of shame and indignation with which they view the acts of a small minority of traitorous irreconcilables.'[37]

It has been something of a commonplace, in view of the impact of the executions on Irish public opinion, to ascribe General Maxwell the moniker: 'the man who lost Ireland'.[38] More recent appraisals have suggested that the Prime Minister, Herbert Asquith, is deserving of an analogous title.[39] As executor to the military regime over which Maxwell briefly presided, Asquith should be apportioned culpability alongside the cabinet-appointed 'military governor'. If nothing else, Asquith's languid political style allowed Maxwell to exert his own military mindedness on public perception of the British State. His official remit had been to 'take such measures as may in your opinion be necessary for the prompt suppression of the rebellion'.[40] Maxwell determined to move swiftly against what he conceived to be Irish sedition. By 1 May, personnel for the implementation of field general court martial in Dublin was being assembled. One day later, house-to-house searches were instituted across Dublin. On 3 May, Maxwell ordered that 'Sinn Feiners' across Ireland be rounded up without recourse to their involvement in the Rising. Although cautioning discretion in later memoranda, Maxwell's directive was underlined, it would seem, on a fundamental view of the position: 'it is in the Irish character to loudly proclaim loyalty, and such protestations are pouring in, but this in my opinion is a reason we should be all the more watchful'. In total, 3,430 men and seventy-nine women across Ireland would be swept up in Maxwell's internment scheme.[41] Sampling the growing discontent in Dublin, John Dillon wrote to Maxwell on 8 May: 'it really would be difficult to exaggerate the amount of mischief that these executions are doing ... I very much doubt the wisdom of instituting searching and arrests on a large scale in districts in which there has been no disturbance.'[42] Asquith, however, demurred only slightly as the executions and widespread arrests came into effect, and did not intervene. Maxwell's military hold over British rule in Ireland was further entrenched with the resignations of the Chief Secretary for Ireland, Augustine Birrell, on 2 May and Under Secretary for Ireland, Matthew Nathan, one day later. 'The Government of Ireland,' Maxwell would remark days later, 'is rotten from A to Z.'[43] Asquith's announcement of a Royal Commission of Inquiry into the Irish administration's handling of the Rising implicitly supported Maxwell's view. Asquith, however, continued to reaffirm his belief that 'these sentences ... are passed under the authority of the Defence of the Realm Act (DORA) by tribunals which have statutory jurisdiction.'[44]

The activation of courts martial procedure under the Defence of the Realm Act did not allow for the institution of the death penalty, with one legal proviso, where proof could be established that breach of DORA was carried out 'with the intention of assisting the enemy'.[45] Although the Proclamation had explicitly alluded to 'gallant allies in Europe', this was no more than circumstantial evidence as physical signature to the document on the part of Pearse and the other six could not be proven. In the midst of this legal quagmire, Patrick Pearse provided an unlikely out. In a letter to his mother on the evening of 1 May, Pearse added a damning postscript at the top of the page: 'I understand that the German expedition on which I was counting actually set sail but was defeated by the British.'[46] Seizing upon this as evidence of 'intention of assisting the enemy', Pearse was court-martialled the following day. In his short trial Pearse made a brief but vainglorious statement, of what the prosecuting counsel W.E. Wylie later termed 'a Robert Emmet type', in which he again declared his reason for surrendering to save civilian lives and that he sought German military support.[47] It has been suggested that the latter testimony was a further attempt by Pearse to secure execution.[48] A comparable but more polished version of Pearse's speech was circulated at the time, the only statement then in the public domain.[49] Pearse was sentenced to 'death by being shot'. Presiding over his court martial, Brigadier General Blackadder later recorded: 'I have had to condemn to death one of the finest characters I have ever come across.'[50]

None of Thomas Clarke, Joseph Plunkett or Seán Mac Diarmada made political speeches in the dock. All were sentenced to death by firing squad. Éamonn Ceannt vigorously contested the charge of 'assisting the enemy' across two days of trial deliberation, cross-examining witnesses and calling two of his own: John MacBride and Thomas MacDonagh. The latter had already been executed by the time of his request. Despite his careful defence, Ceannt too was sentenced to death.[51] James Connolly, conversely, did make a prepared political speech. In his trial on 10 May, held at the Hospital Wing of Dublin Castle on account of the seriousness of his injuries, Connolly denied the charges against him, declaring that Easter Week had been a 'hurried uprising against long established authority' during which any injury to British Army prisoners was entirely 'unavoidable'. He reiterated the sanctity of their actions, denouncing the continued British presence in Ireland.[52] He was sentenced to death. An ornate speech purporting to have been that of Thomas MacDonagh during his court martial of 2 May, meanwhile, was widely published in Dublin in the days that followed. However, the official court-martial record evidences that MacDonagh, who had pleaded 'not guilty' to the charges, made only a curt statement that he assisted the British officers in effecting the surrender. Wylie, perhaps euphemistically, recorded: 'He was the only prisoner who said absolutely nothing.'[53]

The issue of disparities between the court-martial record and alternative accounts has elsewhere been more contentious. Countess Markievicz was tried at Richmond barracks on 4 May. She pleaded not guilty to the charge of colluding with Germany but 'guilty' of 'causing disaffection among the population'. In the official account Markievicz made the following short statement: 'I went out to fight for Ireland's freedom and it doesn't matter what happens to me. I did what I thought was right and I stand by it.'[54] W.E. Wylie's memoir recalled a drastically different scene:

'I'm only a woman. You cannot shoot a woman, you must not shoot a woman.' She never stopped moaning the whole time … We all felt slightly disgusted. She had been preaching rebellion to a lot of silly boys, death and glory, die for your country etc. And yet she was literally crawling. I won't say anymore. It revolts me still.[55]

The two portrayals are irreconcilable. Brian Barton has described Wylie's presentation as a 'wilful and scurrilous distortion' of her response, suggesting that it may have been rooted in 'sexual prejudice and rank misogyny'.[56] Charles Townshend, however, has countered that Wylie's account more broadly is 'very frank and self-deprecating', adding: 'had

5.8
Countess Markievicz, handcuffed, is transported from Richmond barracks in a Red Cross ambulance following her court-martial.
HE:EW.1742

such a scene occurred, it would probably not have been recorded'.[57] The significance of contemporary reports which support Wylie's claim has also been disputed.[58] Although Markievicz was sentenced to death, her execution was commuted to penal servitude 'solely and only on account of her sex', according to the court. The Prime Minister, Herbert Asquith had personally interceded in the matter, a ruling which General Maxwell was to concede.[59]

Writing to the Prime Minister on 11 May, Maxwell classified all those court-martialled and sentenced to death under three headings:

> (a) Those who signed the proclamation on behalf of the provisional Government and were also leaders in actual rebellion in Dublin. (b) Those who were in command of rebels actually shooting down troops, police and others. (c) Those whose offence was murder.[60]

The executions that followed did not strictly adhere to these conventions. William Pearse, Edward Daly, John MacBride, Con Colbert, Michael Mallin, Seán Heuston and Michael O'Hanrahan were all placed in category (b). The misfortunes of war were at play in at least three of these sentences. Michael O'Hanrahan, who was tried on 3 May, denied the charge against him, to which the only supporting evidence was a statement from a Major J.A. Armstrong of the Royal Inniskilling Fusiliers, that he had been in the area of Jacob's factory where shots had been fired; had been armed with pistols on surrender and had himself confirmed that he was an officer. O'Hanrahan, who, in actuality, held the position of a clerk at Volunteer Headquarters, said of his experience during Easter Week: 'As a soldier of the Republican Army … I acted under the orders of my superiors.'[61] Con Colbert, who was tried one day later, also denied the charge against him, to which Major J.A. Armstrong again stated that Colbert was one of several men who had surrendered dressed in Volunteer Captain's uniform at Jacob's Factory. Colbert was, in fact, attached to the Marrowbone Lane Garrison and as a junior officer.[62] Seán Heuston, was tried on 4 May and denied the charge. The evidence presented against him included a document signed by James Connolly, dated 24 April 1916: 'Captain Houston (sic) to seize the Mendicity at all cost'. Other military papers, without signature, were ascribed to Heuston, thereby bulking up the case. The latter, it has been argued convincingly, did not bear resemblance to Heuston's writing.[63] These three men were sentenced to death by the field general court martial. The reasons in these instances, however, are unclear, given that dozens of other rebels were simultaneously charged using similarly inconclusive evidence and avoided execution.[64] Seventy-five death sentences, in total, would be commuted, to life imprisonment and other, lesser, prison terms.

In the case of William Pearse and John MacBride, however, the prosecution appears to have been determined. Pearse, was later described by Maxwell, in his *A Short history of rebels*, as a Commandant. This was not the case. He held no higher position among the rebel force than Captain. Pearse's behaviour during his trial, however, did little to mitigate the apparent pre-prepared verdict. Faced with the familiar charge of taking part in the rebellion 'with the intention and for the purpose of assisting the enemy', Pearse pleaded 'guilty'. The evidence presented in trial amounted to a statement by Lieutenant S.L. King that he was convinced that William Pearse was an Officer, although he did not know his rank. Pearse made a sparse reply, including the following remarks: 'I was throughout only a personal attaché to my brother P.H. Pearse.'[65] It has been suggested that William Pearse's restrained opposition to the limited evidence against him derived from his unwillingness to live on without his brother.[66] Tried one day later, meanwhile, John MacBride denied the charge against him. Two prosecution witnesses, including the ubiquitous Major J.A. Armstrong, testified that they had seen MacBride surrender with the Jacob's Factory garrison. More incriminating were the letter cuttings from Thomas MacDonagh, later found on his person, which named him as a Commandant. This, it has been argued, must have been a clerical error, as MacDonagh only instructed the former to serve as Vice-Commandant during the rebellion itself.[67] However, it is also true that MacBride did not actively contest the charge in court. 'The accused' Brigadier General Blackadder would later write 'wished to die';[68] he was sentenced to death by the field general court martial.

Maxwell's description of Edward Daly and Michael Mallin as 'leaders in actual rebellion in Dublin' held more weight. Both men denied the charge. Daly, who was tried on 3 May, directly denied the charge of 'with the intention and purpose of assisting the enemy', and presented the prosecution with the challenge of presenting evidence to support that specific claim. His astute interpretation of the charge, however, did not save him from the death penalty.[69] Michael Mallin, court-martialled on 5 May, offered a much less impressive defence:

> I had no commission whatever in the Citizen Army. I was never taken into the confidence of James Connolly. I was under the impression I was going out for manoeuvres on Sunday … Shortly after my arrival at St Stephen's Green the firing started and the Countess of Markievicz ordered me to take command of the men as I had been so long associated with them.[70]

Mallin's claims were untrue and unsettling. In an attempt to escape execution, he had put Countess Markievicz's life at risk. There have been suggestions that Mallin anticipated Markievicz's reprieve from the death penalty and consequently presented himself as subordinate to her in his evidence.[71] However, given his later apprehension as to his young family's welfare without him, it is much more likely that this burden of concern drove him to a desperate form of defence. Mallin's pleas proved unsuccessful. He was sentenced to death by firing squad. To judge by Maxwell's criteria, Éamon de Valera should also have met that fate. As the Commandant of Boland's Mill, which had inflicted large casualties on British Forces at Mount Street, de Valera was indeed court-martialled on 8 May. Of the fragmentary evidence available, it is clear that he was identified as a Commandant during the trial and sentenced to death.[72] That this was not, in the end, carried out, has been the source of considerable public intrigue. One view, popularised after the Irish Civil War, was that de Valera's exemption was on account of his American citizenship, particularly his family's diplomatic appeals to this effect. This has been downplayed in more recent academic analyses which have underlined the timing of de Valera's court martial in relation to political concerns over the continuing executions.[73] In this case, W.E. Wylie's account is insightful. On receiving Asquith's telegram to curtail the executions, Wylie informed Maxwell that Éamon de Valera was next on the list: 'Who is he? I've never heard of him before … I wonder would he be likely to make trouble in the future?' 'I wouldn't think so, sir,' Wylie replied, 'I don't think he's important enough.'[74]

'The blood of martyrs is the seed of martyrs.'

*Fr Columbus Murphy of
the Capuchin Order,
to General Maxwell,
29 April 1916*

THE EXECUTIONS

Cold-faced, grimly lit and structurally neglected, Kilmainham jail was a suitably darkened scene for the executions. Those sentenced to death were removed to cells within the formerly abandoned building only hours before. Lacking running water and adequate bedding, the rooms were illuminated only by candles. Names of previous inmates were scratched on the walls. It was here, in their final hours, that the rebels met family members for the last time. They were also permitted to receive members of the Capuchin Order in the closing moments. Fr Augustine OFM, Fr Aloysius OFM and Fr Albert OFM tended to the men before their execution. However, it was only after the first three executions, on Aloysius' complaint, that they were then allowed to be present at the Stonebreakers' Yard to bless the dead bodies. The executions were supposed to follow a set procedure. Not all did. The first man on each date was to be brought before a firing squad of twelve men at 3.45 a.m. The prisoner, hands tied behind his back and a piece of white cloth placed over his heart, was then blindfolded and stood or was seated against the wall. Twelve shots, including one dummy round, would then be fired on command. After each execution the body was removed to a newly dug grave at Arbour Hill and quicklime added to speed decay, before the next body arrived. The remains would never be returned to the families.[75]

5.9
(Opposite page)
The entrance to
Kilmainham jail.
HE:EWT.423.2

Mrs. Pearse
St. Enda's College
Rathfarnham;
or Cullenswood House,
Oakley Road,
Ranelagh

Kilmainham Prison,
Dublin.
3rd / May 1916.

My dearest Mother,

I have been hoping up to now that it would be possible for me to see you again, but it does not seem possible. Good-bye, dear, dear Mother. Through you I say good-bye to Wow-wow, M.B., Willie, Miss Byrne, Micheál, Cousin Maggie, and everyone at St. Enda's. I hope and believe that Willie and the St. Enda's boys will be safe.

I have written two papers about financial affairs and one about my books, which I want you to get. With them are a few poems which I want added to the poems of mine in MS. in the large bookcase. You asked me to write a little poem which would seem to be said by you about me. I have written it, and one copy is at Arbour Hill Barracks with the other papers, and Father Aloysius is taking charge of another copy of it.

I have just received Holy Communion. I am happy except for the

Patrick Pearse
3 May 1916

Patrick Pearse spent his last hours writing to his mother and to Ireland. His parting letter was suffused with affectionate remembrances to his family and surety of his place in Irish history. His final poem, *The Wayfarer,* also composed within the walled confines at Kilmainham, was a melancholic ode to more innocent times. Unbeknownst to Pearse, his mother was travelling across the city to be with him as he wrote. Resigned to a night of solitude he took confession and Holy Communion from Fr Aloysius after midnight. He showed no fear or anxiety, but rather contentment. The news that James Connolly had converted to Catholicism brought further peace of mind. Fr Aloysius was forced to leave the cell between 2.00 a.m. and 3.00 a.m. Somewhere in north Dublin the car conveying Mrs Pearse was stalled by a military picket. At 3.45 a.m. Pearse was marched to the Stonebreakers' Yard. William Pearse, who had been escorted to his cell for one last goodbye, missed his brother by minutes. He was to hear the fatal shots. Blindfolded and hands tied, Patrick Pearse faced the firing squad alone. He was thirty-six.[76]

5.11
Patrick Pearse.
Charcoal drawing by
Seán O'Sullivan.
HE:EW.2012.14

5.10
(Opposite page)
Patrick Pearse's last letter,
to his mother Margaret
on 3 May 1916.
HE:EWL.232a

5.12
Thomas Clarke's empty
spectacle case, pencil and
book of postage stamps.
HE:EW.444.1; HE:EW.444.2;
HE:EW.444.3

Thomas Clarke

3 May 1916

Against his life-long conviction, Thomas Clarke spent his last night in a British military prison. It was on this subject that his wife Kathleen Clarke confronted him when she first entered his cell at Kilmainham jail. He confided that the surrender had been the will of the Provisional Government, to which he was bound. His execution, he assured her, would still be a soldier's death. Over the course of two hours, Thomas Clarke spoke exultantly of Ireland's future and asked his wife to convey his aspirations to the Irish people in the form of an open letter. She decided against mentioning her pregnancy in their final moments together. Within hours Thomas Clarke was marched to the Stonebreakers' Yard. His request to take his execution without blindfold was rejected. At 4.15 a.m. the firing squad took aim. He was fifty-eight.[77]

5.13
Thomas Clarke.
Charcoal drawing by
Seán O'Sullivan.
HE:EW.2012.15

~~Thomas McDonagh~~ Bell   Kilmainham Jail
                                            Midnight. Tuesday 2/5/16

I Thomas McDonagh having now heard the sentence of a
Court Martial on me to-day declare that in all my acts all the
acts for which i have been arraigned i have been actuated by
one only motive the love of independant State. i still hope and
~~pray that my acts may bring~~
i am to die at dawn 3.50 a.m. i am ready to ~~die~~ die in so holy a cause my
Country will reward my deed richly. on April the 30th i was astonished to
recieve by message from P H Pearse (Comanding General of the Irish Republic)
an order to surrender unconditionally to
the British General i did not obey this order as it came from a Prisoner i was
then in Supreme command of the Irish Army and i then consulted with my
second in command and decided to conform to this order i knew that it
would involve my death and the death of other leaders i hoped it would
save many True Men among my followers good lives for Ireland Thank
God it has done so and God approve of our deeds for my self i have no
~~regret~~ for my wife and my loving Children Donagh and Barbara my Country will take them
in hands i know i allowed too much of my time to the National cause and too
little to Money Making to leave them a competence God help and support them
and give them a Happy and Prosperous life for ther was never a Better or
Truer Woman than my Wife Muriel or more adorable Children than Donagh and
Barbara it Breaks my Heart to think i shall never see them again but
i have not wept or murmered i counted the cost of this and i am ready to
pay for it. Muriel has been sent for But i do not know if she can come she
may have no one to take care of the children while she is coming my
~~money affairs~~ are in a bad way i am insured for Three Hundred Pounds
But i have Borrowed one Hundred Pounds from the Alliance Company i have
a Banking difference of Eighty Pounds that Brings to one Hundred &
Twenty Pounds from ther funds if they Pay anything in addition i have
insured my Children for 100 each in the united Company Payment of my
Premiums to end at my death Money to be Paid to my Children at the age of
21. i ask my Brother Joseph McDonagh and my good kind and constant
friend David Huston to help my Poor Wife in these Money Matters my
Brother John who came with me and stood by me all last Week has

Thomas MacDonagh
3 May 1916

Thomas MacDonagh suffered his final hours at Kilmainham without seeing his wife Muriel, son Donagh or daughter Barbara. Attempts to locate them, on the part of the military authorities, had proven unsuccessful. Disconsolate, he penned a last heartfelt letter to them all as the night slipped away. Around his neck was a pair of rosary beads, given to him by his sister, Sr Francesca of the Sisters of Charity, who had visited him only hours before. He took confession and Holy Communion with Fr Aloysius before he was left alone in his cell somewhere between 2.00 a.m. and 3.00 a.m. He was described as calm, happy, even buoyant, in those final moments. MacDonagh is reported to have whistled as he was led from his cell to the Stonebreakers' Yard. Sensing the nervousness of the twelve-man firing squad, he offered each a cigarette. Blindfolded and hands tied behind his back, Thomas MacDonagh faced the firing squad at approximately 3.30 a.m. 'They all died bravely,' it was observed, 'but MacDonagh died like a prince.' He was thirty-eight.[78]

5.15
Thomas MacDonagh.
Charcoal drawing by
Seán O'Sullivan.
HE:EW.2012.13

5.14
(Opposite page)
Thomas MacDonagh's
handwritten last
testament (3 May).
HE:EW.4220

5.16
The rosary beads
given by Joseph
Plunkett to Sergeant
W. Hand, a member
of the firing squad,
before his execution.
HE:EW.5368

Joseph Plunkett
4 May 1916

Joseph Plunkett's dying wish, that he be married to Grace Gifford, was granted. At 8.00 p.m. on the evening of 3 May, they were brought before Fr Eugene McCarthy, in the prison chapel. Two soldiers doubled as witnesses. At the close of the ceremony, Plunkett's handcuffs were refastened and he was led back to his cell alone. It was only after midnight that Grace Plunkett was permitted to see her husband again, this for the last time. Supervised by a prison guard, they spent ten minutes in conversation before she was forced to leave. Joseph Plunkett was afterwards attended by Fr Sebastian O'Brien of the Capuchin Order, to whom he entrusted his spectacles and wedding ring, before being marched to the Stonebreakers' Yard. He was described as calm, assured and courteous as he faced the firing squad. He was twenty-eight.[79]

5.17
Joseph Plunkett.
Charcoal drawing by
Seán O'Sullivan.
HE:EW.2012.18

To   Mrs Clarke   Kilmainham Prison
        10 Richmond Rd.
                Dublin.   May 3rd 1916.

        Madam.
                I beg to inform you that your brother

is a prisoner in the above prison & would like to see

you tonight. I am sending a car with an attendant to

bring you here.

                I am, Madam
                        Your obedient servant,
                                W S Linnon.
                                     Major
                                     Commandant.

11-30 P.m.
11 55 arrived Kilmainham
12.33 a.m.
Got to house with Pat.
Pat & personal down for
they take her to
in delay.

Edward Daly
4 May 1916

Kathleen Clarke was returned to Kilmainham jail on the night of 3 May, to see off her only brother, Edward Daly. She was joined by two other sisters, Madge and Laura. They found him lying on the floor. In a meeting lasting barely fifteen minutes, they discussed the Rising and his place in Irish history. Daly spoke glowingly of Patrick Pearse, Thomas MacDonagh and Thomas Clarke. Hours before he had insisted on seeing and saluting Clarke's dead body. Embracing his three sisters at the end, he calmly bade them goodbye. Daly was later attended in his cell by Fr Columbus Murphy, whom he had met previously during the surrender. Just after 4.00 a.m. Edward Daly faced the firing squad. He was twenty-five.[80]

5.19
Edward Daly.
Charcoal drawing by
Seán O'Sullivan.
HE:EW.2012.12

5.18
(Opposite page)
Letter from Major
W.J. Lennon, British
commandant at
Kilmainham jail, to
Madge Daly giving
permission to visit her
brother (3 May).
HE:EW.148

5.20
A button from Michael
O'Hanrahan's uniform
given by him to his
sisters at Kilmainham
jail. Inscribed are the
words 'Capt. Micheál Ó
hAnnracháin. Executed
4th May 1916'.
HE:EW.1053a

5.21
A button from Michael
O'Hanrahan's uniform
given by him to his sisters
at Kilmainham jail.
Inscribed are the words
'Micheál 4-5-16'.
HE:EW.1053b

Michael O'Hanrahan
4 May 1916

5.22
Michael O'Hanrahan.
Charcoal drawing by
Seán O'Sullivan.
HE:EW.2012.13

On the eve of his execution, Michael O'Hanrahan solicited a final visit from his family. Suspecting that the military authorities were intent on arresting them, only two of his sisters, Eily and Áine, followed their order to travel to Kilmainham. Upon their arrival they were informed by Kathleen Clarke of their brother's likely fate. Michael O'Hanrahan confirmed their worst fears moments later. Surrounded by six soldiers and two officers, he stoically prepared a hand-written Will before embracing his sisters for the final time. Eily fainted on leaving the cell. Assured in his final hours, he took confession and the last rites from Fr Augustine, who accompanied him to the Stonebreakers' Yard. Dressed in military uniform, Michael O'Hanrahan was executed by firing squad between 4.00 a.m. and 4.30 a.m. He was thirty-nine.[81]

2859

₊ The Person who registers the Death **MUST BRING THIS CERTIFICATE TO THE REGISTRAR (if not already sent).**

BIRTHS AND DEATHS REGISTRATION ACT (IRELAND), 1880.

MEDICAL CERTIFICATE of the CAUSE of DEATH.

[To be signed and given by the Medical Attendant to some person by the Act required to give information concerning the Death to the Registrar of the District in which the Death occurred, and to no other person.]

I HEREBY CERTIFY that I ~~attended~~ *was present at the execution of William Pearse* ~~whose age was stated to be~~ ; *that I last saw h* on the *4th* day of *May* 19 *16*; ~~that he died*~~ ~~on the~~ ~~day~~ of ~~19—~~, at† *Detention Barracks Kilmainham* ; and that to the best of my knowledge and belief the cause of h *is* death ~~and duration of h~~ ~~illness were~~ as hereunder written.

* Should the Medical Attendant not feel justified in taking upon himself the responsibility of certifying the *fact* of Death, he may here insert the words, "*as I am informed.*"

† In case the death occurred in a Public Institution, the person filling the Certificate is requested to state also the particulars as under.

‡ The duration of each form of Disease or Symptom is reckoned from its commencement until death occurs.

Cause of Death.	Duration of Disease ‡			
	Years	Months	Days	Hours
~~(a) Primary~~ *Shooting, by order of*				
~~(b) Secondary~~ *Field General Court Martial*				

† Former stated Residence of deceased.

Witness my hand, this *2nd* day of *June* 19 *16*

Signature *M. Stanley Capt R Amc*

Registered Qualification *M B; B Ch Dub Univ.*

Residence *King George V Hosp Dublin*

N.B.—This Certificate is intended solely for the use of the Registrar. The person to whom it is given by the Medical Attendant must deliver it or cause it to be delivered to the Registrar within five days of its receipt, and in default of such delivery is liable to a penalty not exceeding £2.

Entered at No. , in Register of Deaths, District of Union of

Registrar.

Date.

[OVER

5.23

William Pearse's death certificate.

HE:EW.796.4

William Pearse
4 May 1916

Just after midnight on the morning 4 May, William Pearse received his sister and mother, both called Margaret, for the last time. Surrounded by three soldiers and little light, the three spoke briefly about personal matters and Patrick's execution. Anxious that he should receive the sacraments before his death, they left his cell after 2.00 a.m. Her brother, Margaret remembered, gazed sadly as they disappeared from view. Fr Aloysius arrived just as Pearse was being led out to be executed. Hands tied behind his back, he received confession and Holy Communion, before being marched to the Stonebreakers' Yard. He was thirty-four.[82]

5.24
William Pearse.
Charcoal drawing by
Seán O'Sullivan.
HE:EW.2012.11

5.25
A silver cigarette case
inscribed by John
MacBride during Easter
Week: '25th April 1916
Major John MacBride For
Ireland's honor 25/4/16'.
HE:2012.1.2

John MacBride

5 May 1916

John MacBride was attended in his last hours by Fr Augustine Hayden of the Capuchin Order, to whom he entrusted his rosary beads and watch for delivery to his mother, and his remaining money for the benefit of the poor. He took confession and Holy Communion with Fr Augustine in his cell before being marched to the Stonebreakers' Yard. Described as being calm, quiet and good-natured in his closing moments, he was reported to have told the twelve-man firing squad: 'I've been looking down rifle barrels all my life. Fire when I bow my head.' His request neither to be blindfolded, nor to have his hands bound, was denied. Fr Augustine remained at his side. John MacBride was executed at 3.45 a.m. He was forty-seven.[83]

5.26
John MacBride.
Charcoal drawing by
Seán O'Sullivan.
HE:EW.2012.8

Cell 88,
Kilmainham Gaol
7 May 1916

I leave for the guidance of other Irish Revolutionaries who may
tread the path which I have trod this advice, never to treat
with the enemy, never to surrender at his mercy, but to fight
to a finish. I see nothing gained but grave disaster caused,
by the surrender which has marked the end of the Irish
Insurrection of 1916 — so far at least as Dublin is concerned. The enemy has not cherished one generous thought
for those who, with little hope, with poor equipment, and
weak in numbers, withstood his forces for one glorious week.
Ireland has shown she is a Nation. This generation
can claim to have raised sons as brave as any that went
before. And in the years to come Ireland will honour those
who risked all for her honour at Easter in 1916. I bear
no ill will towards those against whom I have fought. I have found
the common soldiers and the higher officers human and companion-
able, even the English who were actually in the fight against us.
Thank God soldiering for Ireland has opened my heart and made me
see poor humanity where I expected to see only scorn and reproach.
I have met the man who escaped from me by a ruse under the Red
Cross. But I do not regret having withheld my fire. He gave me cakes!
I wish to record the magnificent gallantry and fearless, calm
determination of the men who fought with me. All, all, were
simply splendid. Even I knew no fear nor panic and shrunk
from no risk even as I shrink not now from the death
which faces me at daybreak. I hope to see God's face even
for a moment in the morning. His will be done. All here are
very kind. My poor wife saw me yesterday, and bore up — so
my warden told me — even after she left my presence. Poor
Áine, poor Ronan. God is their only shield now that I
am removed. And God is a better shield than I. I have just
seen Áine, Nell, Richard and Mick and bade them a conditional good
bye. Even now they have hope!

Éamonn Ceannt

Éamonn
Ceannt
8 May 1916

Upon learning of his death sentence on the afternoon of 7 May, Éamonn Ceannt fastidiously prepared for his execution. From his barely lit cell, he wrote a series of carefully thought-out letters to his wife and son, and prepared another, open letter to the Irish people. That evening just after 10.00 p.m. he was able to receive his wife Áine, sister, Nell, and two of his brothers, Michael and Richard, in his cell, for only twenty minutes. He described himself as having presented a cold military exterior in his final hours. In the hours before and during his execution he was attended by Fr Augustine Hayden. He was thirty-four.[84]

5.28
Éamonn Ceannt.
Charcoal drawing by
Seán O'Sullivan.
HE:EW.2012.1

5.27
(Opposite page)
Éamonn Ceannt's letter
to the people of Ireland
(8 May).
HE:EWL.147

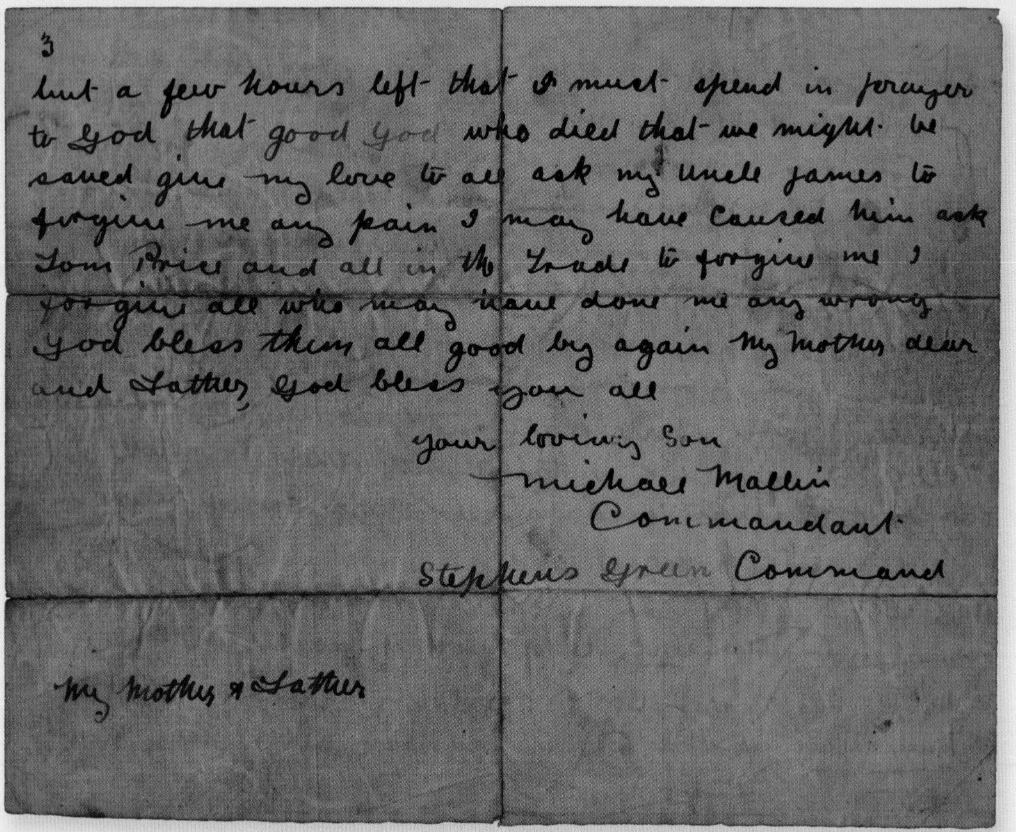

3

but a few hours left that I must spend in prayer
to God that good God who died that we might be
saved give my love to all ask my uncle James to
forgive me any pain I may have caused him ask
Tom Price and all in the trade to forgive me I
forgive all who may have done me any wrong
God bless them all good by again my mother dear
and father, God bless you all
                              your loving Son
                                Michael Mallin
                                  Commandant
                        Stephens Green Command

my mother & father

5.29
Michael Mallin's last
letter to his parents
(8 May).
HE:EW.1233

Michael Mallin

8 May 1916

The journey on which Michael Mallin was brought when he was transferred from Richmond barracks to Kilmainham jail took him past his home in Inchicore. He noticed the family dog wandering freely. It would not be until just before his execution, however, that he saw his family. Waiting for them in his cell, he wrote a trembling letter to his wife agonising over their future without him. Shortly after midnight Mallin was visited by his mother Sarah, his wife Agnes, his four children – John, Séamus, Úna and Joseph, his sister Katie, and his brother, Thomas. It was an emotional scene. Agnes Mallin collapsed on the floor as she learned his sentence. Her husband then presented her with his hopes for their children; one, Maura Constance, as yet unborn. In a quiet moment with his brother, Mallin expressed his preparedness to die for Ireland, and disdain for Irishmen who were fighting and dying in the British Army. On their departure he was attended by Fr Augustine, who followed him to the Stonebreakers' Yard. At 3.45 a.m. Michael Mallin faced the firing squad. He was forty-one.[85]

5.30
Michael Mallin.
Charcoal drawing by
Seán O'Sullivan.
HE:EW.2012.3

Whatever I have done I have done it as a soldier of Ireland and what I believe to be in, my country's best interests.

I have (Thank God) no vain regrets, after all it is better to be a corpse than a coward.

Wont you see that my mother gets all the assistance you can give her, and refund her the salary due to me, also the money & from the superannuation fund she will badly need it all.

Faithfully yours
signed J. J. Heuston.

Seán Heuston

8 May 1916

In his final hours, Seán Heuston asked his family to be with him at Kilmainham jail. Writing honestly to his brother Michael, he conceded: 'I am to be executed in the morning. If the rules of the order allow it, I want you to get permission at once and come in here and see me for the last time in this world.' His brother was joined at Heuston's side by his mother, Maria, his sister, Theresa, his cousin, Lil, and his aunt, Theresa McDonald. Heuston was described as serene and determinedly stoic in their final meeting. The soldier guarding his cell, by contrast, was crying. The family were led away at 3.00 a.m. He was visited, finally, by Fr Albert, who found him kneeling beside a table with rosary beads in his hands. Awaiting his execution in the Stonebreakers' Yard, Heuston kissed a crucifix in the priest's hand. The firing squad assembled just after 3.45 a.m. He was twenty-five.[86]

5.32
Seán Heuston.
Charcoal drawing by
Seán O'Sullivan.
HE:EW.2012.2

5.31
(Opposite page)
Seán Heuston's last letter,
to Mr Walsh, on 8 May
1916.
HE:EW.1271

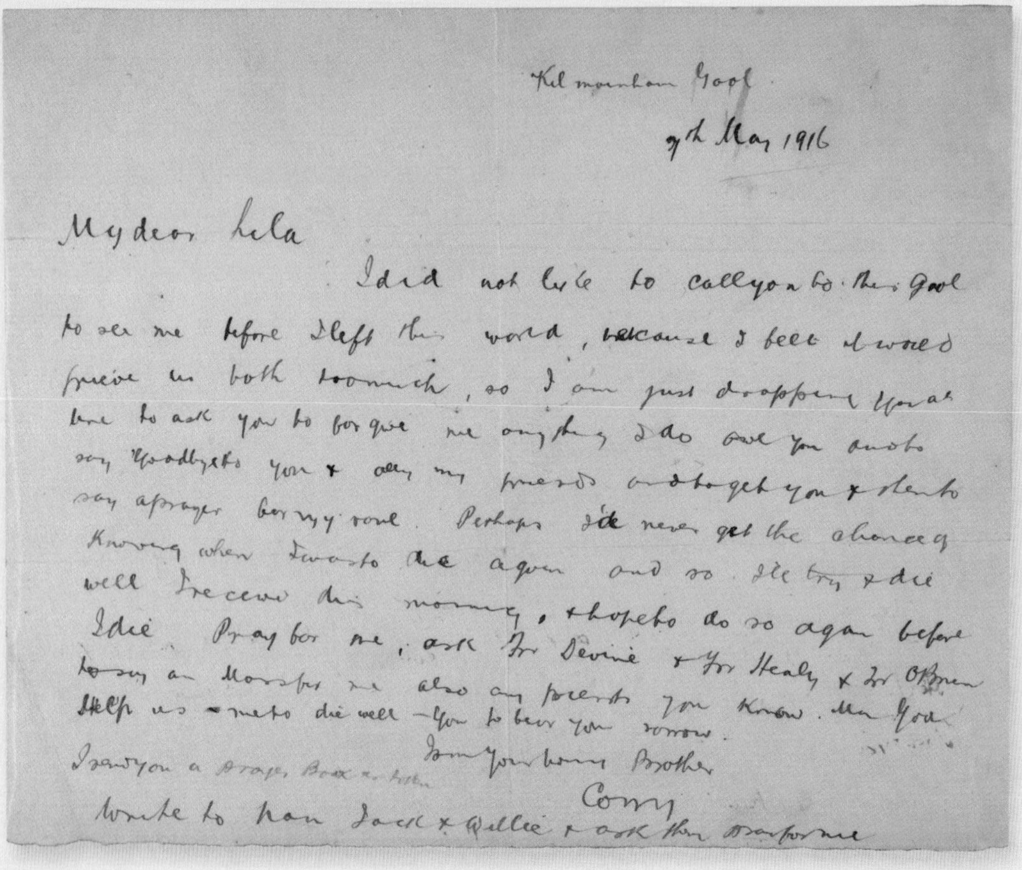

Kilmainham Gaol.

9th May 1916

My dear Lila

I did not like to call you to this Gaol to see me before I left this world, because I felt it would grieve us both too much, so I am just dropping you a line to ask you to forgive me anything I do owe you and to say Goodbye to you & all my friends and to get you & them to say a prayer for my soul. Perhaps I'll never get the chance of knowing when I was to die again and so I'll try & die well. I received this morning, + hope to do so again before I die. Pray for me, ask Fr Devine & Fr Healy & Fr O'Brien to say a Mass for me also any priests you know. May God help us — me to die well — you to bear your sorrow.

I am your loving Brother

Cozy

I sent you a Prayer Book in token

Write to Han, Jack & Willie & ask them to pray for me

5.33
Con Colbert's last letter,
to his sister Lila, on 8
May 1916.
HE:EW.501

Con Colbert
8 May 1916

Con Colbert did not send for his family to visit him lest the meetings 'would grieve us both too much'. Instead he wrote ten letters, one each to his sisters Lila, Nora, Gretta and Katty, his brothers Mack and Jim, his aunt Mary, his cousin Máire, friends Annie and Lily, and the Daly family in Limerick. He was accompanied to the Stonebreakers' Yard by Fr Augustine, who noted 'his lips moving in prayer'. In the final moments before he was shot, Colbert suggested to the soldier pinning the white target paper to his chest: 'Wouldn't it be better to pin it up higher – nearer the heart?' He was twenty-seven.[87]

5.34
Con Colbert.
Charcoal drawing by
Seán O'Sullivan.
HE:EW.2012.4

Thomas Kent

9 May 1916

Despite not having taken part in the Rising, Thomas Kent was tried and executed in Cork detention barracks on 9 May 1916. He held in his hands rosary beads lent to him by the military chaplain, Fr John Sexton. Kent was buried in the grounds of the barracks, requests by his family for burial in the family vault being denied. He was fifty.[88]

5.36
Thomas Kent.
Charcoal drawing by
Seán O'Sullivan.
HE:EW.2012.9

5.35
(Opposite page)
A sketch by Matthew
Barry of Thomas
Kent's prison cell at
Cork military detention
barracks.
HE:EW.48

Kilmainham Prison
Dublin
May 11th 1916.

My Dear Daly

Just a wee note to bid you Good Bye.
I expect in a few hours to join Tom and the other
heroes in a better world. I have been sentenced to
a Soldier's death — to be shot tomorrow, morning.
I have nothing to say about this only that I look
on it as a part of the days work. We die
that the Irish nation may live. Our blood will
re baptise and reinvigorate the old land. Knowing
this it is superfluous to say how happy I feel. I
know now what I have always felt, that the Irish
nation can never die. Let present day place hunters
condemn our action as they will, posterity will judge
us aright from the effects of our action.

I know I will meet you soon, until then
Good Bye. God guard and protect you and all in
no 15. You have had a sore trial, but I know
quite well that Mrs Daly and all the girls
feel proud in spite of a little temporary and
natural grief. that her Son, & the girls, their brother
as well as Tom are included in the list of honours.
Kindly remember me specially to Mrs Clarke and
tell her I am the same Seán that she always
knew.

God Bless you all
As ever Sincerely Yours.
Seán mac Diarmada

Seán Mac Diarmada

12 May 1916

Seán Mac Diarmada requested the company of close friends and associates in his final hours. His visiting party comprised Phyllis Ryan, his accountant John Reynolds and his landlady Elizabeth Dunne. Most intimate of all was Josephine Mary ('Min') Ryan whom Mac Diarmada had described as: 'she who in all probability, had I lived, would have been my wife.' The five warmly discussed mutual friends, places and memories for three hours, staving off thoughts of the impending execution. His final letters to John Daly, and his brothers and sisters respectively, illuminate the convivial mood. As a parting gift, Mac Diarmada initialled buttons and coins for various friends; his pocket-watch he left for Barney Mellows. At 3.00 a.m. the group was escorted out of the cell. Embracing Min Ryan he confided 'We never thought that this would be the end.' Before the execution, he was attended to by Fr Eugene McCarthy. At 3.45 a.m. Seán Mac Diarmada faced the firing squad. He was thirty-three.[89]

5.38
Seán Mac Diarmada.
Charcoal drawing by
Seán O'Sullivan.
HE:EW.2012.7

5.37
(Opposite page)
Seán Mac Diarmada's
last letter, to John Daly,
on 11 May 1916.
HE:EW.145

Statement.

(To the Field General Court Martial held at Dublin Castle on May 9 1916. The evidence mainly went to establish the fact that the accused James Connolly was in command at the _____ of _____ and casualties. The Government pressed for the _____ sedition. Two of the witnesses however, swore to bring an alleged instance of wantonly _____ this body of prisoners. The Court held that these charges were evident and could not be placed against the prisoner.)

I do not want to make any defense except against charges of wanton cruelty to prisoners. Those trifling allegations that have been made if they really ever that really happened deal only with the almost unavoidable incidents of a hurried uprising against long established authority and nowhere show evidence of set purpose to wantonly injure unarmed persons.

We went out to break the connection _____ between this country and the British Empire, and to establish an Irish Republic. We believed that the call we then issued to the people of Ireland was a nobler call in a holier cause than any call issued to them during this war, having any connection with the war. We succeeded in proving that Irishmen are ready to die endeavouring to win for Ireland those national rights which the British have been asking them to die to win for Belgium. As long as that remains the case the cause of Irish freedom is safe.

Believing that the British Government has no right in Ireland, never had any right in Ireland, and never can have any right in Ireland, the presence in any one generation of Irishmen of even a respectable minority ready to die to affirm that truth makes that government forever a usurpation and a crime against human progress.

James Connolly
12 May 1916

James Connolly was court-martialled in Dublin Castle Hospital because of the leg fracture he had received during Easter Week. It was there, at 11.00 p.m. on 10 May, that he received his wife Lillie and daughter Nora for the last time. The sudden realisation that he was to be executed shattered his wife who choked away tears: 'Don't cry Lillie, you'll unman me.' Connolly slipped a written copy of his court-martial statement into the trusted hands of his daughter. 'But your life James, your beautiful life,' his wife lamented. 'Well, Lillie,' he answered, 'hasn't it been a full life, and isn't this a good end?' His wife and daughter were shown out of the room. At 1.00 a.m. Connolly took confession and Holy Communion from Fr Aloysius. Unable to walk, he was stretchered in his pyjamas to a waiting ambulance and brought to the Stonebreakers' Yard at Kilmainham jail. On account of his injuries, Connolly was seated on a kitchen chair, his hands untied. At dawn the firing party took final aim. His body fell forward in the hail of bullets, left hand grasping the chair. He was forty-seven.[90]

5.40
James Connolly.
Charcoal drawing by
Seán O'Sullivan.
HE:EW.2012.6

5.39
(*Opposite page*)
James Connolly's hand-
written court-martial
statement.
HE:EW.1016

THE EXECUTIONS AND PUBLIC OPINION

The Irish public was removed from the poignant scenes at Kilmainham jail. Public opinion, paradoxically, was at a premium in the days immediately following the surrender. Of the Dublin-published dailies, only the *Irish Times* went to press before the executions began. Its reappearance on Dublin streets on 2 May prompted immense public interest. William Cant reported the paper to be 'doing a roaring trade' while Marie Louisa Norway observed that the paper boys 'had a ready sale for their papers at three times their value'.[91] Its editorial, entitled 'The Government's duty', advocated a 'stern policy of suppression and punishment'.[92] Its line on 3 May, before news of the first executions, was more clinical:

> The country has no desire that punishments should be pushed to the point of mere revenge, but in the interests of national peace and safety, it demands that stern justice shall be inflicted on the authors of one of the most deliberate and far-reaching crimes in Irish history.[93]

Was the *Irish Times* representative of a prevailing sentiment in Dublin and further afield? Fergus Pyle and Owen Dudley Edwards have noted perceptively: 'The *Irish Times* obtained a far wider public than that catered to by its editorial columns … a large readership which heartily cursed its editorial views.'[94] Scepticism, indeed, was registered by some in Dublin. Sending copies to his brother on 6 May, Alfred Fannin advised: 'You will make allowances for the view taken.'[95] Keeping John Redmond informed from Dublin, meanwhile, John Dillon wrote exasperatedly: 'Its leaders are most bloodthirsty and wicked and they ought to be dealt with.'[96] The *Irish Times*, however, was only one forum of Dublin opinion. Its readers were just as likely to have been influenced by the views of other civilians as they trawled through the Dublin wreckage. It is in this latter respect that it more certainly chimed with public opinion: 'This tragic insurrection threatens to kill all our hopes. It has dealt a cruel blow at Dublin's trade and industry … the economic and social life of our city, which has been in abeyance for a week, must be resumed under sound and permanent conditions.'[97]

In an important intervention on the debate over the executions as tipping point, Joe Lee has asserted: 'The real historical challenge is to reconstruct reactions in the light of information actually available to the public at the time.'[98] This is paramount but problematic. As has been noted, a disproportionate number of civilian accounts published recorded the experiences of unionists bearing a certain social status. Moreover, public support for the Rising and the rebels was heavily proscribed by censorship.[99]

The Rising was not fully understood as of 4 May 1916; nor were the executions. The slim four-page issues of the *Irish Times* on 2, 3 and 4 May contained fragmentary reports on the rebellion, which added to the public record with each edition: 2 May (surrenders at South Dublin Union, Sackville Street, Jacob's Factory; scenes at Fairview, Portobello, Cork), 3 May (death of The O'Rahilly; fighting at Ballsbridge, the Magazine Fort and Ringsend; military operations at Trinity College Dublin), 4 May (shelling of Liberty Hall; fighting at Ashbourne; rebels' capture of British prisoners).[100] The *Freeman's Journal* and *Irish Independent* returned to press on 5 May, each now offering readers the 'complete story of the Sinn Fein insurrection' across multiple pages. The former was notable for its reprint of the Proclamation of the Irish Republic, while the latter compiled pen pictures of the Rising's leading figures.[101] News of the Rising was even slower to percolate through provincial Ireland. While many households increasingly took a Dublin newspaper, many more relied on regional weeklies. The majority of these went into circulation on Saturday 6 May. Building on information from the national dailies, these titles tended towards chronological surveys of Easter Week in addition to features on the men, women and movements behind the Rising.[102]

Rebels considered suitable for trial are being tried by Field General Courts Martial under the Defence of the Realm Act in Dublin. As soon as the sentences have been confirmed the public will be informed as to the result of the trial.

So read a press announcement from General Maxwell on 30 April.[103] News of the first executions was presented through a perfunctory government communiqué in the *Irish Times* on 4 May.[104] Ernie O'Malley remembered the notice as jarringly spare: 'a brief announcement: three men had been shot at dawn'.[105] The executions were announced in national newspapers as statements of facts and were not subject to scrutiny or analysis. The *Freeman's Journal* of 5 May recorded: 'Convicted and sentenced to death – Joseph Plunkett, Edward Daly, Michael O'Hanrahan, William Pearse. The above were shot this morning after confirmation of the sentences by the General Officer Commanding in Chief.' The adjoining editorial assessed the impact of capital destruction not capital punishment: 'Such a reckless and barren waste of the courage, property and the historic beauty [of Dublin] … It was brought about by men without authority, representative character or practical sanity.'[106] The *Irish Independent* similarly reproduced the official announcement of John MacBride's execution one day later while editorialising at length about the economic and political problems facing the Irish administration.[107] Provincial newspapers on 6 May instanced similar disconnect. The *Ulster Herald* offered brief bulletin news of the first three executions and thumbnail biographies of Pearse, Clarke and MacDonagh. Its editorial, however, did not comment adversely on the executions, focusing instead on the loyalty of the Irish people during the War: 'Ireland is no more responsible for the recent insurrection than for eruptions of Vesuvius.'[108] The *Kerry Weekly Reporter*, similarly, announced the first three executions and précised the lives of Pearse, Clarke and MacDonagh, but did not comment on the executions policy, editorialising instead over the war economy.[109] The executions, it would seem, were an accepted if not expected aftermath of the Rising. Then followed Ceannt, Mallin, Heuston and Colbert. On 9 May, the *Freeman's Journal* published a new editorial: 'There will be the gravest disappointment and uneasiness occasioned throughout Ireland by this drastic severity.'[110]

CHANGING PUBLIC OPINION

Traditional historical interpretations have tended to the Yeatsian thesis that the executions 'transformed' public opinion in the aftermath of the Rising.[111] Joe Lee, conversely, has suggested that the executions may have 'crystallised' an already emerging feeling of sympathy for the rebels.[112] More recent scholarship has allowed for a 'fluid' and 'subjective' public opinion in the days and weeks which followed.[113] There is much to recommend this cautious approach. As has been submitted, news of the Rising reached the public irregularly across time, location and source. Individuals in Dublin, moreover, had unique first-hand experiences and, therefore, interpretations of the Rising. Appraisals of public opinion regarding the executions, thus, can never be absolute. It can, however, be profiled in outline by exploring contrasts and correspondences between public opinion during Easter, and succeeding, weeks.

The bravery of the ordinary rebels, remarked upon by some civilians during the Rising, remained a popular theme in public comment throughout the executions period. Upon its return to press, the *Freeman's Journal* judged the rebels to be 'youths of high principle, bravery and character'.[114] The *Irish Independent*, meanwhile, observed: 'To the credit of the insurgents it must be said that they took no part in looting the city, but, on the contrary, made some efforts to prevent it.'[115] The rebels were further acknowledged for their courage in the provincial papers. The *Kildare Observer* remarked: 'They were brave, no doubt, but bravery so divested of common sense can never accomplish anything.'[116] The *Nenagh News* concurred: 'Brave they were, without doubt, but they are the victims of misguided judgement.'[117] Most prominently of all, John Dillon made an impassioned speech to the House of Commons on 11 May, averring: 'I know they [the rebels] were wrong; but they fought a clean fight, and they fought with superb bravery and skill.'[118] The recurrent empathy with ordinary rebels suggests that identification with aspects of the Rising was not exclusive to the onset of the executions.

Writing his memoir twenty years after the fact, Ernie O'Malley recalled a swelling of emotion upon having learned of Major John MacBride's execution: 'I had felt resentment at the death of the others; now a strange rage replaced it. I had known MacBride.'[119] The vast majority of the Irish people did not know the rebel leaders. Indeed it is striking how many contemporary diarists recorded the passage of executions without acknowledging their acquaintance.[120] The leaders had inherited the eponymous 'Sinn Feiner' label in early reports and were consistently denounced for having instigated the Rising.[121] The first executions, accordingly, passed without noticeable public complaint. Biographical details of the anonymous leaders, including profession, family and political affiliation, however, began to appear from 5 May. Their open address to the Irish people, in the form of the Proclamation, was now simultaneously published in the national press. James Stephens commented on this timing: 'We know the names of the leaders now. They were recited to us with the tale of their execution; and with the declaration of a republic we learned something of their aim.'[122] Did the restoration of the leaders' lives and written legacy transform public opinion? It is an attractive proposition, given the deification of the seven signatories through Masses, photographs and mourning badges soon after. O'Malley again evoked the mood: 'Names of men who had been practically unknown two weeks before were now on the lips and in the hearts of many.'[123] His timing, however, places the rehabilitation of the leaders after the final executions. This is further suggested by contemporary sources. John Dillon's House of Commons speech, for example, did not praise the seven signatories; editorials in the provincial press did not attempt to recast the leaders; RIC county reports for the month of May failed to mention popular reappraisal.[124] The belated realisation of the signatories' political and personal respectability may have softened public criticism of the 'insane leaders' as individuals but it is unlikely to have recast views of their actions, in the immediate aftermath of the Rising. Emergent opposition to the executions was much more about the process of the executions.

The timing of the *Freeman's Journal*'s editorial intervention is significant: 9 May. The execution of Éamonn Ceannt, Michael Mallin, Seán Heuston and Con Colbert one day earlier was a stark aberrant to the scale and scope of the most recent punishments. John MacBride had been the only figure executed on 5 May and there had been no further shootings on 6 and 7 May. In the absence of government information to the contrary, it may have been assumed that the executions had slowed if not ceased. The sharp announcement of four fresh executions certainly arrested public opinion. The *Freeman's Journal* commented in the same issue: 'the executions have already been too numerous and that more than enough blood had been shed'.[125] Allusions, moreover, were now made to the Maritz rebellion in South Africa two years earlier, for which only one rebel had been shot.[126] The protracted nature of the executions, the so-called 'dribbling effect', was perhaps less impactful than the sudden inflation effect. The abrupt change in the apparent scope of the executions policy was also inauspicious. Neither Mallin, Heuston or Colbert had signed the Proclamation. Moreover, their names had not featured

5.41
John Dillon.
HH:1998.62

to date in national press narratives of the Rising. To the majority of citizens, therefore, it appeared that ordinary rebels were liable to suffer the ultimate punishment, on the concealed directives of British 'martial law'.[127] This view was timely. Information on the secret execution of Francis Sheehy-Skeffington and the discovery of civilians buried along North King Street was just emerging in the national press.[128] Rumours of mass shootings of rebels, consequently, abounded.[129] There were eighty prisoners still at Richmond barracks and thousands more were being arrested around the country. Editorial opinion closely reflected these concerns: 'The wildest rumours are already in circulation … that secret executions have taken place of unarmed prisoners without trial and are still taking place'; 'let the worst of the ringleaders be singled out and dealt with as they deserve; but we hope that there will be no holocaust or slaughter'.[130] The Prime Minister, Herbert Asquith, concerned as to misapprehensions in Ireland, now urged upon Maxwell the release of a public statement.[131] None was forthcoming. On 9 May, Thomas Kent, another relative unknown, was executed in Cork detention barracks, followed by the execution of Seán Mac Diarmada and James Connolly at Kilmainham jail three days later.

It was amid this political disarray that John Dillon addressed the House of Commons on 11 May:

> You are washing out our whole life work in a sea of blood … there is no Government in Ireland except Sir John Maxwell and the Dublin clubs … Ireland is a very much harder country to rule than Egypt, and I refuse, and the Irish people will refuse, to accept the well-known high character of Sir John Maxwell as the sole guarantee of their liberty … I declare most solemnly, and I am not ashamed to say it in the House of Commons, that I am proud of these men … if you were not so dense and so stupid, as some of you English people are, you could have had these men fighting for you, and they are men worth having.[132]

Dillon's speech, which was met with heckling from the benches, was met with popular acclaim in nationalist Ireland. Over the course of the next ten days, the provincial press covered the speech, reprinting it in full as the main news story and publishing resolutions extolling its virtues.[133] It had become an instant classic of pseudo-republican vintage. Dillon's remarks have been widely regarded as an attempt to capture the popular mood of disaffection in favour of the Irish Parliamentary Party, what Alvin Jackson has termed as a 'belated and dangerous lunge towards neo-Parnellism'.[134] However, an examination of the speech beyond the analytical framework of the Home Rule movement, reveals that Dillon's combative remarks may have been an underrated influence in the creation and transition of that mood. This was certainly the view of Maxwell himself, who, as early as 20 May confided: 'if Dillon had not made that unfortunate speech I think things would have very nearly got back to normal … he has provoked a good deal of racial feeling'.[135] Tasked with assessing the public mood in mid-June, the RIC Inspector General made a similar observation:

Undoubtedly many Nationalists who at first condemned the Rising and those who took part in it, have changed their attitude towards the latter and now consider that unnecessary severity is being used. This undesirable attitude has probably been stimulated by such pronouncements as that of Mr Dillon in the House of Commons, Colonel Moore's statement to the Rebellion Commission, and the Bishop of Limerick's letter to General Sir John Maxwell.[136]

End of year RIC reports for counties Galway, Monaghan, Meath and Tyrone also cited Dillon's speech as instrumental in the formation of public dissent although the May monthly reports do not attach to it the same significance.[137] Persuasive or otherwise, Dillon's address could be perceived to have been politically provocative; on 12 May, the Prime Minister Herbert Asquith finally arrived in Ireland. Writing of the impact of the Rising and its immediate aftermath on civilian life, the writer Katharine Tynan recalled tortured memories:

> I can safely say that the Rebellion, for many weeks, was never out of my thoughts. The shootings, the deportations, the peculiar trouble as it affected me personally, were with me all day, going on at the back of my mind as I wrote, lying down with me, haunting my dreams, rising up with me, treading the daily round with me: I was Rebellion-ridden.[138]

6

INTERNMENT AND IMPRISONMENT

Between 1 May and 16 June 2,519 internees were deported from Richmond barracks to British detention centres. Arbitrarily removed from their holding cells, groups of men were marched under armed guard to Dublin port where cattle boats awaited to transfer them. Speculation was rife. 'Some more serious minded of the prisoners were of the opinion that the British were taking us out to sea to sink us' Michael Kelly remembered 'and others said we were put on the cattle boat so that the Germans, if they sank the boat, would take it for what it was and would not make any attempt to rescue us.'[1] Word circulated among other passengers that they would be shipped to France to be used

6.0
(Page 190)
Watercolour by Cathal
MacDowell of a Frongoch
South Camp dormitory.
HE:EW.371a

6.1
Prison biscuits given to
Kathleen Lynn at Ship
Street barracks before she
was deported to England.
HE:1998.63 (Allen)

as hard labour for the war effort.[2] The journey across the Irish Sea was
dreadful. Most accounts mention rough waters, severe hunger and thirst
– deportees had been given two hard biscuits ('dog biscuits') and a tin
of bully-beef at Richmond – and the suffocating experience of sharing,
with hundreds of others, the below deck enclosure. The internees were
forced to either sit or sleep in the unclean cattle pens; seasickness was

frequent in these open plan quarters.[3] Meanwhile, at least one shipment
of deportees actually shared a journey with livestock.[4] 'Many of us
were hoping we would meet a submarine', Michael Brennan later
recorded, 'to end our misery.'[5] The journeys usually lasted between
eight and fifteen hours. Docking at Holyhead, the internees were then
transferred by train to one of eight prison centres: Perth, Barlinnie,
Lewes, Knutsford, Stafford, Wakefield, Wandsworth or Woking.[6] Five
female internees were transferred to British detention centres, three of
whom (Winifred Carney, Helena Molony, Ellen Ryan) would remain
interned at Aylesbury prison.

Their experience of the first month (May) in these detention centres
was by all accounts miserable. The British prison authorities were given
little guidance on how to treat the internees and so applied a stringent
daily regime.[7] Solitary confinement was the predominant experience.
At both Knutsford and Wakefield, the internees were kept in their
individual cells for up to twenty-three and a half hours a day. The men
were not allowed to write, have books, see visitors or meet clergymen.[8]
The cells at Knutsford were particularly bad. Here the detainees were

issued with a single blanket and slept on bare boards.[9] A single thirty-minute period of exercise offered reprieve from the desolation of daily life in one's cell. This too, however, was to be conducted in silence. The internees could not come within five feet of each other as they moved around their respective prison yards: 'in single file around the ring we trod the fool's parade'.[10] The quality and quantity of food was an enduring issue for the internees. Breakfast at Knutsford comprised a wedge of bread, a ration of butter and a 'skilly' of oatmeal cooked on water 'a thick sickly mess'.[11] Dinner at the prison was even less palatable: a stew of beef, bones and a couple of blackened or greened potatoes.[12] 'I could not eat the slightest morsel of it,' Michael Lynch remembered.[13] At Stafford the internees' soup contained meat, fat or gristle, depending on one's portion.[14] Evening meal at Wakefield, meanwhile, consisted of tea, bread and butter.[15] The rations exasperated the internees. 'At the end of a week I was wetting my thumbs and picking up crumbs off the ground', Liam Tannam commented, 'the diet was practically starvation'.[16] Others spoke of constantly dreaming and daydreaming of food.[17] Rumination could easily become pre-occupation: 'we were given just enough to keep up in that state of acute hunger in which thoughts of food became an obsession of the mind'.[18]

6.2
Wakefield prison.
HE:EWL.227.56

6.3
An internee's sketch of his
cell at Knutsford prison.
HE:EWL.296

The psychological imprisonment of internees was potentially most injurious to their health. The prolongation of the First World War, and the attendant captivity of prisoners-of-war, directed public attention to the impact of internment on the mental health of detainees. In 1919 the German psychologist Adolf Vischer published his observations of German prisoners of war, suggesting that camp internment could lead to a neurosis which he termed 'barbed wire disease'. The monotony of camp life, confined space and boredom could trigger the slide into depression, irritability and, ultimately, insanity.[19] The Irish internees were acutely exposed to this condition given their essential solitary confinement in the initial weeks. 'I am afraid we were a despondent lot', Seamus Kavanagh recalled, 'sitting on our little stool or pacing the cell practically all day, we had plenty of time to think.'[20] Thomas Leahy remembered the effect of the continued silence: 'some began shouting and dancing in their cells and the hunger was affecting them as well'.[21] Seán Prendergast relived the continuous pacing up and down the cell: 'one performed it mechanically, by impulse rather than design. At other times it had the effect of soothing the evil workings of one's mind, helped to keep one's thoughts and mental facilities alive and active'.[22] Writing of 'Fenian narratives of confinement', William Murphy has commented: 'prison memoir had attained a prominent place in nationalist culture' by the early twentieth century.[23] This is discernible in the internees' later testimony of their experience. Several referred to Fenian prison accounts as having prepared them for the rigours of internment.[24] Drawing on his prior reading of Thomas Clarke's *Glimpses of an Irish felon's life*, for example, Michael Lynch concluded: 'a man could keep sane, under these conditions, only as long as he was able to keep his mind revolving on something or other. If the mind got blank, or if you started worrying about your loved ones at home, madness was staring you in the face.' Lynch attempted to overcome his ennui by counting bricks on the wall, remembering music and calculating the population of the Tribes of Israel from accounts in his Bible.[25] James Kavanagh fashioned a deck of cards out of toilet paper.[26] Frank Robbins recalls doing handstands in his cell as a means of alleviating the boredom.[27]

Towards the end of May (prisons differed on timing), the prison regime for Irish internees was relaxed. The men and women began to be treated as de facto prisoners of war. Freedom of association was instituted including the right to converse (censored) letters could now be written and received, rations were increased and foodstuffs could be purchased.[28]

6.4
Internees enjoying free association at Stafford prison.
HE:EW.302

The sense of liberation experienced by the internees is vividly recalled in retrospective testimony. More pertinently this release is frequently delineated in the form of objects. Daniel Tuite, interned at Wakefield, captured his tangible sense of relief: 'Each day in Wakefield saw a gradual relaxation of prison discipline; visitors came in, tobacco, cigarettes, newspapers, cakes and eatables of all kinds whilst Nuns came in with beads, medals, prayer books, religious magazines, pens, pencils and writing paper.'[29] Thomas Leahy at Knutsford similarly remembered the moment in terms of artefacts: 'It was a welcome change … allowed to give us some cigarettes, papers and other welcome gifts such as pencils, writing papers and stamps.'[30] Writing of his time in Stafford jail, meanwhile, Darrell Figgis itemised his definition of prisoner-of-war status: 'I wanted tobacco and pipe, I wished any books that I might order or that might be sent in to me, daily papers, free communication with my fellow-prisoners and the opening of cell doors by night and by day.'[31] Scholars of what has been termed the 'archaeology of internment', notably Harold Mytum and Gilly Carr, have drawn attention to the potential palliative effect of objects on an individual's internment experience.[32]

These goods were often furnished by sympathetic members of the Irish community in Great Britain. As early as Easter Week itself the Irish National Relief Fund had been formed by Art O'Brien and other London-Irish nationalists in anticipation of the internment of rebels. Further relief committees were later formed in Liverpool, Manchester and Glasgow. By June the INRF was co-ordinating the supply of food,

6.5
Members of the Irish
community in Great
Britain visit internees
at Wakefield prison.
HE:EWL.227.8

clothes and reading material for the internees.[33] Seán T. O'Kelly would later praise the 'herculean work' carried out by the INRF and Art O'Brien in particular: 'I personally am most deeply thankful to you for standing so gallantly in the bearna baoghail ['gap of danger'] at a time when so few men were prepared to recognise us much less to hold out a hand of friendship.'[34]

By early June the internees were on the move. Asquith's directive for the 'combing out' of innocents had already seen 650 men released and returned to Ireland.[35] Joseph McCarthy observed the departures from Wakefield: 'A few spoons and cell discs were smuggled as souvenirs by some of the prisoners who were among the first batch to be released. The warders were reprimanded for this neglect by the prison authorities and, as a result, those on the later parties were subject to a careful search and it was very difficult for anyone to retain such souvenirs.'[36] Twelve internees who were judged 'specially dangerous', including Arthur Griffith and Darrell Figgis, were moved to Reading jail.[37] The Home Office had identified an internment camp in north Wales as a more manageable site for the other Irish internees. From 9 June, the remaining 1,863 detainees were relocated under Regulation 14B of the Defence of the Realm Act. Rumours of an impending transfer to an internment camp were prevalent among the internees; the Isle of Man, Colwyn Bay and an obscure place called Frogmore were mentioned as destinations. W.J. Brennan-Whitmore would remark of these allusions: 'in prison every event is surrounded by a burlesque sort of secrecy'.[38] Confirmation, however, arrived in the form of an internment order for Frongoch.

Frongoch Internment Camp, located near the Welsh town of Bala, comprised two adjacent camp structures. The South Camp, to which internees were first transferred, was based on the site of a former whiskey distillery. The five floors of the distillery had been converted to dormitories. Initially created for German internees during the war, they now housed the first 936 Irish internees to arrive at Frongoch. A further 896 men were moved to the North Camp which consisted of thirty-five wooden huts along two lanes which were named Pearse Street and Connolly Street by their incumbents. A path connected the two camps and internee movement between them was initially permitted.[39] Unlike the clinical regimes, the Frongoch authorities expected the Irish internees to regulate the day-to-day running of

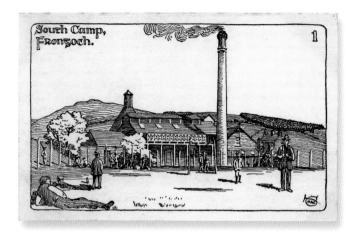

6.6
Postcard image of
Frongoch South Camp.
HE:EWL.227.102

6.7
Postcard image of
Frongoch North Camp.
HE:EWL.227.103

their camps. 'Messes' (groups) of thirty to forty were to be organised by a mess leader, responsible to a head leader, who in turn was to answer to the camp authorities.[40] Political power among the Irish internees was, as Peter Hart noted, highly contested.[41] A 'general council', assembled by mess leaders, attempted to constitute itself a 'civil government' in representations to the camp authorities. Its influence, however, was quickly overtaken by the extant senior Volunteer officers who formed a military staff to run the internees' affairs led by M.W. O'Reilly (North Camp) and J.J. O'Connell (South Camp).[42]

Military discipline was soon in evidence. The staff officers assembled the internees for first count by the camp authorities at 6.00 a.m. After breakfast at 7.30 a.m. they allocated men to carry out fatigue duty in the dormitories and other facilities ahead of a camp inspection at 11.00 a.m. The officers formally lined up the detainees again at 9.00 p.m. each night for last count.[43] Frank Robbins explained the internees' adherence to these regulations: 'this was something that we were doing for ourselves, that at least we should show discipline and do nothing that would prove to the British authorities that our officers could not control us'.[44] Military training was encouraged during the day. Between 11.00 a.m. and 12.00 midday military drill was carried out on the camp's recreation field. In the afternoons, particularly from August, the internees gained permission to engage in route marches through the Welsh countryside supervised by camp authorities. Meanwhile, in the evenings, lectures were prepared for the internees on military strategy and tactics, notably on the use of guerrilla warfare on Irish terrain.[45] 'The military staff had raised Frongoch camp into a military academy', W.J. Brennan-Whitmore would remark.[46] Frongoch, however, also bore the trappings of what the psychologist John Davidson Ketchum has termed 'a prison camp society'.[47] Unconfident of early release, but encouraged by their relative liberation within the camp, the detainees set about creating and maintaining a normal existence at Frongoch. Disused rooms in the inner yard of the South Camp formed a mall of shops: barber, tailor and shoe maker.[48] Internees themselves provided essential services: 'Our postman was Mick Brennan … Jimmy Mallon was our barber … "Comrades" O'Mahony was a kind of welfare officer.'[49] The men could initially write letters to, and receive letters from outside the camp as prisoners of war but this censored correspondence was later changed by the camp authorities.[50] Community activists offered other amenities. Henry Dixon established a library; Jeremiah Purcell introduced a course in shorthand while Michael Lynch formed a choir of between seventy and eighty.[51] The latter performed at weekly mass in a hut on the North Camp. Afternoons could be spent at 'Croke Park', which the internees named their recreation field. Gaelic football matches were played daily on this green patch but hurling was not allowed by the camp authorities on account of the potentially dangerous use of the camán. The 'pitch' was also used for a sports day on 8 August in which internees competed in track and field

6.8
A letter posted home from a Frongoch internee.
HE:EW.829

events such as running, long jump and shotput.[52] Evenings were to be devoted to study. A litany of classes was provided by the internees including architecture, chemistry and bookkeeping, in addition to the provision of French, German and Spanish language tuition.[53] However, the most popular subject was the Irish language. The prevalence of Irish teachers at Frongoch has often been commented upon but statements from the internees attest to the widespread interest in learning the language.[54] In his study of German internment on the Isle of Man during the First World War, meanwhile, Panikos Panayi has pointed to refashioned gender roles as part of the internees' illusory 'substitution' of civilian life behind barbed wire for the normality of their previous lives.[55] This was also illustrated at Frongoch. The emphasis on camp maintenance by the internees brought about a male domesticity at variance with the expected gender roles of the period. The men did their own washing, cleaning and some cooking, practices which were frequently noted within later accounts.[56] One veteran of Frongoch, Joseph McCarthy, would comment: 'Some of the prisoners became expert at housekeeping and were the envy of the others. Their laundry was spotless and their work with the needle was tailor-like in workmanship, and the meals they were able to provide at night-time on top of the hut stoves with meagre resources were appetising fare.'[57] Frongoch functioned for many as an internment camp society.

6.9
A rugby ball used by the internees at Frongoch.
HE:EW.1617

6.10
The internees' chapel at Frongoch.
HE:EW.2882

However, the Frongoch experience was not entirely functional for all internees. The onset of 'barbed-wire disease' was always a possibility and two men were declared insane during their time at the camp. Did the Frongoch regime account for such mental breakdown? Seán McConville has pointed to the potential impact of the fighting during Easter Week on frayed nerves, while it might be noted that the earlier confinement in British prisons was a more difficult experience for most internees, particularly those who had not been involved in the Rising.[58] Nonetheless, the conditions at Frongoch may have been a significant factor underlying an internee's mental distress. Studies of First World War internment have noted the psychological impact of confined space on detainees, particularly those from middle-class backgrounds.[59] The early months at Frongoch were a particularly claustrophobic experience. The South Camp dormitories contained between 150 and 250 beds on each floor, which measured 150 feet long and fifty feet wide. The ceiling of the ground floor dormitory, meanwhile, reached only nine feet high. Ventilation was very poor in the rooms and internees were known to faint on getting up in the morning on account of the deadened smell from the toilets. The first three floors of the South Camp dormitories, moreover, were infested with vermin. It was not uncommon for internees to wake to the sight of a rat within their sheets. Domhnall O'Buachalla was bitten just under the eye by one while he was asleep.[60] The spatial constraints in particular caused considerable psychological difficulty for some internees. 'It was terrible in Frongoch at the start', Thomas Pugh remembered, 'there was no space between us.'[61] 'It was hard to know how they arrived at calling it that [a dormitory]', Seán Prendergast added, 'it was an over-sized loft.'[62] The poet Brian O'Higgins was particularly affected by his surroundings: 'There is absolutely no privacy. A man cannot say to himself that he will go off and be alone for five minutes. Nerves become frayed, tempers out of control, and all the little meanness of man comes to the surface … After Frongoch when I was arrested I hoped and prayed that I might be kept under lock and key in a cell rather than be given the "freedom" and intercourse of my fellows in some hut or dormitory of a prison camp.'[63] The internees were bound to their quarters between 8.00 p.m. and 6.00 a.m.

6.11
A lone internee reflects on life behind barbed wire. Portrait by Cathal MacDowell.
HE:EW.361

6.12
(Opposite page, top)
A macramé bag made by Domhnall O'Buachalla.
HE:EW.529

6.13
(Opposite page, bottom)
A sculpture in memory of Seán Connolly made out of cattle bone.
HE:EW.5013

It was during these hours, within the spatial and psychological confines of the dormitories and huts, that internees turned to the creation of internment craftwork. 'Creativity of one form or other', Gilly Carr and Harold Mytum have observed of the internment experience, 'was a central form of survival.'[64] For some the creation of sculptures, jewellery and macramé was an existential practice directly related to the restraints of internment: 'to overcome such heartaching [the confinement] those who could not give their entire energies to sports and games turned to arts and crafts'; 'when locked in the dormitory each night the men used the time in many ways. A number of them started the hobby of doing macramé work with coloured cord and, in a short time, several of them got very expert with it'; 'when the main body of our men in the camp were denied access to playing fields, many turned to carving bones and making rings out of coins. Some larger meat-bones became astonishing sculptures'.[65]

For others the production of craftwork may have been intended to preserve their experience of Frongoch, serving as personal reminder of time and place. In his examination of First World War 'trench art', Nicholas Saunders has pointed to the proliferation and preservation of craftwork from battlefields as an important tool used by veterans to remain 'in the landscape' years later.[66] Frongoch veterans too recalled the materials used as a metonym for their internment camp experience: 'wood or bone carvings … a broken dinner knife ground into shape on the sandstone window sill was, in most cases, the only tool available for such work'.[67] 'Many prisoners in Frongoch' Seamus Fitzgerald observed decades later 'cherish mementoes of these places, such as little hand craft models, hand-made brooches, rings'.[68]

In time Frongoch became a much more manageable existence for internees. Between the end of June and the beginning of August, the Home Office-appointed Sankey Commission sat in London to adjudicate over the release of less troublesome internees. The Frongoch detainees were transferred to Wandsworth or Wormwood Scrubs prisons ahead of their interview before the Commission. Many were un-cooperative with the process. Nonetheless, by early August only about six hundred internees remained at Frongoch. The majority had been returned to Ireland following the Sankey Review. A further thirty, including camp leaders such as J.J. O'Connell, Terence MacSwiney and Seán T. O'Kelly, had been transferred to Reading jail on 11 July to prevent dissension among the ranks.[69] The remaining internees, who had been moved to the South Camp in the late summer, were ostensibly a cohesive group. Many of the later accounts attest to the inculcation of a comradeship and connectivity at Frongoch among those who had been geographically dislocated in pre-Rising Ireland.[70] This was borne out in the wealth of autograph books signed, rhymed and designed by the internees. Seán Prendergast would later term Frongoch the 'enforced Mecca'.[71] While acknowledging the significance of this collective experience, recent scholarship has drawn attention to the differences which also existed among the internees. As William Murphy has noted: 'neither uniformity nor unity should be assumed'.[72]

6.14
Internees removed to Reading jail. Darrell Figgis (second from left) and Seán T. O'Kelly (sixth from left).
HE:EW.1615

6.15
Page from an autograph book, Frongoch.
HE:EW.3692

6.16
The mysterious 'Black
Hand gang' at Frongoch.
Domhnall O'Buachalla
(seated, third from left).
HE:EW.534b

One of the potentially divisive issues among the detainees at Frongoch
was the influence of the IRB. Although the Rising was discussed during
the men's time at the camp, many of the internees later maintained that
blame was not apportioned to the Organisation for its failure. However, a
number of accounts reveal a suspicion that the Fenians were the guiding
hand behind organisation at Frongoch. Collins and Richard Mulcahy
were among a group of young conspirators to have formed an IRB
circle without the Organisation's authority in late 1916.[73] Others were
similarly clandestine. Mystery still remains over the activity of the 'Black
Hand gang' fronted by Domhnall O'Buachalla at Frongoch.

Contemporarily, however, it was solidarity which appeared to
define the detainees at Frongoch. Two major confrontations emerged
between the internees and the camp authorities in the autumn of 1916.
In September the men were ordered by Heygate Lambert, the camp
commandant, to remove ashes from the refuse bins outside the camp
officers' quarters. When the initial group of internees refused, as this was
beyond the scope of their administration, they were punished by removal
to the North Camp without letters, newspapers or cigarettes. Fellow
internees also refused to carry out this task and by early October 136

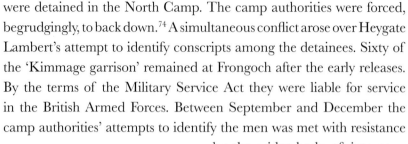

were detained in the North Camp. The camp authorities were forced, begrudgingly, to back down.[74] A simultaneous conflict arose over Heygate Lambert's attempt to identify conscripts among the detainees. Sixty of the 'Kimmage garrison' remained at Frongoch after the early releases. By the terms of the Military Service Act they were liable for service in the British Armed Forces. Between September and December the camp authorities' attempts to identify the men was met with resistance

6.17
Uniform worn by convicts in Lewes prison.
HE:1998.189 (Allen)

by the wider body of internees. Morning and evening roll calls went unanswered, representations were made to the Home Office and letters were sent to the press. Meanwhile, 200 internees went on hunger-strike over the issue between 2 and 4 November. Fifteen of its leaders were court-martialled while Heygate Lambert ordered that those refusing to answer their name should not receive medical treatment. In the ensuing standoff, the camp medical advisor, Dr David Peters, committed suicide. By December, the strain of the protest had begun to show on the internees themselves. Upwards of 184 were beginning to respond positively during the roll call.[75] Michael Collins would call the compliers 'cowards'.[76] The eventual release of the detainees under a Christmas amnesty prevented further displays of disintegration within the population at Frongoch.

The Christmas amnesty also had implications for another

set of Irish detainees: those court-
martialled in the immediate aftermath
of the Rising. In total 122 men and
one woman (Countess Markievicz)
had been sentenced to penal servitude
in May. Sixty-five were transferred to
Dartmoor prison while a further fifty-
seven were imprisoned at Portland.[77]
Countess Markievicz was removed
from Mountjoy prison to Aylesbury
prison on 8 August.[78] The prisoners
were categorised by the penal system as
convicts and accordingly were forced
to wear prison uniform. In December,
however, they were collectively
transferred to Lewes prison (with
the exception of Markievicz) where
regulations were relaxed: civilian
clothes could be worn in addition to
prison clothes.[79]

6.18
Thomas Ashe's Lewes
prison cap.
HE:EWL.390

It was here that Éamon de Valera's leadership of the imprisoned
rebels was consolidated. As the senior surviving commandant of
the Rising, he had brought the prisoners to attention to salute Irish
Volunteer Chief of Staff Eoin MacNeill as he passed, at Dartmoor.
Although Thomas Ashe could claim more successful military service
during Easter Week, it was de Valera who emerged as the most natural
spokesperson for the prisoners at Lewes: 'he became the leader of us
all, without any consultation, debate or election … the first question
everyone asked was "what does Dev think of it?" … he had become "the
chief".'[80] De Valera's commanding influence was further demonstrated
when, on his orders in late May 1917, the prisoners began to destroy
their cells as a strike action for their not being recognised as 'prisoners
of war'. Their release in June, however, would be much more about
political developments beyond prison walls.

7

AFTER THE RISING

'All changed, changed utterly: a terrible beauty is born.' W.B. Yeats'
elegiac 'Easter, 1916' has often been presented as literal reader to Irish
opinion in the aftermath of the 1916 Rising. In gestation between May
and September 1916, the poem gives form to Yeats' 'vertigo of self-
sacrifice', the disconcerting realisation-in-writing of a surrounding
transformation in the political legacies of MacDonagh, MacBride,
Connolly and Pearse: 'now and in time to be'. By this reading the fifteen
executions immediately and irrevocably changed Irish public opinion
on the Rising and fatally undermined the constitutional politics of Irish
Home Rule. Yeats' second fall and decline thesis has traditionally been

accepted by early scholars of the period .[1] Recent scholarship, however, has suggested the need for a broader historiographical view.[2] This chapter profiles the impact of the Rising across a 'long' 1916, between 'Sinn Fein rebellion' and Sinn Féin Convention, arguing that all did change, changed otherly.

The executions portended not the death of Irish Home Rule but rather its resurrection. More specifically, the Rising and executions revived Irish Home Rule as Redmondite project. John Redmond's reaction to events in Ireland, underexplored within the historiography, suggests a posturing towards British political opinion, in keeping with a wartime strategy, with the view to best positioning Nationalist Ireland in Home Rule negotiations on partition. Addressing the House of Commons on 27 April, following a speech by Edward Carson, Redmond issued a short statement describing his 'detestation and horror' at events in Dublin, adding: 'I join most cordially with the Right. Hon. Gentleman in hoping that no set of newspapers or public men in this country will attempt to use what has happened in Ireland as a political weapon against any party that may exist.'[3] His statement to the international press, first published on 29 April, again appeared to be aimed at British opinion. Speaking of Ireland in the third person singular, Redmond presented a lengthy exposition of the country's contribution to the imperial war effort, concluding 'Home Rule has not been destroyed. It remains indestructible.'[4] Ensconced in his Dublin home, John Dillon advised Redmond of his inclination not to make any public statement at this juncture.[5]

The London–Dublin divide within the Irish Parliamentary Party leadership, it has been argued, created a 'comprehension gap' between Redmond and Dillon on Irish current affairs.[6] This was undoubtedly heightened during the Rising itself where the London-based Redmond had limited, and often delayed, access to information on events in Dublin and Dillon's own views. However, this does not explain Redmond's continued courting of British opinion after the full restoration of order in, and communication from, the Irish capital. On 1 May a letter from Dillon, dated 30 April, reached Redmond:

> You should urge *strongly* upon the Government the day after the *extreme* unwisdom of any wholesale shooting of prisoners … If

7.0
(Page 206)
Countess Markievicz is transported past tricolour-waving crowds on Sackville Street in a horse-drawn carriage following her release from prison (June 1917).
HE:EWP.35

there were … the effect on public opinion throughout the country might be disastrous in the extreme. So far the feeling of the population in Dublin is against the Sinn Feiners – But a reaction might easily be created.[7]

Redmond's biographers have pictured an Irish Parliamentary Party leader '[working] hard to secure clemency for the [rebel] leaders'; '[making] incessant personal intervention[s]' and issuing 'frantic pleas for leniency' during the executions.[8] The evidence does not support this caricature. His attempts to prevent executions can be more accurately divided between private and public.

On 1 May, he recounted to Dillon Asquith's personal view on the executions with which Redmond, implicitly, agreed: 'while the recognised ringleaders who may be captured alive must be dealt with adequate severity, the greatest possible leniency should be shown to the rank and file'.[9] Joseph Devlin, having been briefed by Dillon in Dublin, now joined Redmond in London. Redmond made a second visit to Asquith on the afternoon of 3 May: 'Saw Asquith today and urged him to prevent executions. He said some few were necessary but they would be very few. I protested.'[10] Redmond's public position in the House of Commons earlier that day, following the execution of Pearse, Clarke and MacDonagh, however, had been noticeably more restrained. At the end of a lengthy speech in which he praised the outgoing Chief Secretary for Ireland, Augustine Birrell, Redmond declared: 'This outbreak, happily, seems to be over. It has been dealt with with firmness, which was not only right, but it was the duty of the Government to so deal with it … I speak from the very bottom of my heart and with all my earnestness, not to show undue hardship or severity to the great masses of those who are implicated, on whose shoulders there lies a guilt far different from that which lies upon the instigators and promoters of the outbreak.'[11] Redmond, however, made no public statement in the House of Commons the next day, following the execution of Plunkett, Daly, O'Hanrahan and William Pearse. In a highly suggestive letter to Dillon that afternoon, Redmond confided: 'Saw Asquith again and told him if any more executions took place I would feel bound to denounce them and probably retire.'[12]

A further five executions were to take place (MacBride (5 May); Ceannt, Mallin, Heuston, Colbert (8 May)) before Redmond made his views on the executions known publicly.

Redmond's reluctance to publicly denounce the executions, it is argued, was grounded in his determination to remain on the right side of British political opinion, as future determinants of any Home Rule settlement. The timing of his statements reflects this. On Friday 5 May, Liberal opinion transitioned into criticism of the continued executions. A *Manchester Guardian* editorial recorded: 'Court-martialling and shooting in Ireland have already created a reaction of feeling here … The feeling is that there is no political need for these hurried executions. They might be justified if rebellion were still raging … Further executions can only create martyrs and the shrines of martyrs to refresh and renew the old bitterness between England and Ireland.' On the same date, the *Daily Chronicle* added: 'We felt that nothing could be said against the first three shootings of Irish rebel leaders … but the list of four more shootings which occurred yesterday – only one of them that a signatory to the manifesto – will make most people with memories feel a little anxious lest the process should be carried too far.'[13] The British regional press, meanwhile, widely republished these leaders on 6 May.[14] It was on the next sitting of Parliament, 8 May, that Redmond shifted public position, in sync with but not ahead of British political opinion. Addressing Asquith in the House of Commons, Redmond asked:

> Whether he is aware that the continuance of military executions in Ireland has caused rapidly increasing bitterness of exasperation amongst large sections of the population who have not the slightest sympathy with the insurrection; and whether, following the precedent set by General Botha in South Africa, he will cause an, immediate stop [sic] to be put to military executions?[15]

John Dillon's speech to the House of Commons just three days later, conversely, resulted in widespread condemnation from the British press.[16] 'It would be futile to deny … or to conceal' Stephen Gwynn later admitted 'Redmond's view that the effect was most lamentable.'[17]

However, within weeks, the British government had initiated new Home Rule talks, Asquith deputing David Lloyd George to take charge of the negotiations. Lloyd George met Edward Carson and James Craig in London on 26 May, followed by discussions separately with T.P. O'Connor and John Dillon one day later. In further talks with Carson and Redmond respectively, Lloyd George addressed the keystone issue: partition. Finally, Redmond, supported by Devlin and O'Connor, agreed to abandon their 1914 position of county plebiscites and to concede the Ulster demand for a block exclusion of six counties, including Fermanagh and Tyrone. For his part, Carson would accept the immediate implementation of Home Rule for nationalist Ireland together with something less than the permanent exclusion he had previously sought. The Home Rule Act, suitably modified by an Amending Act, was to come into operation as a war emergency measure. John Redmond recorded of the Nationalists' last meeting with Lloyd George on 11 June: 'He gave us the most emphatic assurance … saying he had placed his life upon the table and would stand or fall by the agreement come to.'

7.1
David Lloyd George
(Minister of Munitions
in May 1916).

The Irish Parliamentary Party and Ulster Unionist Party had, through the mediation of David Lloyd George, achieved in under two weeks in 1916 what they had failed to do in over two years between 1912 and 1914: negotiate a 'provisional' agreement for the implementation of Home Rule in Ireland. Term and conditions, however, applied. The entire accord hinged on the ambiguous expression: 'provisional'. John Redmond, and the Irish Parliamentary Party delegates, were led to believe verbally that the 'provisional' agreement meant that six county partition would no longer remain in effect after the duration of the war. In a letter dated 29 May, however, Lloyd George advised Carson in writing that 'at the end of the provisional period Ulster does not, whether she wills it or not, merge in the rest of Ireland'. Neither side was privy, formally, to the other's discussions.

The differences in Lloyd George's dealings with nationalist and unionist representatives has given rise to the prevailing view that a duplicitous David Lloyd George sold out nationalist Ireland. Alvin Jackson has argued of Carson, Redmond and Lloyd George: 'It is hard to believe that they did not uniformly appreciate the need to keep the partition arrangement as open as the demands of political statesmanship would allow.' Asquith had informed the Attorney General in Dublin of his intention to impose 'a workable modus vivendi … something which all reasonable men approved and which under existing conditions, patriotic duty required them both to accept'. On 10 June Carson was confronted with their double dealing by A.W. Samuels, a leading Unionist lawyer: 'Asquith and Lloyd George are deep tricksters. For you the exclusion is to be permanent, for Redmond provisional.' Carson did not press the particulars. Similarly, the Irish Parliamentary Party leadership did not demur when presented with the equivocation of the proposals. Speaking to a Lloyd George aide, Joseph Devlin confirmed: 'As to the apparent difference of opinion between Mr. Redmond and Sir Edward Carson whether exclusion is permanent or temporary, he [Redmond] thinks that this is more apparent than real, that it actually represents two legitimate views of the same proposal, and may easily be cleared up afterwards.'

The proposed settlement appeared in the press on 12 June. On the same date unionists from Cavan, Donegal and Monaghan reluctantly agreed to the Ulster Unionist Council's proposals. The Irish Parliamentary Party leadership set out to convince Nationalist Ireland as to the merit of the articles. Devlin had strong misgivings over the abandonment of his Nationalist constituents in Ulster but agreed, ultimately, that 'there must be some sacrifices about Ulster'. Dillon and Redmond accompanied Devlin to Belfast on 23 June. Following a forty-five minute speech from Devlin in which he promised temporary partition, the end of the Defence of the Realm Act under a new Home Rule government and an amnesty for the interned rebels, the vote was taken. 475 delegates voted in favour of the amended Home Rule settlement and 265 against. Redmond exulted in the news: 'Joe's loyalty in all this business has been beyond words. I know well what it has cost him to do as he has done.' On 3 July, meanwhile, the United Irish League accepted the Lloyd George proposals 'for the temporary and provisional settlement of the Irish difficulty'. The Irish Parliamentary Party formally had their mandate.

Between 23 June and 22 July 1916, Lloyd George's Home Rule settlement collapsed. Southern unionists, such as Lord Lansdowne and Walter Long, who had been marginalised from the talks, lobbied strongly against the proposal. On 19 June Conservative Cabinet ministers, Andrew Bonar Law excepting, sent Asquith a collective message protesting the implementation of Home Rule during the war. Lloyd George offered Asquith and Long an ultimatum, the amended Home Rule Bill or his resignation. By 24 June, with the outcome of the Nationalist Convention in Belfast revealed, tensions were acute within the Cabinet. T.P. O'Connor, alone in London, reported the settlement to be 'trembling in the balance' and requested the attendance of Devlin, Dillon and Redmond on Lloyd George's request. Further wires were sent from Asquith on 29 June but to no avail. Later that day Lord Lansdowne announced in the House of Commons that the Lloyd George proposals were being examined by the Cabinet and that no agreement had been reached on their details. Tensions within the Cabinet remained and Asquith attempted to stave off Unionist resignations with the forceful argument that they would be 'not only a national calamity but a national crime'. A four-man committee was formed, including Asquith and Lloyd George, to review Unionist concerns over the wartime effects of the bill on defence measures. In July, Redmond wrote a letter responding to each of their points in turn, to the satisfaction of Long and Lansdowne who withdrew their threats to resign.

Ten days later, on 11 July, Redmond and his peers were rocked by an unexpected intervention. Speaking in the House of Lords, Lord Lansdowne announced that the amending bill would make 'structural alterations' to the Home Rule settlement and that its terms would be 'permanent and enduring in character'. In a coup de grâce, Lansdowne added that he was speaking on behalf of the Cabinet. Shocked, Redmond demanded a response from Asquith and Lloyd George to negate the perception that the Irish Parliamentary Party had ceded the permanent partition of six Ulster counties. In a statement published on 21 July, Redmond vehemently opposed 'any proposal to depart from the terms agreed upon, especially in respect of the strictly temporal and provisional character of ALL the sections of the bill, [this] would compel us to declare the agreement, on the faith of which we obtained the assent of our supporters in Ireland, had been departed from and was at an end'. At the Cabinet meeting of

19 July, Lansdowne and Long influenced the changing of the agreement to the effect that partition would indeed be permanent. Three days later Redmond was presented by David Lloyd George with the fait accompli. In a strongly worded letter to Asquith, Redmond repudiated the agreement as now constituted on behalf of the Irish Parliamentary Party. Asquith replied understandingly and understatedly: 'There can of course be no question of introducing a bill to which you and your friends are not prepared to assent.' The Lloyd George negotiations and for the moment, the Home Rule settlement, were dead.[18]

The brothers Gwynn have storied the conclusion of the Lloyd George negotiations as the end for the Irish Parliamentary Party and John Redmond: 'That day really finished the constitutional party and overthrew Redmond's power'; 'Redmond's influence in Ireland was irreparably broken … faith in his judgment as a political leader had all but vanished.'[19] More pertinently perhaps, Redmond's faith in his own judgement as a political leader had all but vanished. He retired to his estate in Co.Wicklow, ruminating over his failed wartime policy. A promise to draft a new party manifesto never materialised and he remained *hors de contact* to Dillon, Devlin and O'Connor for much of the autumn.[20] Tellingly, Redmond did not appear again at Westminster until mid-October; he decided further against reading the papers. If the demise of Redmondism has been dated, what of the Irish Parliamentary Party? Recent scholarship has detected a residual rural support for the IPP in late 1916 and even 1917.[21] This careful parsing of public opinion, paradoxically, is perhaps the best indicator of the Party's fateful decline. The silence of the Home Rule movement during this period resounded with political resignation. The Irish Parliamentary Party, as per Lloyd George's conditions, did not make public statements on the proposals during the negotiations. The RIC Inspector General noted accordingly:

> I have to report that Ireland was in an unsettled condition during the month of June, due in a great measure to sympathy with the Sinn Fein insurgents, and divergence of opinion with regard to the Home Rule proposals … Nationalist opinion was divided respecting the Home Rule proposals, and the exclusion of six Ulster Counties was unpopular … neither the advantages of the proposed settlement

nor the necessity for accepting it has yet been explained by local members of parliament to their constituents.[22]

Irish Parliamentary Party restraint, however, was uncharacteristically evident after the failed partition negotiations. The emergence of dissidents in Ulster (the Irish Nation League) noticeably did not move the Party into takeover mode. The UIL national directory, further, did not meet for almost two years.[23] More significantly still, the Irish Parliamentary Party did not attempt to re-launch itself through that most established of nationalist campaigns: amnesty for prisoners.

Fearghal McGarry has perceptively judged the hasty arrest of almost 3,430 men and seventy-nine women across Ireland as an underrated contributing factor to the shift in public opinion.[24] Their potential significance was borne out contemporarily by two very public interventions. On arrival at Richmond barracks on 12 May Asquith offered an implicit critique of Maxwell's military policy, reviewing the internees and ordering a process of 'combing out' innocent from guilty. Within two weeks 1,424 of the arrested men were released.[25] A more explicit appraisal of the military governor's regime appeared in the national press only five days later. In an open letter to Maxwell on 17 May, following the latter's request to discipline local priests for their public support of the Rising, the Bishop of Limerick, Edward O'Dwyer, penned a piercing commentary of his 'work as a military dictator of Ireland'. Although the executions were highlighted in O'Dwyer's note, internment was given greater attention:

> The deporting of hundreds and even thousands of poor fellows without a trial of any kind seems to me an abuse of power, as famous as it is arbitrary, and altogether your regime has been one of the worst and blackest chapters in the history of misgovernment of this country.[26]

Maxwell would remain in Ireland until November 1916.

7.2
Bishop of Limerick Edward O'Dwyer.
HE:EW.2153

7.3
A postcard portrayal of General Maxwell disturbed by the reaction to the executions.
HE:EWL.275.23

Coming on the heels of Dillon's vituperative speech in the House of Commons, O'Dwyer's statement continued the theme of unjust arrest, internment and deportation in the press.[27] This was a much more pressing and personal concern in provincial Ireland than the executions. Weekly newspaper columns for the month of May were full of local council resolutions protesting at the arraignment of known, and indeed reputable, local community members.[28] The early release of 1,424 men

7.4
Alderman James Kelly of Dublin Corporation was not involved in the Rising but was mistakenly arrested in its aftermath. This photograph was taken before his arrest.
HE:EWL.227.41

7.5
Between 26 April and 8 May, Kelly was detained at Richmond barracks before being deported on a cattle boat to Wandsworth prison. He was released on 12 May. This photograph was taken after his release.
HE:EWL.227.42

was unlikely to have mitigated such grievances, given the effects of even short-term internment on the individual. Internment, regardless, was a current issue within many local communities. The Irish Parliamentary Party, significantly, was not seen as the organisation behind an amnesty campaign for internees and prisoners.

Support for those directly impacted by the Rising swiftly took organisational form. In May 1916 the Irish National Aid Association (INAA), was assembled by a Dublin-based collective of well-known figures associated with the IPP and other, advanced, nationalists, with the view to securing financial assistance for the families of those killed or executed because of the Rising and for the families of those imprisoned or interned in its aftermath.[29] In the same month Kathleen Clarke established a separate Volunteer Dependants' Fund (VDF), centred on the widows of republican leaders, with the view to supporting families of

7.7
(Opposite page, bottom)
INAAVDF catalogue of memorabilia associated with the 1916 Rising on view for auction at the Mansion House.
HE:EW.1281

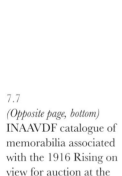

Irish Volunteers and, more ambiguously, advancing the ideals of the Rising.[30] Although Clarke was suspicious of the INAA as a vehicle for the Irish Parliamentary Party, the Home Rule leadership evidenced little inclination of their pre-War tendency to annex rival nationalist groupings. The two bodies, thus, were amalgamated in August 1916 as the Irish National Aid Association and Volunteer Dependants' Fund (INAAVDF). The organisation would increasingly reflect a republican 'hierarchy of victims'; special financial provision being made for the dependants of Irish Volunteers.[31] As of October 1916, the INAAVDF had raised up to £41,000 and was collecting, on average, £1,400 per week.[32] The significance of these associations, however, extended beyond benevolent political life. They reinforced the Irish Party's disengagement from popular politics in late 1916. Caoimhe Nic Dháibhéid's careful analysis has suggested that the national expansion of the INAA may have served as an associational and political framework for later republican organisation, to the further diminution of local UIL activity.[33] Senia Pašeta, meanwhile, has drawn attention to the visibility of female activism within these organisations until late 1916, contemporarily suggestive of a changing nationalist politics.[34] More persuasively still, the INAAVDF remained in existence, beyond Irish Parliamentry Party takeover.

'On every level' R.F. Foster has cogently observed 'martyrolatry had taken over'.[35] Public opinion, which recognised the bravery of the ordinary rebels, and had begun to recognise the respectability of their leaders, effectively sacralised their memory in the summer of 1916. Timing was a contributory factor. The Catholic tradition of a month's mind mass for the dead brought members of the public to Catholic churches across the capital in late May. Ritual attendance at these

7.6
Irish Volunteer Dependants' Fund collecting card.
HE:EWL.275.49

7.8
Mass card for those executed after the Rising.
HE:EW.1022c

7.9
Memorial card for Charles D'Arcy (15) who was killed at City Hall on the first day of the Rising.
HE:EW.4147

7.10
Memorial locket commemorating Roger Casement.
HE:EW.2237

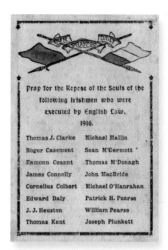

ceremonies often involved the purchase of mass cards, recital of prayers and displays of reverence towards the deceased. 'Public sympathy' the RIC Inspector General noted frustratingly 'has been stimulated by the sale of photographs of the rebel leaders'.[36] The beatification of the dead rebels continued apace within the pages of the *Catholic Bulletin*. Between May and July, this overtly nationalist periodical evaded the rigours of the censor by publishing obituary biographies of those who had been killed as a result of the Rising with particular emphasis on their 'Catholic and social' lives. Photographs of the widows and children left behind by the Rising's dead evoked natural sympathy.[37] The fate of Roger Casement, concurrently, reinforced the Rising as sacrificial cause. The issue of the 'black diaries' (charging Casement with homosexual activity) during his London trial was widely perceived to have been an attack on the morality of Irish nationalism.[38] Casement's conversion to Catholicism on the day of his execution (3 August) enshrined him as nationalist martyr.

Shrines to the 1916 Rising also came in the form of objects, iconography and materials. The exposition of 'Sinn Féin' colours among the general population in the months after the 1916 Rising has long been noted by researchers. Members of the public increasingly wore badges, pins and insignia bearing the tricolour while GAA teams occasionally adopted green, white and gold/orange apparel in matches. This 'wearing of the colours' is often explained simply as political fashion; a popular style of identifying with the Rising. 'Sinn Féin' was 'in' during the summer of 1916.

7.11
Tricolour ribbon.
HE:1998.260 (Allen)

This, however, is to depoliticise what was contemporarily understood as a popular political movement. Both participants and observers of the emerging movement referred to it as such. Ernie O'Malley wrote of the 'strange rebirth' of politics in late 1916: 'it was manifest in flags, badges, songs, speech, all seemingly superficial signs'.[39] C.S. Andrews commented similarly of a nascent movement: 'these little badges … evoked mutual recognition and sympathy among a large section of public opinion'.[40] Writing of public opinion on 14 August, meanwhile, the RIC Inspector General estimated that over 36,000 people were broadly sympathetic to the rebels, but reported concernedly 'about 7,000 persons … [who] have been noticed wearing Irish republican and mourning badges'. The purchase and display of 'Sinn Féin' materials, he considered, was sufficiently widespread to be considered 'organised disloyalty'.[41] In his seminal study of the American revolution, T.H. Breen has discussed the significance of consumer culture under the political censorship of the 'Intolerable Acts': 'shared experiences as consumers provided them [the colonists] with the cultural resources needed to develop a bold new form of political protest … consumer choices

communicated personal loyalties … [and] provided a means to educate and energize a dispersed populace'.[42] In Ireland in 1916, the rigours of the Defence of the Realm Act (and the potential enforcement of Martial Law) prohibited the holding of political meetings, the publication of seditious literature and the carrying of arms. 'Buying into' the Sinn Féin movement, thus, may have provided the cultural resources to develop a collective form of political protest in Ireland in late 1916. Material culture indeed, as Breen suggests, provided a means to educate and energise a dispersed populace. Between 14 and 22 October the American-based Irish Relief Fund opened a bazaar at Madison Square Garden in which Irish-American patrons were encouraged to purchase artefacts from the 1916 Rising. Back in Ireland, meanwhile, rebel ballads such as the recently adopted 'Soldier's Song' were purchased as songbooks and widely sung at 'Sinn Féin' events. Rising veteran Seán Prendergast would later recall: 'people too had learned to sing *our* songs – songs of praise "for the gallant men of Easter Week" and "the Felons of *Our* Land". Our songs, *their* songs, *Ireland's* songs … a "new spirit" had come.'[43]

7.12
Programme of the Great Irish Relief Fund bazaar held at Madison Square Garden, New York.
HE:EW.473

7.13
Peadar Kearney's 'Soldier's Song' was popularised after the Rising.
HE:EW.564

Prendergast was one of those released early from Frongoch in July 1916. The remaining six hundred internees were released from the internment camp in December as part of a Christmas amnesty introduced by new British Prime Minister David Lloyd George. Returning to this 'new' Ireland many rebels were faced with a more prosaic and (de)pressing reality: securing financial support after eight months of internment. Michael Collins, it became quickly established, held the key to vital emergency funding. Collins, who had been released with the rest of the Frongoch internees, found early employment in Dublin, through his IRB connections, as secretary of the INAAVDF. 'It was here', Peter Hart suggested, 'that the legend of Michael Collins, Superclerk, was born.'[44] The fastidiously maintained ledgers and registers of the INAAVDF attest to Collins' bureaucratic proficiency and his expanding range of contacts: Monaghan, Manchester, Melbourne.[45] In sum, it has been estimated that he administered over £100,000 to two thousand applicants, on behalf of its many committees, during his eighteen months at 10 Exchequer Street.[46] The Frongoch internees were also faced with the choice of rejoining the Irish Volunteers on their release. A Provisional Volunteer Council convened by Cathal Brugha in November 1916 had secured the structural continuity of the Irish Volunteers after the Rising while Volunteer companies began to re-emerge on local initiative in the winter of 1916/17.[47] Some rebels did

7.14
Michael Collins.
HE:EW.5720

7.15
Michael Collins' key for the INAAVDF's office at 10 Exchequer Street, Dublin.
HE:EW.491

not seek any further involvement in the movement; many others did. The protracted war in Europe also provided returned rebels, Collins included, with more unexpected opportunities to mobilise the post-Rising politics.

The North Roscommon by-election of February 1917 was cumulative and confirmative of the change in popular politics which had materialised since the Rising. The death of the IPP's James Joseph Kelly, who had been waiting to retire on the conclusion of the war, created an opening for an alternative nationalist candidate to run against the Irish Parliamentary Party. Count George Plunkett, significantly, was nominated by local activists. Plunkett's candidacy and campaign were symbolic of the 'new nationalism'. Although widely cited as the 'Sinn Féin' contestant, Plunkett ran as an independent, acquiring support from a spectrum of alternative nationalists including the Irish Nation League and Irish Volunteers. This electoral affinity was underpinned

7.16
Count Plunkett (seated in back of car) on the election trail during the later Longford by-election, May 1917.
HE:EWP.37

by a 'negative' political manifesto. Plunkett's platform was built around criticisms of the Irish Parliamentary Party and the British State. Voting for Plunkett, it was argued, was a vote of solidarity with his family's 1916 sacrifice.[48] Constituents were identified, and self-identified, with Plunkett's candidacy, through displays of material culture. Kevin O'Shiel, one of his campaigners, noted the proliferation of tricolour buttons and badges at Plunkett's meetings; his platforms were draped by tricolour flags in contrast to the IPP candidate's green Home Rule flag, while tricolours, it was widely reported, were flown from the cars of celebrating supporters travelling back to Dublin.[49] These scenes followed Plunkett's successful polling of 3,022 votes, to the nearest candidate's 1,708. Only after his by-election victory did Plunkett

SINN FEIN ABU.

announce a policy of abstention from Westminster. The United Irish League's dysfunctional campaign pronounced the Irish Party's local dissolution and John Redmond's despair for the Home Rule cause: 'Let the Irish people replace us by all means, by other and, I hope, better men, if they so choose.'[50] Only on T.P. O'Connor's pleading did Redmond decide against issuing this public resignation.[51] John Dillon's speech in the House of Commons neatly bespoke politics in Ireland since the Rising: 'the British government have been manufacturing Sinn Feiners by tens of thousands'.[52]

The popularity of the 'Sinn Féin' brand, however, was not sold on all advanced nationalists. The mercurial Count Plunkett had designs on leading an alternative, republican organisation: the Liberty League. Writing from prison, meanwhile, Éamon de Valera expressed concern for any 'reversion to the old Sinn Féin *political* movement'. The majority of the republican leadership interned at Lewes, moreover, were opposed to the idea of contesting further elections against the Irish Parliamentary Party, lest 'what has been purchased by our comrades' blood should be lost on a throw with dice loaded against us'.[53] However, the emerging Sinn Féin party, nominally under Arthur Griffith's leadership, was becoming a skilled electioneering machine. This would be increasingly

7.17
A postcard capturing the iconic image of the Sinn Féin movement in 1917.
HE:EW.2291

223

in evidence during the South Longford by-election. The death of the IPP MP John Phillips on 2 April prompted an almost immediate response from a group of advanced nationalists, including Plunkett, Collins and Griffith, to select Joseph McGuinness, the Longford-born Lewes prisoner, as their candidate. The Home Rule candidate was only selected one week before the election. Sinn Féin canvassers, meanwhile, had descended on Longford within days. Marie Coleman has drawn attention to the 'intensity' of the party's campaign, in contrast to the 'lethargic' application of the United Irish League, allowing the former to dictate the issues of the election: conscription, partition, prisoners.[54] The party also evinced an increasingly sophisticated approach to electioneering. Contemporary reports documented the volume and diversity of print material circulated by Sinn Féin campaigners: handbills, pamphlets, posters, postcards, journals.[55] The party's literature also denoted a carefully organised strategy of stratified

7.18
South Longford
by-election handbill,
May 1917.
HE:EW.275.54

7.19
South Longford
by-election handbill,
May 1917.
HE:EW.275.59

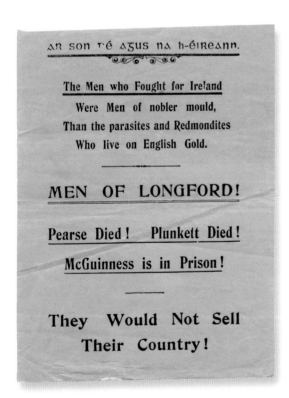

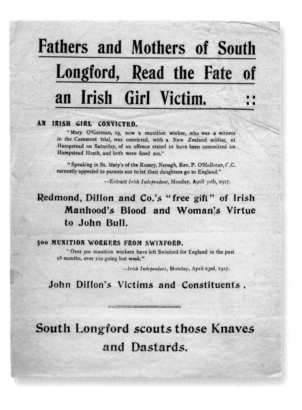

electioneering. Perhaps the most influential example of the party's propaganda nous arrived on polling day itself when organisers reprinted comments from the Archbishop of Dublin decrying partition in the form of Sinn Féin handbills. In a remarkably tight election, McGuinness polled just thirty-seven more votes than the Irish Party candidate. McGuinness' victory, however, was significant for its solidification of 'Sinn Féin' as the party of opposition to the IPP. Michael Laffan's invaluable study has indicated that the organisation began to 'take-off' from April onwards, reaching 336 cumann by the end of July: 'Sinn Féin was the fad or the craze of 1917.'[56]

Recognition of Sinn Féin's political ascent came from unlikely sources. On 11 June 1917 the Prime Minister announced the composition of an Irish Convention which would be assembled to reach a settlement on the issues of Home Rule and partition in Ireland. Members of the Irish Parliamentary Party would be joined by representatives of northern and southern unionism, local councils, the churches of Ireland and other nationalist affiliations. Five of the 101 seats at the Convention were allocated for representatives of 'separatist doctrines'.[57] Lloyd George had initially suggested four seats for the 'Sinn Feiners' while John Dillon pushed for six, to ensure 'no plausible excuse for staying out [of the Convention]'.[58] The Sinn Féin party, however, refused to attend on the premise of fundamental opposition to partition.[59] Dillon himself declined to take part in the proceedings, becoming entrenched in the view that Redmond's acquiescence to yet another British proposal could only further damage the Party.[60] The Irish Convention opened at Trinity College on 25 July and would remain in session until 5 April 1918. It has been judged by R.B. McDowell as a 'brilliant failure'.[61] Its proceedings, which were conducted in private, cast further silence on the leadership of the Irish Party; Dillon writing privately: 'The curse that is hanging over us in Ireland is that the great mass of *our friends* are bewildered and do not know where they are. They have got it firmly fixed in their heads

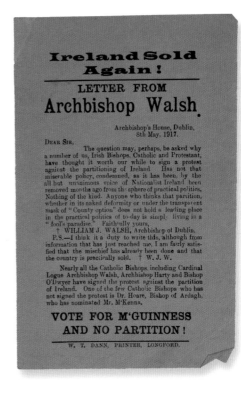

7.20
The Sinn Féin handbill presenting the Archbishop of Dublin's comments on partition.
HE:EW.1891

7.21
Countess Markievicz's
return at Westland Row.
HE:EWL.227.68

that Redmond has no more fight in him.'[62] The announcement of the Convention, moreover, was coincided with the release of the republican leadership from Lewes prison.

Éamon de Valera, Thomas Ashe and, more familiar faces such as Countess Markievicz, arrived at Westland Row Station on 17 June to scenes of popular acclaim. 'Tens of thousands of the citizens lined all the main streets', Simon Donnelly remembered, 'it was with the greatest difficulty that their earlier released comrades got them through to their hotel where an official reception awaited them.'[63]

7.22
Postcard image of
Éamon de Valera in Irish
Volunteer uniform.
HE:EW.2637

IRISH REBELLION, MAY 1916.

ED. de VALERA
(Commandant of the Ringsend Area).
Sentenced to Death;
Sentence commuted to Penal Servitude for Life.

In the pocket of his military uniform de Valera carefully held onto a telegram received one day earlier informing him of his nomination by Sinn Féin for the East Clare by-election.[64] The vacancy had arisen following another casualty of the War, Willie Redmond (John's brother), who had been tragically killed leading an offensive at the Battle of Messines Ridge. As the senior surviving commandant of the Rising, and emergent leader of the prisoners at Lewes, de Valera had a strong republican profile but his political repute was less established. He would consciously blur the lines between militant and constitutional politician during his campaign. Speaking from platforms he declared 'you have no enemy but England, and you must be prepared to fight against England' but later advised that 'every vote you give now is as good as the crack of a rifle in proclaiming your desire for freedom'. Local professionals canvassed on his behalf beside armed Volunteers while de Valera frequently wore his Volunteer uniform on the election trail.[65] His biographers Lord Longford and T.P. O'Neill would remark: 'politics and soldiering were not yet fully sorted out in his mind'.[66] The campaign, however, further clarified Sinn Féin and Éamon de Valera's political credentials, with the resounding defeat of the Irish Parliamentary candidate by 5,010 votes to 2,035. Charting the development of Sinn Féin branches in the county following de Valera's by-election victory, David Fitzpatrick has discerned a preponderance of former UIL organisers among its new activists. By extension, Fitzpatrick argued, Sinn Féin at local level fortified 'old wine in new bottles'.[67]

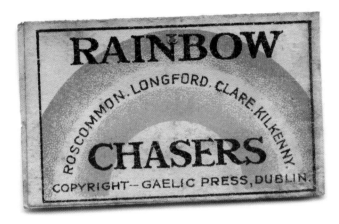

7.23
Sinn Féin activists were popularly labelled 'rainbow chasers'. This badge lapel was issued to mark the Party's by-election victories in 1917. In September William T. Cosgrave had won Sinn Féin's fourth successive contest, at Kilkenny City.
HE:EWL.227.39

It also fortified the Irish Volunteers. County studies of Longford and Clare have indicated the revitalisation of Irish Volunteer activism through by-election campaigns.[68] The intersection between Sinn Féin and Irish Volunteers organisers at local level has also been noted.[69] Where did politics end and political violence begin? In an arresting counter-factual essay, Peter Hart has questioned 'the necessity for violence' during the Irish revolution arguing, in part, that 'Sinn Féin never used – and never needed – violence to achieve its successes of 1917–18' leading to his suggestive conclusion: 'if a non-violent Sinn Féin had evolved, revolutionary in its aims but akin to the Land League in its militancy and methods, it might well have got just as many votes, been just as successful and made the IRA unnecessary'.[70] A number of Rising veterans, however, did feel that violence was necessary. Later statements to the Bureau of Military History evince the persistence of an early twentieth-century militarisation of minds which has been

termed the Irish 'soldiery ideal'.[71] Seumas Robinson expressed his relief at being invited to Tipperary to reorganise the Volunteers upon his release from Frongoch 'because I had taken a solemn resolution on Easter Monday morning … that I'd soldier for the rest of my life or until we had our freedom'.[72] Frank Thornton was even more resolute on his return from Lewes: 'We were back in Dublin with a determination. The surrender of 1916 was only a breathing space between that and the commencement of the war proper.'[73] Others were moved towards violence by their underlying conviction in the 'Fenian ideal'. In June 1917, a new IRB Supreme Council, presided over by Thomas Ashe, decided on the removal of the clause in its constitution which had vested the Irish people with sole power to decide on the moment to begin an armed conflict with Britain. A Military Council was established, further, to acquire arms for the Irish Volunteers. Ashe's protégé, Michael Collins, became a member of both the Supreme Council and the Military Council.[74] Although a new military order in July had prohibited drilling, some activists continued to parade with rifles. Others encouraged 'public defiance' through seditious speeches.[75] Following one too many such addresses, Thomas Ashe was arrested and incarcerated at Mountjoy prison in August, whereupon

he and other Volunteers began a hunger-strike in search of prisoner-of-war status. The prison authorities' practice of forcibly feeding the hunger-strikers resulted in Ashe's agonising death on 25 September 1917. His burial at Glasnevin cemetery five days later, though skilfully organised by fellow Frongoch returnee Richard Mulcahy, was defined by the performance of Michael Collins. Emerging from the funeral crowds after Volunteer rifles were fired over Ashe's graveside, he pronounced ominously: 'Nothing additional remains to be said. That volley which we have just heard is the only speech which it is proper to make above the grave of a dead Fenian.'[76]

7.26
Thomas Ashe.
HE:EW.2902

In post-Rising Ireland, a man must have upon his side the Volunteers or the Fenians. Éamon de Valera consciously decided against the latter. In the aftermath of the East Clare by-election he discontinued his nominal membership of the IRB, believing that open organisation was paramount to safeguarding the nascent 'Sinn Féin' movement. This public path, according to Ronan Fanning, further strengthened de Valera's 'asumption of power'.[77] On 27 October, at its Croke Park convention, de Valera was elected president of the Irish Volunteers. Those in attendance pledged to carry on the reorganisation of the Volunteers throughout the country and put them in a position to complete, by force of arms, the work begun by the 1916 Rising, on the proviso that there was a reasonable chance of military success. This deviation from the IRB's more principled committment to offensive action was indicative of different strategic approaches to political violence within the Volunteer leadership. Michael Collins and other 'turbulent spirits' would assume executive roles within the Irish Volunteers.[78] Two days earlier de Valera had also been elected president of Sinn Féin at its national convention; Griffith and Plunkett having decided, ultimately, not to contest the leadership. The Convention, which was attended by over 1,700 delegates representing over 1,200 clubs, was assembled to decide, almost eighteen months after the Rising, what Sinn Féin stood for. Addressing its congregation of long-standing dual monarchists, recent Home Rulers and veteran republicans, de Valera announced Sinn Féin's new manifesto: 'we say it is necessary to be united under the flag under which we are going to fight for our freedom: the flag of the Irish Republic'.[79]

8

COMMEMORATION

'The past is a foreign country: they do things differently there.'[1]
Inherent in L.P. Hartley's irrepressible opening line is an aphorism on
commemoration, memory and history: the existential distance, and
therefore difference, between past experienced and past remembered.
An examination of any historical event must reconcile itself to this
fundamental disjunction; we are all, by definition, revisionists now. The
1916 Rising, significantly, has transitioned commemoration, memory
and history in twentieth-century Ireland. It is beginning to transition
debates between practitioners of the same.[2] Its impact, for example,
can be projected through state ceremonies; profiled through museum

8.0
(Page 230)
A group of schoolchildren
are directed to a case
of guns in the National
Museum of Ireland's 1941
exhibition.

exhibitions; and penetrated through historiographical review. This multi-disciplinary approach is apposite. The centenary of the 1916 Rising has encouraged unprecedented knowledge exchange between the academy and cultural institutions; to the successful creation of new exhibitions, archival programmes and public events. The late twentieth century 'turn towards memory' within international scholarship, further, has originated new conceptual frameworks within which to understand commemorative presentation.[3] The open access movement, meanwhile, has digitally restored objects as sources of historical interpretation.[4] Concepts of commemoration, memory and history are being remapped and reconceptualised. The legacy of the 1916 Rising, correspondingly, is expectantly primed for fresh interrogation. Three essential questions suggest themselves. How have public commemorations of the 1916 Rising been integrated into the political life of modern Ireland? To what extent has cultural or social memory self-distinguished from collective memory of the 1916 Rising? In what ways can material culture establish 'new histories' of Ireland, 1916?

COMMEMORATION

1923–34

The Irish State has had an identifiable relationship with the legacy of the 1916 Rising in the late twentieth and early twenty-first centuries. Official commemoration ceremonies, or lack thereof, have purposed legitimation of Irish sovereignty, presenting the Rising in and out of focus accordingly. It has not always been publicly defined as Ireland's national moment. In the first decade of independence, commemoration of the Rising was distinctly party political.

Successive Cumann na nGaedheal and Fianna Fáil administrations marked the 1916 Rising with annual ceremonies at Arbour Hill, beginning in 1924. These proved Civil War events. Attendance was both proscribed and prescribed by association with its politics. Several anti-Treaty republicans were debarred from attending the Cumann na nGaedheal-led ceremonies in 1924. Conversely, all but one of the 1916 relatives declined their invitation.[5] Party, army and civil service officials were annual attendees.[6] Fianna Fáil's ascent to power in 1932 cultivated an equally partisan commemoration of the 1916 Rising. Attendance at Arbour Hill was confined to party designates and relatives of the rebels.[7] Meanwhile, over 200 civil servants previously invited were removed from the list, prompting parliamentary debate in Dáil Éireann. In his survey of early commemoration in the Irish State, Diarmaid Ferriter has adjudged the issue of the 1916 Rising to have been used 'to create political capital … and emphasise the divisions that existed within the Irish body politic'.[8] The very constitution of ceremonial commemoration is of relevance here. In his volume on the cultural impact of the First World War, Jay Winter has observed: 'After 1914 commemoration was an act of citizenship. To remember was to affirm community, to assert its moral character, and to exclude from it those values, groups, or individuals that placed it under threat.'[9] Converging on Arbour Hill, according to such an analysis, was less about the inculcation of the Rising as the foundational national memory, than the political legitimation of those present. Both governments, indeed, excluded the general public from the commemorative ceremonies.[10] Was Arbour Hill a site of memory, site of mourning?

The state commemorations at Arbour Hill between 1924 and 1934 were ritualistic. A requiem Mass was held at the Church of the Sacred Heart followed by a solemn procession to the graveside of the executed rebels for the recitation of the rosary and other prayers. The Irish Defence Forces, subsequently, would fire three rifle

8.1
President Éamon de Valera and members of the Executive Council attend a commemoration ceremony at Arbour Hill.

shots over the graves before the official ceremony was concluded with the last post. Renditions of *De Profundis* and the Soldier's Song were occasionally performed.[11] The form of commemoration chosen is of interest. Writing on collective memory, Paul Connerton has noted the restriction of such rites: '[these] are formalised acts … they are not subject to spontaneous variation, or at least are susceptible to variation only within strict limits'.[12] The circumscribed commemorations at Arbour Hill suggest an uncertainty as to how to cultivate the memory of the 1916 Rising to the legitimation of the state. Ceremonial stages were stoically adhered to without attempts to reconstitute the Rising in the contemporary image of the state. Indeed participants were concerned for any deviation in the established choreography lest the commemoration be seen as legitimating a particular historical memory of the Rising. In advance of the 1925 ceremony, for example, the Cumann na nGaedheal government expressed disquiet over the suggestion that they, and not the army, would lay wreaths on the graves of the executed.[13] This was not the case at their Glasnevin ceremonies for Michael Collins and Arthur Griffith.[14] Silent, stoic and consciously straightjacketed, the official commemoration of the 1916 Rising in early independent Ireland ritualised party ascendancy. The Rising had yet to be formally conceptualised as national collective memory.

1935

The 'invented tradition' of a state military parade to commemorate the 1916 Rising, first took place outside the General Post Office, Dublin, on 21 April 1935.[15] Its occurrence has since become synonymous with official commemoration of the 1916 Rising in the public mind. This construction of collective memory requires attention, not least because it marks the first attempt by the Irish State to openly involve the people in the process of remembering. Why that commemorative practice was created in 1935 and why it was maintained, against the emergency backdrop of the Second World War, in 1941, is significant to understanding the 1916 Rising as national memory.

Nineteen years after the events of Easter Week, the Irish State returned to the scene of the GPO. The occasion, nominally, was to mark the opening of a specially designed memorial to the 1916 Rising, 'the death of Cuchulainn', within the building's main hall.[16] The commemoration at the General Post Office, however, was imbued with much greater spatial significance. Probing the extents of collective memory on modern France, the historian Pierre Nora has famously discerned the prevalence of '*lieux de memoire*', literally translated as 'sites of memory'.[17] The commemorative purpose of creating *lieux de mémoire*, Nora asserted, was to 'stop time, to block the world of forgetting, to establish a state of things, to immortalize death, to materialize the immaterial'.[18] The GPO, following a break of almost two decades, was being established as a collective 'site of memory' to the 1916 Rising. The process of 'remembering' was strengthened through the arrangement of a military parade outside the GPO, simultaneous to the grand opening of the memorial inside. The ceremonies were elaborately staged. The mobilisation of participants was carefully rehearsed while the order of events was well publicised in the national press.[19] Cordons, stretching from Abbey Street to Nelson's Pillar held back thousands of cheering onlookers. The events of Easter Week, meanwhile, were narrated repeatedly over loudspeaker.[20] The parade itself constituted an attempt to impress upon the public a memory of the Rising, through ceremonial re-enactment. Veterans of the GPO, Four Courts, South Dublin Union and Bolands' Mills garrisons assembled outside the Post Office, in the very uniforms worn during Easter Week. Upon the arrival of de Valera, just before midday, the ex-combatants entered the GPO, for the opening of the memorial. Minutes later, former rebels, armed with original Howth mausers, fired their rifles from the roof of the GPO. This was met with artillery gunfire from the direction of O'Connell Bridge. The sequence was consecutively repeated, concluding with the sound of rifles over the Post Office and de Valera's re-emergence onto O'Connell Street.[21] The ritual re-enactment of past events, Paul Connerton has suggested, is 'a quality of cardinal importance in the shaping of communal memory'.[22] The

8.2
Members of the Irish
Defence Forces parade
past the GPO during the
1935 ceremony. President
of the Executive Council
Éamon de Valera observes
from the stand.

commemorations outside the GPO remembered a contemporary story of the 1916 Rising. It also remembered the 'story of Ireland'.[23] Immediately following the ceremonies involving veterans of the Rising, the Irish Defence Forces paraded before de Valera and the GPO. The procession, consisting of some 2,000 regular troops and 4,500 volunteers, would take a full hour and a half to pass through the centre of Dublin.[24] The juxtaposition of Irish military personnel with the veterans of the Rising, was an attempt to represent the 1916 Rising as the foundational moment and memory of the Irish State.

1941

The centrality of the GPO, and military victory, to the collective memory of the 1916 Rising was perhaps most sharply represented during the 1941 state commemoration. Ireland's engagement with the Second World War was premised on political and military neutrality. The Irish people further experienced the 'emergency' through censorship, economic rationing and social restraints.[25] In this supremely charged hour, the continued celebration of the Rising was not necessarily politically correct. Still less so, potentially, was a military commemoration. Such doubts were present within state administrative and government circles.[26] The ceremonies did take place; their cultivation of military memory was emphatic.

8.3
Taoiseach Éamon de Valera, Ministers of State and the Irish Defence Forces stand to attention before the GPO in 1941.

The commemorative sequence was almost identical to that of 1935. On Easter Sunday morning, veterans of the 1916 Rising formed a guard of honour outside the GPO and were reviewed by the Taoiseach, Éamon de Valera. The tricolour above the building was lowered to half-mast, followed by speeches from the Taoiseach, and President Douglas Hyde, before it was then restored to full-staff. Former rebels interchanged rifle fire from the roof of the GPO with artillery fire from the O'Connell Bridge direction, before de Valera emerged onto O'Connell Street to oversee the military parade. Tens of thousands of Irish people witnessed the procession of the Irish Defence Forces from Collins Barracks to College Green. The 20,000 trained troops, volunteers and non-military personnel took over two and a half hours to pass the General Post Office, overlooked by three squadrons of army planes in the skies above. It was widely reported as the largest military ceremony ever seen in the capital city.[27]

1966

Reflecting on halcyon days in Ireland, the poet Dermot Bolger has remarked: 'For anyone who grew up in the 1960s, the Easter Rising meant 1966 and not 1916.'[28] This generation of communal memory was significant, not only because it marked the Rising's Jubilee commemoration, but because official commemoration impressed '1916' upon Irish political, cultural and social life. For one full week in April 1966, Ireland collectively remembered the Rising. On collective memory; the French sociologist Maurice Halbwachs has pioneered scholarship on the essentiality of 'social frameworks' to the construction and continuation of memory, positing that the 'memory' of an event is shaped by contemporary societal influences and needs.[29] Halbwachs' approach is resonant of Ireland's official 1966 programme. Remembering 1916 in 1966 presented, above all, a highly sociable event.

8.4

The scenes outside the GPO on the occasion of the jubilee commemoration of the Rising in 1966.

The Irish State's commemoration of the fiftieth anniversary of the 1916 Rising was participatory and diverse. The Easter Sunday parade outside the GPO set the tone. Two hundred thousand people crowded the centre of Dublin to observe the ceremony.[30] The, by now, familiar sight of military personnel marching in their thousands past the political stage was followed immediately by a distinctly unfamiliar sight: a civic procession of 5,000 people representing language, labour, sporting and cultural interests.[31] The official programme encouraged active communal engagement with the legacies of the 1916 Rising across recognisable themes. The spirituality of the Rising was emphasised through ecumenical services and the opening of the Garden of Remembrance to the public on Easter Monday.[32] The literary and linguistic contributions of the signatories were publicly extolled through the arrangement of eighteen competitions for the composition of contemporary music, art and literature in their honour, while official concerts were staged at the Abbey and Gaiety theatres. Children, in particular, were encouraged to draw inspiration from the cultural leaders of the Rising.[33] Meanwhile, the social centrepiece of the week, the bilingual pageant entitled *Aiséirí* (Insurrection), was performed five times at Croke Park to crowds of thousands.[34] Halbwachs' delineation of collective memory is pertinent: 'it is in society that people normally acquire their memories. It is also in society that they recall, recognize, and localize their memories'.[35] The official programme attempted to cultivate a 'collective effervescence' through commemoration of essential themes in social spheres.[36] Was this, however, a collective memory of 1916 or 1966?

8.5
A performance of *Aiséirí* at Croke Park during Easter Week 1966.

Remembering the Rising, under the guidance of official commemoration, did not particularly encourage differentiation. Indeed constants between 1916 and 1966 were repeatedly advanced. Carole Holohan has noted the commemorative pressures exerted on young people to emulate the seven signatories, advocated through universals such as achievement, co-operation and initiative.[37] Roisín Higgins, meanwhile, has discerned the 'resuscitation' of the Rising's leaders as 'individuals' in commemorative pageants with the view to bringing the lives of Connolly, Pearse, Plunkett, etc, to present-day application.[38] Maurice Halbwachs' position on this subject was seminal: 'The past is not preserved but is reconstructed on the basis of the present.'[39] The 'presentism' of 1916 in 1966 was perhaps most evident in the commemorative emphasis on Ireland as a modern economy and society. Tourist bodies identified 1916 trails for international visitors; a specially commissioned documentary juxtaposed images of the Rising with footage of contemporary Ireland, while all the major ceremonial events were screened, for the first time on Teilifís Éireann, the national broadcaster.[40] The 1916 Rising could, quite literally, be remembered through the lens of Ireland 1966. Mary Daly has, quite correctly, attributed the modernising impulses of the official commemoration to the 'intellectual character' of Seán Lemass.[41] Lemass' tenure as Taoiseach, which ended in 1966, had seen the attempted reorientation of Irish economic policy from a protectionist self-sufficient model towards a more free-market internationalist approach, denoted neatly by membership of the General Agreement on Tariffs and Trade (GATT) in 1960 and attempted membership of the European Economic Community (EEC) in 1961.[42] The commemorations, Lemass concluded, were about showcasing the Ireland of today. The 1916 Rising, he asserted accordingly, had proven 'the birth pangs of modern Ireland'.[43]

The fiftieth anniversary was formally brought to a close with a commemorative ceremony outside the GPO on 16 April. President de Valera was given the honour of delivering the final address. Surveying the success of the 1966 commemoration, he turned optimistically to the state of Ireland: 'Thanks be to God the dissensions and differences we have had down here are now past. We are all on the straight road marching again side by side and we can look forward to the people of the North also wishing to be with us.'[44]

1967–2005

In the late 1960s the North began, again. The collapse of the Northern Ireland administration, under immense internal socio-political pressures in 1972, and the devastation of Northern Ireland society across a further quarter-century of political violence, negated the Irish State impulse to commemorate the 1916 Rising. The Irish State's 1966 official commemoration of republican violence in 1916, it was argued, could be misconstrued as tacit approval of republican violence in 1969. Some, indeed, had already judged the Irish State guilty by commemorative association. In an influential treatise on 'the cult of 1916' in 1966, Irish politician and cultural commentator Conor Cruise O'Brien suggested that 'the great commemorative year [was] a year in which ghosts were bound to walk, both North and South'.[45] Successive generations of Ulster unionist leaders publicly subscribed to this view.[46] More recent scholarship has rejected the corollary of commemoration in southern Ireland with inter-communal conflict in Northern Ireland.[47] The impact of the 'Troubles', as the violence was collectively referred to, on Irish State commemorations, however, was 'inevitable'.[48]

Between 1972 and 2005 inclusive, the annual military ceremony outside the GPO was discontinued, resumed only briefly for the seventy-fifth anniversary in 1991. National commemorative events elsewhere in Europe were being slowly transitioned out of the public sphere by the late 1960s.[49] The Irish State, however, attempted to systematically repress collective memory of the 1916 Rising. Alternative state commemorations on Easter Sunday were disavowed while the commemorative space outside the GPO remained unused.[50] Benedict Anderson has termed this process of absolution from memory: 'collective amnesia'.[51] Successive Irish governments attempted, in this tradition, to subsume the memory of the 1916 Rising within more benign collective and commemorative events. In 1972, a suggestion was considered for the introduction of a single day of remembrance for those who had died during the 1916–21 period. In 1973, meanwhile, Conor Cruise O'Brien himself was central to discussions on the reformulation of St Patrick's Day as a National Day of Reconciliation. The proposals were announced as part of President Erskine Childers' St Patrick's Day speech one year later but not formally introduced.[52]

Sigmund Freud once observed of the human mind: 'it is our belief that it is time that makes memory uncertain and indistinct ... there can really be no question of a direct function of time ... the unconscious, at all events, knows no time limit'.[53] The extent to which the state could successfully 'repress' the 1916 Rising from the 'public mind' during the Troubles was undermined by its seventy-fifth anniversary in 1991. On 31 March 1991, President Mary Robinson and Taoiseach Charles Haughey stood before the GPO, flanked by senior members of the Irish Defence Forces. Neither formally addressed the lowly 600 in attendance. The tricolour was lowered from the roof of the Post Office and the Proclamation read aloud. The tricolour was then reinstated to full mast, before the national anthem was played. The entire ceremony was begun and concluded within fifteen minutes.[54] 'Acting out' a minimal ceremony outside the GPO was, in Freud's terms, a resistant form of remembering the Rising.[55] The Irish State was not ready to fully communicate a collective memory of 1916.

2006

Official commemoration of the Rising in 2006 was less about Ireland as Irelands. The ninetieth anniversary saw the return of the military parade to O'Connell Street which, ostensibly, reclaimed the 1916 Rising as Ireland's foundational memory, violence and all. Contemporary comment questioned the continued relevance of the Easter Sunday commemoration, to the Irish public, as military display. Historiographical critiques have followed similar lines of enquiry.[56] Southern Ireland's preoccupation with parading military history, however, belied the Irish State's broader commemorative imperative, to reflect upon 'the shared history and shared experience of the people of this island, from all traditions'.[57] The 2006 commemoration was a Peace Process event. Constructing the collective memory of 1916, in this context, was about sharing commemorative emphases between the Rising and the Somme. Parity of esteem, paradoxically, equated the past through military history.

This pluralist mandate was heavily foregrounded by two speeches in advance of the commemoration ceremonies. At a University College Cork symposium entitled 'The Long Revolution: the 1916 Rising in context', President Mary McAleese opened with a speech, entitled

'1916 – a view from 2006', which treated capaciously of the Rising's legacy through social reform, active citizenship and international statesmanship. Her empathetic analysis of the Rising as a progressive 'intellectual event' drew considerable public criticism, and some praise, from cultural commentators.[58] However, such remarks did not denote the president's speech in its entirety. The leitmotif of Mary McAleese's speech, on closer inspection, was inclusivity. The text, which had been cleared by the Department of the Taoiseach, espoused a 'culture of inclusion' towards 1916 and repeatedly paralleled nationalist and unionist expectations of the past for the future. In the clearest elucidation of this shared commemorative paradigm, the president posited: 'This year, the ninetieth anniversary of the 1916 Rising, and of the Somme, has the potential to be a pivotal year for peace and reconciliation, to be a time of shared pride for the divided grandchildren of those who died, whether at Messines or in Kilmainham.'[59] The commemorative discourse of 'shared past, shared future' was similarly promulgated by the Taoiseach Bertie Ahern. At the opening of the National Museum of Ireland's new exhibition, 'The Easter Rising: Understanding 1916', on 9 April, Ahern delivered an address entitled 'Remembrance, Reconciliation, Renewal'. His advocacy of active citizenship, using the Rising's leaders as exemplars, attracted considerable public attention.[60] However, it was the emphasis on 'shared history' which gave the speech commemorative definition. Repeatedly linking the years 1916 and 1998, the year of the signing of the Belfast/Good Friday Agreement the Taoiseach declared: 'our history is a shared legacy … the culmination of our shared achievement in the twentieth century was the Good Friday Agreement'. Most suggestively, Ahern prefaced the forthcoming state ceremonies: 'the Government has planned this ninetieth anniversary commemoration of the Easter Rising so that Ireland properly remembers her past'.[61]

Properly remembering the past is an anachronism. Pierre Nora's reflections here are again pertinent. In the introduction to his third volume *Les France*, Nora drew attention to the broader conceptualisation of *lieux de mémoire* as 'realms of memory'. Within this interpretative framework, the past comprises a spectrum of distinct memories which can be summarily conjoined in the present to support contemporary historical meta-narratives.[62] In 2006's prerogative for inclusive commemoration, the Irish State remembered the 1916 Rising and Battle of the Somme respectively. Military tradition constituted their shared history. On 16 April 2006, the official ceremonies commemorating the 1916 Rising took place in Dublin. At the wreath laying ceremony at Kilmainham jail, Taoiseach Bertie Ahern spoke partly on the continuation of the Peace Process. He was joined by President Mary McAleese at the GPO later that afternoon to review the military parade of 2,500 army personnel, a figure noticeably smaller than the more triumphalist processions of the 1930s and 1940s. Over 100,000 watched from the city centre. Ulster unionists, significantly, were invited to attend the ceremony, but declined.[63] The situation was different just over two months later. On

1 July 2006, representatives of Ulster unionism joined President McAleese and the Taoiseach Bertie Ahern at the Irish National War Memorial Gardens, Islandbridge, to mark the ninetieth anniversary of the beginning of the Battle of the Somme. The Irish Defence Forces were again present. In a carefully weighted ceremony, the President and a representative of the Northern Ireland administration each laid wreaths at the Cenotaph.[64] Addressing a North–South reception twelve days later,

8.6

Taoiseach Bertie Ahern addressing the launch of 'The Easter Rising: Understanding 1916' at the National Museum of Ireland, Collins Barracks on 9 April 2006.

President McAleese concluded the Somme commemoration to have evidenced: 'a fresh and exciting comprehension of a shared history which had been allowed to become bitterly divisive ... it is a credit to this generation that it insists on telling and commemorating the whole story'.[65]

MEMORY

The memory of the 1916 Rising, as projected by official state commemoration, has never been absolute. Scholars of memory, while indebted to Halbwachs' original concept of 'collective memory', have more recently presented arguments for theoretical stratification. Identifying and defining alternatives to 'collective memory', however, remains the subject of intense inter-disciplinary debate.[66] In one important intervention to the growing appropriation, and misappropriation, of Halbwachs' work as disciplinary paradigm, German Egyptologist Jan Assmann has calibrated memory across three levels: 'individual' (neuro-mental), 'communicative' (social) and 'cultural' (cultural).[67] The first, proffered initially by psychoanalysts such as Freud and Gustav Young, presents memory as an exclusively internal biological process, unique to the individual.[68] Proponents of the second interpretative framework, most commonly termed 'social memory', have built upon Halbwachs' idea of 'social frameworks' to explore the cultivation of individual memory through social interaction. The democracy and diversity of this memory, further, is often presented in contradistinction to state-directed 'collective memory'.[69] Assmann, meanwhile, has distinguished a third category of memory:

> Cultural memory is a kind of institution. It is exteriorized, objectified and stored away in symbolic forms that ... are stable and situation-transcendent ... things do not have a memory of their own, but they may remind us, may trigger our memory ... [cultural memory] exists also in disembodied form and requires institutions of preservation and reembodiment.[70]

Within this classification Jan Assmann, and fellow cultural anthropologist Aleida Assmann, have suggested that 'cultural memory' treats of a past beyond the experience of the individual, through mediated objects and continues to exist long-term through institutions.[71] The history of remembering the 1916 Rising, beyond state-led commemoration, presents similar challenges of description, interpretation and designation. The National Museum of Ireland embodies the complexity of this memory.

CULTURAL MEMORY

The Easter Week collection has, from its very inception, exhibited the 1916 Rising from alternative perspective. Though supported institutionally by the Irish State, the Museum's displays reflect the curator's presentation of the Rising's place in Irish history and, more broadly, donors' impartation of objects, artefacts and ephemera to personal memorial effect. The first 1916 exhibition at the National Museum of Ireland, however, was not necessarily representative of institutional- or individual-directed memories of the Rising. Nellie Gifford-Donnelly, secretary of the Dublin-based 1916 Club, provided the organisational impetus. As a participant in the Rising and a prominent figure among surviving veterans, Gifford-Donnelly contacted the Department of Education and the National Museum of Ireland in 1932 with the view to exhibiting 1916 *matériel* at the latter's Kildare Street site on the occasion of the International Eucharistic Congress and Tailteann Games, both being held in Dublin that year. Although the Department of Education voiced approval for the project, the Museum's Director Adolf Mahr expressed concerns as to the financial implications for the institution of acquiring such a collection and, more philosophically, its role in displaying a 'patriotic relic' which is 'neither scientific nor artistic nor illustrating antiquity or industry'.[72]

8.7

Nellie Gifford-Donnelly.

Gifford-Donnelly's assurances that the Museum would not incur any additional costs for the temporary display of objects appear to have nullified Mahr's formal opposition and from 8 June the general public were directed to send artefacts in parcels to the director's office.[73]

The exhibition, without formal title, opened in the National Museum's Irish Folk Room at Kildare Street on 20 June 1932. Although no official inventory of objects exists, the national media drew attention to a significant number of items on display: the last letters of Patrick Pearse and Seán Heuston, Joseph Plunkett's diary from the GPO, Countess Markievicz's green jacket and wristwatch, correspondence from Thomas

'Data is a cold affair, for the professors. History will be cold on the warm, human motive that impelled them towards their target, or the odd kinks, loves and capabilities — all in short that make the man live on.'

Nellie Gifford-Donnelly

MacDonagh and a sculpture by William Pearse entitled 'Memories'. Other artefacts more exclusively related to the fighting during Easter Week including the Four Courts flag, a shell from the GPO, military orders, Irish Citizen Army uniforms, and rifles, bombs and revolvers used by the rebels.[74] An emphasis on the leaders of the Rising in the exhibition was also discernible although perhaps more circumstantially produced. Nellie Gifford-Donnelly was sister-in-law to both Joseph Plunkett and Thomas MacDonagh and was likely to have had immediate access to their effects for display. She had made often unsuccessful enquiries for ephemera from other, less prominent, participants in the Rising.[75] More tellingly, perhaps, the general public had been given just under two weeks to locate and deliver items for inclusion. The *Irish Press* advised readers: 'The collection does not purport to be in any way complete. It is, however, remarkably good, considering the fact that it was collected in three weeks.'[76] The assortment of objects, it would seem, did little to mitigate interest from the general public. The exhibition which was scheduled to open for just a week remained in place for over a year.

The success of this first, temporary, exhibition prompted the Department of Education to contact Mahr with the suggestion that the artefacts might be presented on permanent display and their intention to solicit Éamon de Valera's support for the same, as then president of the Executive Council. The director of the Museum, however, protested that maintaining such a collection was beyond the remit of the institution as the objects it contained held neither archaeological nor folk value.[77] The artefacts, nonetheless, were to remain at Kildare Street. This had been an underlying premise of the 1916 Club's initial appeal to the National Museum. Nellie Gifford-Donnelly, who was no longer associated with the Museum, however, would quickly become disillusioned by the institution's approach to remembering the 1916 Rising and its participants, writing privately:

> After starting and completing a 1916 relics exhibition – now made a new division of Museum – I am not required and will not ever be permitted to write a book on same. Apparently we 1916 people – the women anyhow – will not be given any encouragement to live. Someone else generally profits by our efforts.[78]

Her sister-in-law Grace Plunkett was less reticent, penning an open letter to the *Irish Press* in 1935 suggesting Kilmainham jail as an alternative site for the 1916 Rising collection:

> The British War Museum of mementoes of mercenary soldiers is splendidly housed. Are we to fall behind in love for our glorious patriots … the collection is now being dealt with by museum officials who had no personal connection with the fighting … I am withholding the collection of objects which belonged to Joseph Plunkett until a guarantee of proper housing is given.[79]

The creation of the Easter Week collection in that same year, under the Museum's Art and Industry Division, thus, was highly significant: marking the institution's formal assumption of responsibility for the conservation and curation of the 1916 Rising as cultural memory.

1935

While 1916 objects continued to be donated to the National Museum, the announcement of a new exhibition in January 1935, as Lar Joye and Brenda Malone have identified more widely, prompted a deluge of new artefacts. In that year alone the Easter Week collection acquired 760 items as gifts and 182 items as loans from the general public.[80] Objects arrived from as far afield as Shanghai and San Francisco while a considerable number of artefacts were sourced from Argentina, Great Britain and South Africa.[81] In sum, almost 1,100 objects were available to Museum and Archives Assistant Tomás Ó Cleirigh who curated the exhibition.

On 16 April 1935 the 'Relics of the struggle for Independence' exhibition was opened in the Ivory Room of the National Museum's Kildare Street premises. The exhibition was framed by the period between the establishment of Sinn Féin in 1905 and the execution of Erskine Childers during the Civil War in November 1922. Over 500 objects were displayed. While the fighting during Easter Week was evidenced through mobilisation orders and a portion of the tricolour flown over the GPO, the exhibits assembled presented the Rising as an influential event within a deeper military history. Ephemera relating to

8.8
Visitors to the National
Museum inspect the
uniforms at the 1916
exhibition (1935).

the early Sinn Féin movement, including a collection of journals from the 'mosquito press', was dwarfed by the mass of military paraphernalia chronologically displayed: rifles from the Larne and Howth gun runnings; Sir Roger Casement's friezecoat; autograph books, handbags and tara brooches made in the internment camps after the Rising; the medical records of the hunger-striking Thomas Ashe; a sculpture of the hunger-striking Terence MacSwiney; last letters from Kevin Barry; Auxiliary caps worn by republicans escaping from Mountjoy prison; the death masks of Arthur Griffith and Michael Collins; Collins' military uniform worn at Béal na mBláth; and Erskine Childers' final letter. This production of the Rising's story differed further from the previous exhibition in the Museum, and indeed the state's commemoration at the GPO five days later, with the noticeable inclusion of British artefacts and narrative. An original Proclamation of the Irish Republic, for example, was displayed for the first time, presented beside the British Proclamation of Martial Law. The exhibition was also notable for its integration of personal histories into the Rising's more public history. Thomas MacDonagh's kilt, Seán Mac Diarmada's watch and cheques written by The O'Rahilly brought the lives of the Rising's dead into greater focus. On its opening day 800 visitors packed into the new exhibition.[82]

Newspaper reviews of the 'Relics of the struggle for Independence' exhibition suggested a positive response to the Museum's more ample interpretation of the Rising as military event. The *Irish Press* commented initially: 'it shows how a period can be reconstructed and fixed in a form easily grasped by future generations'.[83] The *Irish Times* considered that 'this new section of the museum forms an important link in the history of the country and is well worth a visit'.[84] The *Irish Independent*, meanwhile, judged it 'a very noteworthy beginning for a historical museum of the kind but … it is only a beginning, and it is to be hoped that all who can will contribute to make it larger and more comprehensive.'[85] This, it would seem, was given wide consideration; additional 1916 objects continued to arrive at Kildare Street throughout 1935. The exhibition would attract thousands of visitors until its eventual closure in 1941. Within the national media only the *Irish Press* criticised the exhibition's presentation of the Rising as an historical event of short gestation:

> We must not be satisfied even here, for the inspiration of the independence movement is not confined to two decades. The ideals of the men of Easter Week did not originate with them, nor can they be fully understood without reference to the struggle of centuries in which these ideals were shaped.[86]

8.9
Visitors to the National Museum examine a case of arms at the 1916 exhibition (1935).

1941

The National Museum's 1941 exhibition extended the cultural memory of the 1916 Rising. Entitled 'Seachtmhain na Cásca, 1916–41', the exhibition, in fact, charted the lineage of the Rising from the end of the eighteenth century to the beginning of the twentieth century. Statements on this new conceptual approach towards the Rising were released to the press in advance of the exhibition: 'It is intended to illustrate the historic background of the various movements out of which the Republican movement arose and into which various lines of political thought were canalised.'[87] The absence of reference to new source material as curatorial justification was noteworthy. In 1941 alone 754 items had been acquired by donation and a further 241 items had been secured through loan, making this the high-point of 1916 Rising artefact acquisition in the history of

8.10
The Seachtmhain na Cásca exhibition in the National Museum's central gallery (1941).
DF5406

the Museum.[88] G.A. Hayes-McCoy, assistant keeper within the National Museum and curator of the 1941 exhibition, would have almost 3,500 objects to choose from within the Easter Week collection alone.

Seachtmhain na Cásca was opened on 12 April 1941. In contrast to previous attempts, the twenty-fifth anniversary exhibition was given the more spacious surroundings of the central gallery of the Kildare Street museum.

8.11

Cases of uniforms, arms and memorabilia in a gallery at the National Museum, Kildare Street (1941).

DF5411

Although no formal inventory of objects has been preserved within the National Museum archives, press reports of the period highlighted the exhibition's new additions. In the darkened vestibule of the building the historical background to the Rising was suggested: uniforms of Henry Grattan's Irish Volunteers; James Tandy's crimson flag; Theobald Wolfe Tone's death mask; pike heads from the Emmet rebellion of 1803; personal effects of Daniel O'Connell and Young Ireland's John Mitchel; and locks of hair from the Manchester Martyrs Allen, Larkin and O'Brien. The frequency of such 'Fenianana' was widely remarked upon. The visitor was then directed towards the well-lit central hall of the museum which showcased the period 1916–23. Some figures such as Erskine Childers were presented in bespoke presentations while prison artefacts between the Rising and the Civil War appear to have been privileged. Though the exhibition undoubtedly included items of a political and military nature, many reports focused on the objects which revealed personal dimensions to the Rising's public personas: Patrick Pearse's umbrella, Countess Markievicz's watercolours, Roger Casement's morning suit, Sean Milroy's prison cartoons. Writing of the juxtaposition between public and private memories of the Rising induced by the exhibition, one reviewer commented: 'There is not an inch of that Hall where there is not a reminder of death, and yet it is a joyous place of happy pilgrimage for all who had a part in it at any time.'[89]

Speaking at the launch of the exhibition on 12 April, Minister
for Education Michael Derrig declared: 'I hope that the teachers
and pupils will make good sense of this exhibition, not merely
from the point of view of historical lessons but to show their love
and affection for the men who fought for the sake of Ireland.'[90] The
broad chronological scope of the exhibition and diversity of objects
displayed evinces a cultural memory of the 1916 Rising which counter-
balanced the singular collective memory presented outside the GPO
on Easter Sunday. Some citizens indeed appear to have experienced
these respective interpretations of the Rising in close proximity. Nine
thousand people visited the National Museum on the day of the state
commemoration outside the GPO.[91]

1966

Writing in the middle of the Rising's jubilee commemoration, the *Irish Independent* opined: 'Of all the things to be seen or heard or experienced this week, I have no doubt at all that the 1916 exhibition in the National Museum will turn out to be the most affecting and the most memorable.'[92] This was high praise indeed given the panoply of commemorative events taking place across Ireland between 10 and 17 April 1966. Creating a memorable exhibition, above all, required careful reflection on what the 1916 Rising was fifty years after the fact.

The 'Historical exhibition commemorative of the Rising of 1916' opened at the National Museum, Kildare Street, on 12 April 1966. The displays presented the Rising as the central event in the 'long gestation' of an alternative Irish politics between the establishment of the Gaelic League (1893) and the signing of the Anglo-Irish Treaty (1921).[93] An essential feature of the exhibition, in contrast to the state-led programme, was its emphasis on the movements which influenced the emergence of a 'new nationalism'. Of the exhibition's twenty-four cases of objects, fourteen were dedicated to the organisations which defined early twentieth-century Ireland including the IRB, Gaelic League, Sinn Féin, Ulster Volunteer Force, Na Fianna Éireann, Irish Citizen Army, Irish Volunteer Force and Irish Parliamentary Party. Only ten cases attended to the leading figures associated with the Rising.[94] The portrayal of the period as one of collective action was judged particularly important within the National Museum. Replying to Oliver Snoddy, the exhibition's curator, on a draft publication of an accompanying guide, the Museum's Director A.T. Lucas affirmed:

8.13
Taoiseach Seán Lemass is guided through the National Museum's 'Historical exhibition commemorative of the Rising of 1916' (1966).

I think it is our duty to supply this … some idea why material connected with so many movements and bodies takes its place in the exhibition. It is too much to expect that a visitor can piece the story together for himself from the data given about the contents of the individual cases. The inter connections of the various organisations and the partial interlocking of their ideals and personnel should be at least indicated.[95]

Snoddy attempted to showcase the comprehensiveness of the Easter Week collection through the display of costume (ICA, IVF, Fianna and Cumann na mBan uniforms), arms (Mauser single shot rifles and Martini Enfield rifles), insignia (Gaelic League badges and medals), documents (the Roll of Honour) and photographs (IRB activists during the Boer War). Personal effects of the leaders and executed, such as Patrick Pearse's barrister gown and wig, Éamonn Ceannt's bagpipes and handcuffs worn by Thomas Ashe, were also displayed. The *Irish Times* was complimentary of their arrangement: 'the immediate poignancy of the personal relics … the casual ordinary things they wore and used'; the *Evening Press* less so: 'you can't extract emotion out of a glass case'.[96] Most widely reported on, however, was the première exhibition of the Plough and the Stars and Irish Republic flags. The latter had recently been acquired by the Irish State from the Imperial War Museum and was officially donated to the National Museum of Ireland by the Taoiseach Seán Lemass as part of an elaborate opening ceremony.[97] The Irish Republic flag would hold centre-stage in Kildare Street's courtyard exhibition space. The opening was later broadcast across the nation, for the first time, by Radió Teilifís Éireann.[98]

1991

If the 1916 Rising was muted within commemorative-led collective memory during the Troubles, the National Museum provided persistent cultural reminder. Its jubilee anniversary exhibition remained in place for a further twenty-two years. In a letter to the Department of the Taoiseach dated July 1988, the Museum's Keeper John Teahan proposed a new exhibition for the seventy-fifth anniversary of the Rising:

> The display could begin with the 17th century and could follow events since then, coming as close to the present time as sensitivity would allow. As this exhibition would have an all-Ireland compass and would take account of the evolving political situation in the North, I suggest that the Ulster Museum could be invited to co-operate.[99]

Although the Department's reply was not filed within the Museum's archive an exhibition was authorised to be opened in March 1991.[100] Six months before, Teahan cautioned the Museum's staff as to the sensitivity of the arrangement:

> While the Rising should be presented in all its reality it must none-the-less appear as the historical event that it is and in no-way as the 'glorification' or 'incitement to violence' at this time. The goals of the Rising should take precedence over the means used to attempt to reach them. In addition to their revolutionary character, would it be possible to set the leaders or at least some of them – in the context of their other attributes e.g. musical, poetical.[101]

'The Road to Independence' was opened at Kildare Street on 24 April 1991. Consisting of fourteen cases and approximately one hundred objects, the exhibition formally presented the Rising between the end of the nineteenth century and the end of the War of Independence. However, the number of uniforms displayed, covering six full cases, suggested to some visitors that the exhibition's focus was the period of militarisation between 1913 and 1921.[102] The Rising itself was covered chronologically in a single presentation comprising the Fingal Roll of Honour, Citizen Army bugles, Dublin Veterans Corps Cap Badge, a silver cup, a Trinity

College Dublin armlet, a Volunteer hat and a watercolour painting of a Kilmainham jail execution.[103] A case entitled 'personalities' displayed some of the personal effects of the leaders of the Rising although Michael Kenny, the exhibition's curator, privately acknowledged that this had been difficult to assemble as 'the main historical figures are not evenly represented [in the collection] in terms of artefacts'.[104] A separate exhibit showcased weapons from the period including Patrick Pearse's Browning pistol, Con Colbert's Webley and Scott pistol and Countess Markievicz's Mauser automatic.[105] The Museum, however, was keen to disclaim any association with contemporary violence in Ireland. At its launch Museum Director Pat Wallace maintained that the exhibition was not a 'highly charged political event', pointing to the inclusion of uniforms and memorabilia from British and loyalist perspectives.[106] Michael Kenny, meanwhile, countered criticism on his choice of cultural artefacts, replying to one correspondent: 'I have been taken to task by some members of the public for exhibiting a Black and Tan uniform. I have been accused by others of being "pro I.R.A." for including "too many guns" … What I do find unpalatable is the suggestion that I am perpetuating mythology.'[107] The National Museum, by its very embodiment of the Rising through objects, artefacts and ephemera, preserved a niche cultural memory of '1916' during the Troubles, a period in which the Irish State disinclined to remember on the commemorative stage.

2006

The 1916 Rising returned anew to the National Museum in 2006, at Collins Barracks, through 'The Easter Rising: Understanding 1916' exhibition. The display, curated by Michael Kenny and Sandra Heise, adopted the analytical framework of the period 1913–1923, including objects and paraphernalia from the Lockout, the First World War, the War of Independence and Civil War. In contrast to the 1966 presentation, the exhibition was overlooked by a statue of Thomas Clarke. A further disparity with previous displays lay in the exhibition's self-conscious memory of representations of '1916' through commemoration. It explored the appropriation of certain figures from the Rising by political parties, contested narratives and interpretations of the period and the significance of alternative memorial projects to the Rising in the Irish State. One of these was given particular prominence in the Museum's exhibition: *Leabhar na hAiséirighe* ('The Book of the Resurrection').

8.15

(Opposite page)
W.B. Yeats' quote from 'September 1913' frames 'The Easter Rising: Understanding 1916' exhibition (2006).

"Romantic Ireland's dead and gone.
It's with O'Leary in the grave"

W.B. Yeats

The Black and Tans
and Reprisals, 1920–21

8.16
Art Ó Murnaghan.

8.17
(Opposite page)
Leabhar na hAiséirghe,
The 'Sixteen men'
page.
HE:EW.79

THE NATIONAL MEMORIAL

Between 1924 and 1951 this brilliant work of Celtic Revival art was created by a self-taught artist named Art Ó Murnaghan. Its twenty-six vellum pages of illuminated manuscript were intended to honour the memory of those who had died during the Irish independence struggle from 1916 to 1921. Ó Murnaghan was commissioned to create the work by the Irish Republican Memorial Society, which had been established on 5 March 1924 with the aim of promoting 'a national memorial to the memory of the heroes who have given their lives for the attainment of the absolute independence of Ireland since Easter Week 1916'. The society's governing committee included Count Plunkett and also the artists Leo Whelan and Jack B. Yeats. Author and mystic Ella Young was secretary, and Mia Cranwill, one of the great metalworkers of the Arts and Crafts movement, was elected treasurer of the subscription funds. As agreed between the artist and the committee, the work was to be a combination of inscribed lists of those who had died, and an illuminated work of art. It was intended that the writings and sayings of nationalist leaders would be presented alongside emblems associated with particular regions and events, interwoven with Irish symbolism. All of the artwork was done with pencil and brush on vellum, with the artist creating his own paints by mixing pigment with egg-white, parchment glue, fish glue and gum.

In the first phase of the work, from 1924 to 1927, the artist completed seven pages and was in the process of finishing an eighth, although one of the pages, entitled 'The Second Milesians Page', was taken to the United States in 1927 for the purpose of fundraising and was never returned. As a result, the artist later painted a replacement page, using the design for the original work but employing a different colour scheme. Following a lapse in the activities of the Memorial Society, the second phase of the *Leabhar*'s creation began in 1937. With funding from Joseph McGarrity, a wealthy Irish-American republican, Ó Murnaghan would create three further pages, before tensions between the reformed Memorial Society committee and the artist again stalled the project in 1939.

Who is this
that cometh
from Edom with dyed
garments from
Bozrah? This
that is glorious
in his apparel
travelling in
the greatness
of his strength?
wherefore art
thou red in thine
apparel

and thy garments
like him that treadeth
eth in the wine vat?

I have trodden the
wine press alone
and of the people
there was none
with me :

Pádraig mac Piar-
ais quoted this
saying for
Ireland in the
year 1915.

The names here
of the Sixteen Men.

Pádraig mac Piarais.
Tomás mac Donnchada.
Tomás ó Cléirig.
Seósaim m. Pluingcéid.
Éamonn ó Dalaig.
Miceál ó hAnnracáin.
Liam mac Piarais.
Seán mac Giolla Bríġde.
Concobar ó Colbáird.
Éamonn Ceannt.
Miceál ó Meallain.
Seán S. mac Aoda.
Tomás Ceannt.
Séumas ó Conġaile.
Seán mac Diarmada.
Ruaidrí mac Asmuint.

Dream raor,
fá bunara blis,
ba caom cumara.

The Tuata Dé Danann
had four noble jewels
which they brought out
of the North into Éirinn—
namely : A Stone of Vir-
tue, and it is that which
is called Lia Fáil.
The Second Jewel, that
is the Sword which Luġ

Lámfada had used. The
third Jewel — namely the
Spear which the same Luġ
had.
The Fourth Jewel, the Cald-
ron of the Dagda.
The Lia Fáil is the stone
of destiny, and XVI
is the sacred number
of Lia Fáil.

8.18

Leabhar na hAiséirghe,
The 'Men of the
Harbours' page.

HE:EW.1426

Following intervention by Taoiseach Éamon de Valera, Ó Murnaghan resumed his work in a room in the National Library in 1943. Between this year and 1951, he would complete fifteen more illuminated pages, including the replacement 'Second Milesians' page, as well as five pages dedicated to named individuals and six designed to frame the names of those who had died during the independence period. One of the remaining pages would be dedicated to members of the clergy who had supported the movement, while another commented disapprovingly on the Anglo-Irish Treaty. The last remaining page was a record of the details of the artist and of his work on the memorial. Art Ó Murnaghan completed this final page in 1951. He had researched, designed and created the *Leabhar*, but his true contribution goes even further. He had nurtured the project even when the original committee had ceased to exist and the spirit of the memorial book had to be sustained in the face of changing priorities. It was, ultimately, his tenacity and utter belief that he would finish what he had started which brought *Leabhar na hAiséirghe* to fruition.[108]

Art Ó Murnaghan's memorial was fully displayed for the first time in 2006 drawing considerable attention from contemporary commentators.[109] The Museum's displays of 1935 and 1941 had each included folios from his magnum opus but their beautiful arrangement in 'Understanding 1916' visibly illuminated this exhibition's textured presentation of the Rising.[110] Its inclusion, more significantly, was recognisant of the National Museum's broader institutional responsibility, materialised across seventy years of the Easter Week collection: the conservation, construction and re-construction of the 1916 Rising as cultural memory.

SOCIAL MEMORY

However, the National Museum of Ireland is not only a repository of cultural memory. Its collections and archive profile the heterogeneity of social memory on the Rising in Ireland. 'How does one make individual memory social?' anthropologist James Fentress and historian Chris Wickham asked rhetorically in their important study *Social Memory*: 'by talking about it'.[111] Treating of depositing memoirs in archives, more specifically, they have suggested the agency of the individual in creating social memory: 'When we remember we represent ourselves to ourselves and to those around us.'[112] Jan and Aleida Assmann's more narrow construct, 'communicative memory', is complementary: 'The participation of a group in communicative memory is diffuse … it lives in everyday interaction and communication.'[113] While social memory continues to defy fixed definition, the National Museum's Easter Week collection and archive are exemplary of the schema and characteristics outlined within existing scholarship. The Easter Week collection of 15,000 artefacts constitutes, in each effect, the representation of an individual memory of the Rising to a wider social audience. The donation of an object to the National Museum implicitly opened that dialogue with society. In some cases the communication between the individual and society was even more explicit. The Museum's archive contains a register for each item donated in which the donor imparts a memory of the item in the form of a written witness statement, letter or note. The process of presenting an object to the National Museum, practiced by thousands of citizens across Ireland, thus represents a point of transition between individual and social memory. How the 1916 Rising has been remembered therefore requires closer examination of individual objects and the individuals who deposited them.

Individual memories of the 1916 Rising, as judged by donations to the National Museum between 1935 and 1941, chimed with the Irish State's commemorative emphasis on Easter Week as capital military event but also indicated that '1916' was popularly remembered from many different geographical, temporal and thematic perspectives. The Museum's public call for items relating to the 1916–22 period in 1935 and 1941 prompted a rush of military paraphernalia. Gifts to the museum included bayonets from the Royal College of Surgeons garrison, a first-aid kit from Fr Mathew Hall, a water bottle from the Jacob's garrison and ammunition from the fighting at Mount Street Bridge. Individuals who had taken part in the Rising were, in some cases, exclusively represented by their military engagements during Easter Week. The family of fourteen year old John Kelly remembered him to others through the donation of his Fianna Éireann uniform, gun holster and mobilisation order. Within months of his death Robert de Coeur's family had dressed his memory in full Irish Citizen Army regalia: tunic, bandolier, belt, boots and hat. Meanwhile, Rose McNamara presented her Cumann na mBan dress with the following inscription: 'Tunic of Cumann na mBan uniform worn by Miss Rose McNamara in Marrowbone Lane Distillery during Easter Week 1916, and in Kilmainham jail after the Surrender'.[114]

Gifts to the Museum on the part of others, however, suggested a memory of '1916' distant, and indeed discordant, from the military hardships of Dublin: Easter Week. The 'pre-revolution' was heavily represented in the first generation of 1916 Rising material. Badges were received identifying donors variously with the Gaelic League, pro-Boer, Home Rule, anti-Home Rule, Ulster Volunteer Force and Irish Volunteer Force movements. Artefacts relating to the 1914 Irish Volunteers were particularly prevalent within early donations: Limerick Volunteer uniforms, Westmeath Volunteer photographs, Dublin Volunteer rifles. The experience of internment after the Rising, further, was substantively represented in the early Easter Week collection, often through less politicised objects. Tomás O'Reilly's rosary beads, bag and artwork from Wandsworth prison were offered to the Museum, Sean Milroy donated his cartoon sketches from Reading jail while autograph books bearing the names of ordinary internees from Frongoch and Lewes were submitted. The donation of specific items to the National Museum inherently shaped the memory of an individual, an event, an experience.

Some contributors wrote enquiringly as to the relevance of their artefacts to the Easter Week collection. Others were more certain of their importance and sent them in accordingly. Limerick-based republican Madge Daly informed exhibition curator Tomás Ó Cléirigh of letters in her possession from Thomas Clarke, Countess Markievicz and Seán Mac Diarmada: 'I am giving them to the Museum as I feel they will be of great interest in the future and that they should belong to the nation', although she added, 'it hurts to part with them. The writers were all my dearest friends'.[115] Bequeathing personal mementoes was undoubtedly an emotional experience. Many, however, were also concerned with redressing a perceived imbalance in the memory of the Rising. Former Wexford combatant Sean Doyle signalled his intention to submit objects to the Museum because 'the interesting part played by Wexford has not been hitherto adequately represented'.[116] A significant proportion of contributors, meanwhile, gifted objects with the purpose of directing the memory of the subject. Presenting Seán Mac Diarmada's will to the Museum, John Reynolds requested that it be placed beside Thomas Clarke's effects in any exhibition.[117] The family of Francis Macken, who was killed on Moore Street, insisted that his hat be exactly labelled: 'This hat was worn by Lt Francis Macken, E. Co. 4th batt, Dublin Brigade I.R.A. who fell fighting beside the O'Rahilly Easter 1916. It has been presented by his father John J. Macken a "67" man.'[118] An American writer, meanwhile, proposed to donate a portion of a coracle constructed by Patrick Pearse with the view to presenting the latter's 'absorbing interest in the Gaelic way of life'.[119]

The leaders and executed of the 1916 Rising provide an interesting case study of the creation and communication of social memory within the Museum's Easter Week collection. The canonisation of these individuals contemporarily through the *Catholic Bulletin* and retrospectively through state-led commemoration reduced Connolly, Colbert, Casement et al. to figures of public representation without allowance for personal disposition or dimension. The National Museum's collection, containing objects from friends and family as well as the general public, however, constituted an alternative sphere of memory. As a signatory to the Proclamation, Éamonn Ceannt was bestowed posthumously with the memorial expected of any nationalist martyr: memorial card, portrait and militaria. Ceannt's family, however, remembered another aspect of his life. In 1935 Ceannt's widow donated only one item relating to her husband: his piper's uniform. Consisting of Gaelic tunic, breeches, belt, hat and shoes, Ceannt was represented as a person of note independent of his involvement in the Rising. The memory of Countess Markievicz was similarly re-created through her personal effects. While the public image of Markievicz as a forceful participant in the Rising was maintained in the collection with early donations of her Irish Citizen Army tunic, bandolier and weapons, the objects donated by her stepson Stanislas Dunin-Markievicz preserved memories of the person behind the persona. Over the course of twenty-six years Stanislas imparted objects and anecdotes of Markievicz's life for posterity: water-colour self-portrait ('Madame painted of herself at the age of about 16, at Glaslough, Co. Monaghan, the seat of Sir John Leslie'); bible ('she had it 51 years. It was this bible she used to read of evenings at Surrey house'); notebooks ('You know how it would be with her; they would be lying ab[ou]t – or she would be short of paper – and she w[oul]d begin making notes etc … years later').[120] Roger Casement, similarly, was strongly associated in early donations with the failed recruitment of an Irish Brigade in Germany: Brigade uniform, German passport, Casement's German letters. Irish-American friend and confidant, Joseph McGarrity, however, presented the Museum with a more charismatic Casement in the form of a trunk of fashion attire including evening dress coats, waistcoats, shirts, tweed trousers and tweed caps. These items remembered the Casement of soirée, sophistication and sociability. The communication of a fuller memory of the Rising's leaders, however, was not imperative for all it would seem. In the late 1930s the Museum was forced to write to the families of both John MacBride and Patrick and William Pearse in order to source material for them.[121] Brigid Pearse, their sister, chose to donate Patrick's barrister's wig and robe, William's coat, and a tea set they both had used.[122] The Easter Week collection offered family and friends a space in which to remember the distinctive lives of the leaders, to themselves and others, beyond the legacy of the Rising.

The legacy, for those who lived through 1916, was invariably bittersweet. Veterans of the Rising who participated in the later War of Independence and/or Civil War could expect to enjoy political influence and commemorative emphasis on the vicissitudes of a continued Treaty-divided electoral politics. Others who could not reconcile the increasing mono-culturalism of the Rising's afterlife with the pre-Rising's myriad ideological expectations were destined to less public disillusionment.[123] Yet the legacy of the 1916 Rising was not consigned to the memorial impulses of state and society. Individuals retained the ability to dissent against the status quo by preserving conflicting narratives and alternative evidence for posterity. Unlike the Bureau of Military History, Richard Mulcahy interviews or Ernie O'Malley notebooks, the National Museum's Easter Week collection was not perceived as a politicised memorial project by veterans of the 'revolutionary generation'. Diarmuid Lynch praised the Museum's efforts: 'wishing you every success with the admirable work in hand',[124] as did Molly Childers: 'it is a happiness to me to think of the work that you are doing'.[125] Recalcitrant republicans such as Art O'Brien, Count Plunkett and Elizabeth O'Farrell, who declined to offer statements to other enterprises, presented objects to the National Museum. Meanwhile, uniquely among these projects, both W.T. Cosgrave and Éamon de Valera contributed to the Easter Week Collection. Their donations suggest a contrasting approach to the perpetuation of the Rising's memory. W.T. Cosgrave presented just two '1916' items to the National Museum, in 1937: a tricolour flag belonging to Countess Markievicz and a Stars and Stripes flag belonging to Thomas Clarke. Both had been given to him by a British officer who had seized them during Easter Week.[126] Neither object related to Cosgrave's own participation in the Rising nor did he proffer any memory of that period for the Museum's records in the process. Éamon de Valera, by contrast, placed himself central to the memory of the 1916 Rising – donating 304 objects on the occasion of the twenty-fifth anniversary. De Valera's presentation not only included effects evidencing his participation in the Rising – Irish Volunteers membership card, Boland's Mill flag, enlistment forms of 3rd Battalion (Donnybrook) – he also submitted artefacts which suggested his custodianship of the Rising more generally: Patrick Pearse's Irish Volunteer hat, an Irish Volunteer bugle and Irish Volunteer company records.[127] His donation would be heavily publicised in the *Irish Press*.[128]

HISTORY

'History is written by the victors' philosophised Walter Benjamin. Irish historians need write against such fatalism.[129] The heavy historical legacy of the 1916 Rising has the potential to impress a commemorative *Sonderweg* of the 'long' 1916 on public memory, presenting a smooth, singularity of movement towards later signposts of Irish history. Attempts to historical objectivity through academic scholarship, however aspirational, offer empirical checks and balances to the prejudices of public commemoration and individual memory in representations of the past. Beyond the rigours of the academy, historical subjects can be exposed to, and exhibited, as polemic. On this matter, the 1916 Rising has precedent. Historical surveys written in the 1920s and 1930s frequently accounted for the 1916 Rising through the myopia of the Irish Civil War, to the legitimation of party politics.[130] P.S. O'Hegarty's *The Victory of Sinn Féin* (1924) and Piaras Béaslaí's two volume *Michael Collins and the making of a new Ireland* (1926) chronicled the 1916 Rising within founding narratives of the Irish Free State.[131] Dorothy Macardle's *The Irish Republic* (1937), conversely, chaptered the Rising ('The Republic proclaimed') as preface to republican dissolution under Cumann na nGaedheal but eventual restoration under Fianna Fáil.[132] The integration of the 1916 Rising into teleological histories of Irish political parties and state compacted historical memory, removing the Rising from counter-narrative and critical enquiry. The emergence of scientific historical scholarship from the late 1930s, under the aegis of Robert Dudley Edwards, T.W. Moody and their *Irish Historical Studies (IHS)*, contributed a healthy, and necessary, discomfiture to the established historical record.[133]

LOCATING THE RISING

Writing, in 1971, of Ireland since the Famine, F.S.L. Lyons adverted to a recurring problem within early Irish historiography: 'Because the 1916 Rising has lodged itself so firmly in the mythology of the Irish revolution, it has been easy to regard it as inevitable. But it was far from inevitable.'[134] Lyons' cautionary remark was instructive to historians of modern Ireland: locating the significance of the 1916 Rising in the grand sweep of Irish history required attention to time and place. His own survey centred the Rising within a narrative analysis of the period 1914–23, entitled 'The Union Broken', although the events of Easter Week were shallowed in the more immediate context of the First World War.[135]

J.J. Lee's *The Modernisation of Irish Society*, published three years later, offered a different interpretative framework: 'anglicisation or modernisation'. Following the contours of his predecessor at University College Cork, Oliver MacDonagh,[136] Lee charted the 'long gestation' of the Rising from Douglas Hyde's declaration 'on the need to de-Anglicize Ireland' in 1892 to Sinn Féin's declaration of victory at the 1918 general election.[137] Alvin Jackson and Paul Bew, further, have closely adhered to this temporal framework. Jackson's *Ireland, 1798–1998* (1999) situated the 1916 Rising between the Parnell split in 1891 and the Anglo-Irish Treaty of 1921, framed as 'the End of the Union'.[138] Paul Bew, in his *Ireland: the politics of enmity, 1789–2006* (2007), meanwhile, has chaptered the Rising within the period 1891 to 1918, entitled 'Conflict in Ireland'.[139] Both treatments background the Rising as an event in the broader eclipse of the Irish Parliamentary Party and, in Bew's view particularly, conciliatory nationalism. Diarmaid Ferriter's *The Transformation of Ireland, 1900–2000* (2004), meanwhile, has given focus to the 1916 Rising as sharply illustrative of a shorter period of political organisation and agitation, between 1910 and 1918.[140]

In his seminal *Modern Ireland, 1600–1972*, first published in 1989, R.F. Foster pronounced the period 1914–18, not 1916, as twentieth century Ireland's formative moment: 'The First World War should be seen as one of the most decisive events in modern Irish history … it created the rationale for an IRB rebellion.'[141] Foster's influential thesis found contemporary resonance. George Boyce's *Nineteenth Century Ireland: the search for stability*, published one year later, examined the 1916 Rising against the backdrop of the First World War, within a chapter entitled 'The Union Broken, 1914–23'.[142] Charles Townshend's *Ireland: the twentieth-century* (2000), further, positioned analysis of the Rising within the extents of the War.[143] R.V. Comerford's conceptual treatise on Irish nationalism, *Ireland* (2003), meanwhile, juxtaposed the First World War and the 1916 Rising, suggesting that the latter was contingent on the former.[144] More recent surveys by Richard English (*Irish Freedom: the history of nationalism in Ireland* (2006)) and Thomas Bartlett (*Ireland: a history* (2010)) have eroded the single historical influence of the Rising still further, prepositioning the Rising as but one event in a half-century Irish experience of war and conflict between 1900 and 1945.[145] The deliberative location and relocation of '1916' within the metanarrative of modern Irish history has recalibrated the significance of the 1916 Rising as both historical and historiographical event.

DEFINING THE RISING

The events of Easter Week, continuously remembered in memorial if not commemorative spaces, have been the subject of less sustained historical analysis. The Rising has been written differently across the twentieth and early twenty-first centuries, imprinting distinctive 'editions' of the rebellion on generations of historical memory. Desmond Ryan's *The Rising*, first published in 1949, presented Easter Week through Dublin's constituent garrisons and 'the Rising in the country', chronicling the military exertions of the rebels. Though subtitled 'the complete story of Easter Week', it confined the Rising to the discreet experiences of the republican forces, partly derived from Ryan's own memory of the fighting at the GPO and partly from later interview with his peers.[146] Building on Ryan's work, Max Caulfield's *The Easter Rebellion* (1964) detailed the military aspects of the Rising in Dublin through episodic narrative. Drawing on unreferenced interviews with British military personnel as well as republican veterans, Caulfield's 1916 Rising was chaotic, character-driven and highly impressionistic, a presentation the author prefixed: 'it has been my endeavour to retain the atmosphere of events as well as I can'.[147] It would be a further thirty-five years before the Rising received full book-length treatment. Michael Foy and Brian Barton's *The Easter Rising* (1999) provided the first heavily referenced survey of the 1916 Rising. Although again explaining the Rising as a series of garrison experiences and leaning heavily, even optimistically, on the rebels' fighting capability, they interposed civilian testimonies into the military-driven analysis.[148] Claire Wills' *Dublin 1916: the siege of the GPO* (2009), which drew further attention to civilian perspectives on the conflict, was notable for its examination of the Rising through the narrative of the principal garrison.[149] Detailing the Rising through separate garrison analyses has since become a popular historiographical approach.[150] In 2005, meanwhile, Charles Townshend published the most authoritative account of the Rising to date: *Easter 1916: the Irish rebellion*. Drawing on his insurmountable knowledge of British and Irish archives, Townshend expertly adjudicated over the military strategies, tactics and conduct of the participants across Easter Week. Townshend's forensic analysis, further, gave proportionate attention to the British position during the rebellion, scaling the Rising's daily significances against the totality of the ongoing First World War.[151] Fearghal McGarry's *The Rising: Ireland, Easter 1916* (2010) has further reconceptualised what the 1916 Rising was. Drawing extensively on the recently released Bureau of Military History, McGarry explored the Rising 'from within and below'.[152] Examining its voluminous witness statements, he has illuminated the *mentalité* of ordinary rebels during the 1916 Rising, offering a judicious but empathetic analysis of their motivations, mistakes and misguidances during Easter Week. McGarry's penetrative analysis, ultimately, has added historiographical weight to the argument for reading the 1916 Rising beyond narratives of 'leaders and men'.

PERSONIFYING THE RISING

F.X. Martin's edited volume of the same name (*Leaders and Men of the Easter Rising*), published in 1967, was representative of the 'great man' interpretative approach prevalent within the historiography of his time. Countess Markievicz was the sole woman headlined within a collection of nineteen essays which assessed the influence of Carson, Larkin, Redmond and Maxwell, among others, on the Rising. The signatories of the Proclamation dominated proceedings, receiving extensive biographical treatments. Patrick Pearse, however, was uniquely assessed beyond comparative analysis with other leaders and men.[153] The 1916 Rising has been heavily framed through biography, most notably the biography of Pearse. History has preserved different Pearses at different points of historical scholarship. Louis Le Roux's 1932 hagiography *Patrick H. Pearse*, translated from the original French by Desmond Ryan, presented Pearse as a messianic poet, educationalist and revolutionary.[154]

Ruth Dudley Edwards' *The Triumph of Failure* (1979) opened Pearse's early family life to historical interpretation and added the journalistic Pearse to the historical record. Pearse's political radicalisation and rebellion were explained as a consequence of his eventual career failures.[155] Seán Farrell Moran's Pearse (1994) was the skilled propagandist whose stunted psychological development drove him towards the martyrology of violence, a process accelerated by the broader irrationality of early twentieth-century Europe.[156] Joost Augusteijn, conversely, has presented Pearse (2010) as a European intellectual, whose ideas were both of their time and of rational and progressive character.[157] In a later thematic collection of essays, meanwhile, Pearse appeared variously as schoolmaster, poet, *littérateur*, 'Victorian Gael' and 'Irish modernist'.[158] The Rising has also been commonly seen through the lives of James Connolly. C. Desmond Greaves' classic treatment *The Life and Times of James Connolly* (1961) examined Connolly through his public career from American-based socialist speaker to Irish-based union organiser.[159] In a book based on his centenary lecture to the Irish Congress of Trade Unions, however, Owen Dudley Edwards recast Connolly as a public intellectual, drawing on his political papers and writings.[160] Austen Morgan's *James Connolly* (1988) was, for the majority of his life, a 'revolutionary socialist', before becoming a 'revolutionary nationalist' from 1914.[161] Kieran Allen's *Connolly* (1990), conversely, was foremost an international socialist throughout his career, including the lead-up to the Rising.[162] Donal Nevin in his 'full life' biography of James Connolly, finally, has critiqued him as soldier, social democrat, revolutionist, syndicalist, revolutionary socialist-insurrectionist and revolutionary thinker.[163] Although not a signatory, Roger Casement has been the subject of sustained historical analysis, not least because of his enigmatic connections with the Rising. Denis Gwynn's early biography (1931) polarised Casement's career in British/Irish political context: *Traitor or Patriot*.[164] Over the course of three subsequent biographies, Brian Inglis and Angus Mitchell filled out much of Casement's international experiences.[165] B.L. Reid in a further biography (1976) sought to capture the 'daily Casement' through his personal correspondence and writings.[166] Subsequent analysis has presented a variegated Casement. Séamus Ó Síocháin has allowed for Casement as *Imperialist, Rebel and*

Revolutionary (2008) while a later collection of essays edited by Mary Daly variously explored Casement and the international humanitarian movement, the Irish Volunteers and British Intelligence.[167] The other signatories to the Proclamation have drawn less contested biographical portrayal. Louis Le Roux's *Tom Clarke and the Irish freedom movement* (1936) presented his subject as the arch-Fenian and the lead conspirator behind the Rising.[168] This thesis has been advocated most forthrightly by Michael Foy in his *Tom Clarke: the true leader of the Easter Rising* (2014).[169] Gerard MacAtasney, in a thorough biography, meanwhile, has argued for Seán Mac Diarmada's place within the historiography as the 'mind of the revolution'.[170] More recently Éamonn Ceannt, Thomas MacDonagh and Joseph Plunkett have each received their own book-length biographies through the O'Brien Press' 'Sixteen lives' series.[171] In sum, the seven members of the Military Council, and Roger Casement, have been the subject of over one hundred biographical treatments. The individual lives and minds of the Rising's 'leading men' have been central to historical readings of the Rising.

Material culture opens Ireland, 1916 to further reading. Objects such as ceramics, craftwork and clothing bespeak the primacy of the individual like no other historical source, effecting a truly democratic collection. The National Museum's collections thus present the Rising in a unique tapestry of first person perspectives, completing the historical mosaic. Artefacts such as weapons and ammunition supply hard evidence of the damaging realities of the Rising while everyday articles expose the historical record to contemporary contingency and counter-narrative. The National Museum's collections ask afresh of historians what, where and how the Rising was. The donation, curation and conservation of objects, moreover, instance the Rising as live historical event. The National Museum's collections attest to the continued necessity for locating and relocating the Rising's place in history. Writing seventy-five years ago, Keeper G.A. Hayes-McCoy commented on the 'scholastic' potential of the Museum's extensive historical collections to provide 'a realistic basis for book studies of Irish history.'[172] Historians have yet to follow this call to academic enquiry. It is time to think outside the archival box.

Endnotes

Introduction

1   Oliver Snoddy, *Guide to the historical exhibition commemorative of the Rising of 1916* (Dublin, 1966); Michael Kenny, *The road to freedom: photographs and memorabilia from the 1916 Rising and afterwards* (Dublin, 1993).

2   Michael Kenny, *The Fenians: photographs and memorabilia from the National Museum of Ireland* (Dublin, 1994).

3   John Gibney, *A history of the Easter Rising in 50 objects* (Cork, 2016).

4   Toby Barnard, *A guide to sources for the history of material culture in Ireland, 1500-2000* (Dublin, 2005), p. 12.

5   Lisa Godson and Joanna Brück (eds), *Making 1916: material and visual culture of the Easter Rising* (Liverpool, 2015).

6   Lar Joye and Brenda Malone, 'Displaying the nation: the 1916 exhibition at the National Museum of Ireland, 1932-1991' in Lisa Godson and Joanna Brück (eds), *Making 1916: material and visual culture of the Easter Rising* (Liverpool, 2015), p. 187.

7   A.T. Lucas, *The National Museum: its place in the cultural life of the nation* (Dublin, 1969), p. 6.

8   G.A. Hayes-McCoy to Director of the National Museum of Ireland, 3 Jan. 1956 (N.M.I.A.S., Easter Week purchases, 1930s-1950s, A1.EWP.0090.001.00034(2)).

9   Tomás Ó Cléirigh to Robert Brennan, 12 May 1937 (N.M.I.A.S., Easter Week donations, 1935-1936, A1.EWD.0091.003.00032(5)).

10 G.A. Hayes-McCoy to J.J. Burke, 18 October 1940 (N.M.I.A.S., Easter Week donations, A1.EWD.0091.006.00040(4)); G.A. Hayes-McCoy to Cormac MacManus, 1 March 1940 (N.M.I.A.S., Easter Week donations, A1.EWD.0091.004.00012(1)).

11 Liam Gogan to unstated, November 1937 (N.M.I.A.S., Easter Week donations, 1935-1936, A1.EWD.0091.003.00020(5)).

12 Christopher Tilley, 'Introduction' in Chris Tilley et al (eds), *Handbook of material culture* (London, 2006), pp. 2-3.

13 Arjun Appadurai (ed.), *The social life of things: commodities in cultural perspective* (Cambridge, 1986).

14 Alfred Gell, *Art and agency: a new anthropological theory* (Oxford, 1998).

Chapter 1

1   Garry Wills, *Inventing America: Jefferson's Declaration of Independence* (Boston, 1978), p. 341.

2   W.T. Cosgrave speech to the Assembly of the League of Nations, 10 September 1923, Documents on Irish Foreign Policy http://www.difp.ie/docs/Volume2/1923/454.htm [Accessed 22 July 2016].

3   Seán Lemass speech to Dáil Éireann, 16 July 1931, Dáil Éireann debates http://oireachtasdebates.oireachtas. ie/debates%20authoring/debateswebpack.nsf/takes/ dail1931071600055?opendocument [Accessed 25 July 2016].

4   *Irish Times*, 17 May 1945.

5   Ibid, 29 April 1949; ibid, 1 July 1963; ibid, 19 June 1969.

6   *Irish Press*, 3 July 1990.

7   *Irish Times*, 19 March 2016.

8   Ibid, 28 March 2016.

9   Ibid, 16 September 2015.

10 *Irish Independent*, 16 March 2016.

11 *Irish Times*, 4 April 2015. Murphy made a similar argument almost one year later: *The Cork Examiner*, 7 March 2016.

12 *Irish Times*, 16 May 2016.

13 Ibid, 12 March 2016.

14 *Guardian*, 23 January 2015; ibid, 30 May 2015; ibid, 28 June 2015.

15 House of Commons Political and Constitutional Reform Committee 'Consultation on a new Magna Carta?', 3 March 2015 http://www.publications.parliament.uk/pa/ cm201415/cmselect/cmpolcon/599/599.pdf [Accessed 28 June 2016].

16 See David Marrani, *Dynamics in the French constitution: decoding French republican ideas* (London, 2013).

17 Michael Molloy military pension application (M.A.I., Military Pension records, MSP34REF1259).

18 Christopher Brady statement (M.A.I., Bureau of Military History, BMH/WS 705).

19 Liam Ó Briain statement (M.A.I., Bureau of Military History, BMH/WS 323); Joseph Bouch, 'The republican proclamation of Easter Monday 1916' in *Bibliographical Society of Ireland*, v (1936), p. 1; *Irish Press*, 24 April 1934.

20 Christopher Brady statement (M.A.I., Bureau of Military History, BMH/WS 705).

21 Joseph Bouch to Dick [?], 7 March 1935 (N.L.I., Joseph Bouch papers, MS 5442).

22 Liam Ó Briain statement (M.A.I., Bureau of Military History, BMH/WS 323).

23 Michael Molloy military pension application (M.A.I., Military Pension records, MSP34REF1259).

24 W.T. Cosgrave statement (M.A.I., Bureau of Military History, BMH/WS 268).

25   See Seán Enright, *Easter Rising 1916: the trials* (Dublin, 2014).

26   Charles Townshend, *Easter 1916: the Irish rebellion* (London, 2005), p. 160.

27   Christopher Brady military pension application (M.A.I., Military Pension records, MSP34REF20847).

28   Christopher Brady statement (M.A.I., Bureau of Military History, BMH/WS 705).

29   *Irish Press*, 24 April 1934.

30   Christopher Brady statement (M.A.I., Bureau of Military History, BMH/WS 705).

31   For a full discussion of the typographical solutions arrived at by the printing team see: http://the1916proclamation.ie/the-original/ [Accessed 28 June 2016].

32   Joseph Bouch, 'The republican proclamation of Easter Monday 1916' in *Bibliographical Society of Ireland*, v (1936), p. 4.

33   Liam Ó Briain statement (M.A.I., Bureau of Military History, BMH/WS 323).

34   Christopher Brady military pension application (M.A.I., Military Pension records, MSP34REF20847).

35   Martin Daly, *Memories of the dead: some impressions* (Dublin, 1917), p. 20.

36   Sources variously place Pearse at the portico of the GPO, on the 'steps of the GPO' and at Nelson's pillar.

37   Martin Daly, *Memories of the dead*, p. 20.

38   Katharine Tynan, *The years of the shadow* (Boston, 1919), p. 224.

39   Diarmuid Lynch, *The IRB and the 1916 Rising* (Cork, 1957), p. 159.

40   W.J. Brennan-Whitmore, *Dublin burning: the Easter Rising from inside the barricades* (Dublin, 1996), p. 50.

41   'Easter Week 1916', 1957 (N.L.I., Sean T. O'Ceallaigh papers, MS 27, 696).

42   Charles Donnelly statement (M.A.I., Bureau of Military History, BMH/WS 824); Eamonn Bulfin statement (M.A.I., Bureau of Military History, BMH/WS 497).

43   A handful of rebels at Marrowbone Lane and the South Dublin Union recorded hearing the Proclamation being read by Éamonn Ceannt and Edward Daly respectively during Easter Week. See James Coughlan statement (M.A.I., Bureau of Military History, BMH/WS 304); Liam O'Carroll statement (M.A.I., Bureau of Military History, BMH/WS 314).

44   Ina Connolly-Heron statement (M.A.I., Bureau of Military History, BMH/WS 919).

45   Donal O'Hannigan statement (M.A.I., Bureau of Military History, BMH/WS 161).

46   Ernie O'Malley, *On another man's wound* (Dublin, 1936), p. 31.

47   Mick O'Farrell, *1916: What the people saw* (Dublin, 2013), p. 271.

48   Charles Donnelly statement (M.A.I., Bureau of Military History, BMH/WS 824).

49   'Easter Week 1916', 1957 (N.L.I., Sean T. O' Ceallaigh papers, MS 27, 696).

50   Mick O'Farrell, *1916: What the people saw* (Dublin, 2013), pp. 270–1.

51   James Stephens, *The Insurrection in Dublin* (New York, 1916), p. 31.

52   Diary of Edward French, 25 April 1916 (N.L.I., Edward French papers, MS 49, 903); Diary of Alexander Malcolm, 25 April 1916 (N.L.I., Alexander Malcolm papers, MS 46, 081).

53   *Irish Times*, 26 April 1916; ibid, 27 April 1916.

54   See *Freeman's Journal*, 5 May 1916; *Connacht Tribune*, 6 May 1916; *Donegal News*, 6 May 1916.

55   Charles Townshend, *Easter 1916*, p. 160; Fearghal McGarry, *The Rising*, p. 133.

56   Charles Baudelaire, T.R. Smith (ed.), *Baudelaire: his prose and poetry* (New York, 1919), p. 246.

57   Liam Kennedy, *Unhappy the land: the most oppressed people ever, the Irish?* (Dublin, 2015), pp. 147–8.

58   Kennedy, *Unhappy the land*, p. 148; Patrick Geoghegan, *Reinterpreting Emmet: essays on the life and legacy of Robert Emmet* (Dublin, 2007).

59   See Ruth Dudley Edwards, *The Seven: the lives and legacies of the founding fathers of the Irish Republic* (London, 2016).

60   An exception to this is J.J. Lee, *Ireland, 1912–85: politics and society* (Cambridge, 1989), p. 5.

61   Liam de Paor, *On the Easter Proclamation and other declarations* (Dublin, 1997), p. 52.

62   F.S.L. Lyons, 'The Rising and after' in W.E. Vaughan et al. (eds), *A new history of Ireland: Ireland under the Union, 1870–1921*, vi (Oxford, 1989), 214.

63   Paul Fussell, *The Great War and modern memory* (Oxford, 1975), p. 22.

Chapter 2

1   See Alvin Jackson, *Two Unions: Ireland, Scotland, and the survival of the United Kingdom, 1707–2007* (Oxford, 2012).

2   See for example Linda Colley, *Britons: forging the nation, 1707–1837* (New Haven, 1992); Krishan Kumar, *The making of English national identity* (Cambridge, 2003); Peter Gray (ed.), *Victoria's Ireland? Irishness and Britishness, 1837–1901* (Dublin, 2004).

3   Michael Billig, *Banal nationalism* (London, 1995), p. 6.

4   Tom Garvin, *Nationalist revolutionaries in Ireland, 1858–1928* (Oxford, 1987), p. 5.

5   Matthew Kelly, *The Fenian ideal and Irish nationalism, 1882–1916* (Woodbridge, 2006), p. 10.

6   Owen McGee, *The IRB: the Irish Republican Brotherhood from the Land League to Sinn Féin* (Dublin, 2005), pp. 328–9.

7   R.V. Comerford, 'The land war and the politics of distress, 1877–82' in W.E. Vaughan *et al* (eds), *A new history of Ireland vol. 6: Ireland under the Union, II, 1870–1921* (Oxford, 1996), pp. 45–6.

8   For a comprehensive treatment of the Skirmishing campaign see Niall Whelehan, *The dynamiters: Irish nationalism and political violence in the wider world* (Cambridge, 2013), pp. 138–75.

9   Thomas Clarke, *Glimpses of an Irish felon's prison life* (Cork, 1922). For the Fenians in prison in context see Seán McConville, *Irish political prisoners, 1848–1922: theatres of war* (London, 2003), pp. 361–404.

10   Charles Townshend, *Ireland: the twentieth century* (London, 1999), pp. 26–7.

11   P.S. O'Hegarty, 'Introduction' in Thomas Clarke, *Glimpses of an Irish felon's prison life* (Cork, 1922), xiii.

12   Michael Foy, *Tom Clarke: the true leader of the Easter Rising* (Dublin, 2014), p. 78.

13   James McConnel, *The Irish Parliamentary Party and the third Home Rule crisis* (Dublin, 2013), pp. 94–115 *passim*.

14   R.V. Comerford, *The Fenians in context: Irish politics and society, 1848–82* (Dublin, 1985).

15   See also R.V. Comerford, 'Patriotism as pastime: the appeal of fenianism in the mid-1860s' in *I.H.S.*, xxii (1981), pp. 239–50.

16   W.F. Mandle, *The Gaelic Athletic Association and Irish nationalist politics, 1884–1924* (London, 1987); Mike Cronin, 'Fighting for Ireland, playing for England? The nationalist history of the Gaelic Athletic Association and the English influence on Irish sport' in *International Journal of the History of Sport*, xv (1998), pp. 36–56.

17   Matthew Kelly, *The Fenian ideal*.

18   Owen McGee, *The IRB*, pp 327–30.

19   Matthew Kelly, *The Fenian ideal*, p. 5; Fearghal McGarry and James McConnel, 'Introduction' in idem, *The black hand of republicanism: Fenianism in modern Ireland* (Dublin, 2009), xi, xv–xvi.

20   Alan Ward, *The Irish constitutional tradition: responsible government and modern Ireland, 1782–1992* (Washington, 1994).

21   Paul Bew, *Ideology and the Irish Question: Ulster unionism and Irish nationalism, 1912–1916* (Oxford, 1994) p. 20.

22   Michael Wheatley, *Nationalism and the Irish Party: provincial Ireland, 1910–1916* (Oxford, 2005) p. 263.

23   Alvin Jackson, *Home Rule: an Irish history, 1800–2000* (London, 2003), p. 142.

24   Eugenio Biagini, *British democracy and Irish nationalism* (Cambridge, 2007).

25   Arthur Griffith, *The resurrection of Hungary: a parallel for Ireland* (Dublin, 1904).

26   Michael Laffan, *The resurrection of Ireland: the Sinn Féin party, 1916–1923* (Cambridge, 1999), pp. 17–18.

27   James McConnel, *The Irish Parliamentary Party*, pp. 117–22, 131.

28   Michael Laffan, *The resurrection of Ireland*, pp. 27–9.

29   Douglas Hyde, 'The necessity for de-anglicising Ireland' in Charles Gavan Duffy, George Sigerson and Douglas Hyde (eds), *The revival of Irish literature* (London, 1894), pp. 117–61.

30   Timothy McMahon, *Grand opportunity: the Gaelic revival and Irish society, 1893–1910* (Syracuse, 2008), p. 88. This figure, as McMahon discusses, however, may not be absolute.

31   Ibid, pp. 91–3, 185–8.

32   Brian Ó Cuiv, 'Irish language and literature, 1845–1921,' in William Vaughan *et al.* (eds), *A new history of Ireland Vol. 6: Ireland under the Union, II, 1870–1921* (Oxford, 2006), p. 412.

33   Ruth Dudley Edwards, *Patrick Pearse: the triumph of failure* (London, 1977), p. 55.

34   Ibid, p. 26.

35   Regina Uí Chollatáin, '"The history of a century in a generation": the perspective of an Irish journalist, P.H. Pearse' in Roisín Higgins and Regina Uí Chollatáin (eds), *The life and after-life of P.H. Pearse* (Dublin, 2009), pp. 81–98.

36   *An Claidheamh Soluis*, 14 Mar. 1903.

37   Tom Garvin, 'Priests and patriots: Irish separatism and fear of the modern, 1890–1914' in *I.H.S.*, xxv (1986), pp. 67–81; John Hutchinson, *The dynamics of cultural nationalism: the Gaelic revival and the creation of the Irish nation state* (London, 1987).

38   Declan Kiberd, *Inventing Ireland: the literature of the modern nation* (London, 1995), pp. 134–5; Philip O'Leary, *The prose literature of the Gaelic revival, 1881–1921: ideology and innovation* (Pennsylvania, 1994), pp. 15–16.

39   Patrick Pearse, Séamus Ó Buachalla (ed.), *The letters of P.H. Pearse* (Gerrards Cross, 1980), p. 265.

40   See Brian Ó Conchubhair, 'The Gaelic font controversy: the Gaelic League's (post-colonial) crux' in *Irish University Review*, xxxiii (2003), pp. 46–63.

41   Joost Augusteijn, *Patrick Pearse: the making of a revolutionary* (London, 2010), pp. 84–7, 148–54.

42   See Elaine Sisson, *Pearse's patriots: St. Enda's and the cult of boyhood* (Cork, 2004).

43   Joost Augusteijn, *Patrick Pearse*, pp. 82–105.

44   D.P. Moran, 'The battle of two civilisations' in idem *The philosophy of Irish-Ireland* (Dublin, 1905), pp. 94–114.

45   See Ben Levitas, *The theatre of nation: Irish drama and cultural nationalism, 1890–1916* (Oxford, 2002); P.J. Mathews, *Revival: the Abbey Theatre, Sinn Féin, the Gaelic League and the co-operative movement* (Cork, 2003).

46   Fearghal McGarry, *The Abbey rebels of 1916: a lost revolution* (Dublin, 2015).

47   Laura Nym Mayhall, *The militant suffrage movement: citizenship and resistance in Britain, 1860–1930* (Oxford, 2003), pp. 14–24.

48   Senia Pašeta, *Irish nationalist women, 1900–18* (Cambridge, 2013), p. 34.

49   Ibid, pp. 75–6.

50   Marnie Hay, 'The foundation and development of Na Fianna Éireann, 1909–16' in *I.H.S.*, xxxvi (2008), pp. 53–71.

51   Owen Dudley Edwards, *The mind of an activist – James Connolly* (Dublin, 1971), p. 12.

52   Richard English, *Irish Freedom: the history of nationalism in Ireland* (London, 2006), p. 276.

53   R.F. Foster, *Vivid Faces: the making of a revolutionary generation in Ireland, 1890–1923* (London, 2014), xxiii.

54   Ibid, pp. 21, 23.

55   A.T.Q. Stewart, *The Ulster crisis: resistance to Home Rule, 1912–14* (Glasgow, 1967), p. 18.

56   Alvin Jackson, 'Loyalists and unionists' in idem *The Oxford handbook of modern Irish history* (Oxford, 2014), p. 52.

57   Paul Bew, *Ideology and the Irish Question*, p. 27.

58   David Fitzpatrick, *The two Irelands, 1912–1939* (Oxford, 1998), pp. 32–3.

59   A.T.Q. Stewart, *The narrow ground: aspects of Ulster, 1609–1969* (London, 1977), pp. 159–65.

60   John Bowman, *De Valera and the Ulster Question, 1917–73* (Oxford, 1982), pp. 11–19.

61   Joseph Finnan, *John Redmond and Irish unity, 1912–18* (Syracuse, 2004), p. 40.

62   Alan O'Day, *Irish Home Rule, 1867–1921* (Manchester, 1998), pp. 247–9.

63   James McConnel, *The Irish Parliamentary Party*, pp. 222–41 *passim*.

64   Ruth Dudley Edwards, *James Connolly* (Dublin, 1981), pp. 94–7; Ruth Dudley Edwards, *Patrick Pearse*, p. 159.

65   Diane Urquhart, *Women in Ulster politics, 1890–1940: a history not yet told* (Dublin, 2000), pp. 56–63.

66   Paul Bew, *Ideology and the Irish Question*, pp. 92–8; Alvin Jackson.

67   Timothy Bowman, *Carson's Army: the Ulster Volunteer Force, 1910–22* (Manchester, 2007), pp. 15–38, 85–7.

68   Ibid, pp. 62–9.

69   See Padraig Yeates, *Lockout: Dublin 1913* (Dublin, 2000).

70   P.S. O'Hegarty, *A history of Ireland under the Union: 1801 to 1922* (London, 1952), p. 672.

71   *An Claidheamh Soluis*, 1 Nov. 1913.

72   Daithí Ó Corráin, '"A most public spirited and unselfish man": the career and contribution of Colonel Maurice Moore, 1854–1939' in *Studia Hibernica*, lxxi (2014), p. 91.

73   Marnie Hay, *Bulmer Hobson and the nationalist movement in twentieth-century Ireland* (Manchester, 2009), pp. 109–11.

74   William Henry, *Éamonn Ceannt: supreme sacrifice* (Cork, 2012), pp. 53–5.

75   Mary Gallagher, *Éamonn Ceannt* (Dublin, 2014), p. 141.

76   F.X. Martin, *The scholarly revolutionary: Eoin MacNeill, 1867–1945, and the making of a new Ireland* (Dublin, 1973), p. 112.

77   Matthew Kelly, 'The Irish Volunteers: a Machiavellian moment?' in D.G. Boyce and Alan O'Day (eds), *The Ulster crisis: 1885–1921* (Basingstoke, 2006), p. 64.

78   Colin Reid, 'The Irish Party and the Irish Volunteers: politics and the Home Rule army, 1913–1916' in Caoimhe Nic Dháibhéid and Colin Reid (eds), *From Parnell to Paisley: constitutional and revolutionary politics in modern Ireland* (Dublin, 2010), pp. 34–8.

79   Matthew Kelly, *The Fenian ideal*, p. 207.

80   Charles Townshend, *Easter 1916*, pp. 95–6.

81   The phrase is Michael Tierney's: Michael Tierney, *Eoin MacNeill: scholar and man of action, 1867–1945* (Oxford, 1980), p. 119.

82   *An Claidheamh Soluis*, 8 Nov. 1913.

83   R.F. Foster, *Vivid Faces*, p. 180.

84   Daithí Ó Corráin, 'A most public spirited and unselfish man', p. 92.

85   Pat McCarthy, *The Irish Revolution, 1912-23: Waterford* (Dublin, 2015), p. 23; Fergal McCluskey, *The Irish Revolution, 1912-23: Tyrone* (Dublin, 2014), p. 45.

86   David Fitzpatrick, *Politics and Irish life, 1913–1921: provincial experience of war and revolution* (Cork, 1977), p. 86.

87   William O'Brien famously caricatured the AOH as an Irish Parliamentary Party 'Frankenstein of their own raising': William O'Brien, *An olive branch in Ireland* (London, 1910), p. 418.

88   Daithí Ó Corráin, 'A most public spirited and unselfish man', pp. 92–3.

89   Matthew Kelly, *The Fenian ideal*, p. 225.

90   Timothy Bowman, *Carson's Army*, p. 140.

91   Michael Wheatley, *Nationalism and the Irish Party*, pp. 187–8.

92   Matthew Kelly, *The Fenian ideal*, p. 225.

93   For the most comprehensive analysis of the IPP's 'takeover' see James McConnel, *The Irish Parliamentary Party*, pp. 286–9.

94   Charles Townshend, *Easter 1916*, p. 53.

95   Matthew Kelly, *The Fenian ideal*, p. 232.

96   Charles Townshend, *Easter 1916*, p. 59.

97   George Dangerfield, *The strange death of liberal England* (New York, 1935), p. 330.

98   Dermot Meleady, *John Redmond: the national leader* (Sallins, 2014), pp. 281–4.

99   F.X. Martin (ed.), *The Howth gun-running and the Kilcoole gun-running, 1914* (Dublin, 1964).

100   Timothy Bowman, *Carson's army*, p. 106.

101   Charles Townshend, *Easter 1916*, p. 59.

102   Ronan Fanning, *Fatal Path: British government and Irish revolution, 1910–1922* (London, 2013), p. 130.

103   Dermot Meleady, *John Redmond*, p. 301.

104   James McConnel, *The Irish Parliamentary Party*, p. 299.

105   *Hansard 5* (Commons), lxv, col. 1829 (3 Aug. 1914).

106   Redmond had only advised T.P. O'Connor and John Hayden of his speech, at Westminster. Although some Party MPs demurred, both James McConnel and Michael Wheatley have evidenced a groundswell of support for Redmond's 'initiative' within Nationalist Ireland. See James McConnel, *The Irish Parliamentary Party*, pp. 298–9; Michael Wheatley, *Nationalism and the Irish Party*, pp. 202–3.

107   Dermot Meleady, *John Redmond*, p. 304.

108   *Freeman's Journal*, 17 September 1914. The core of Redmond's argument had first been made in the House of Commons on 15 September following Asquith's announcement.

109   See Paul Bew, *Ideology and the Irish Question*, pp. 118–23; James McConnel, 'John Redmond and Irish Catholic loyalism' in *E.H.R.*, cxxv (2010), pp. 109–11.

110   James McConnel, *The Irish Parliamentary Party*, p. 312.

111   *Freeman's Journal*, 21 September 1914.

112   F.S.L. Lyons, *John Dillon: a biography* (London, 1968), p. 359.

113   See R.F. Foster, *Modern Ireland, 1600–1972* (London, 1988), pp. 472–3.

114   Michael Laffan, 'John Redmond and Home Rule' in Ciaran Brady (ed.), *Worsted in the Game: losers in Irish history* (Dublin, 1989), pp. 133–42.

115   John Bruton, 'September 1914: Redmond at Woodenbridge' in *Studies: an Irish quarterly review*, ci (2012), p. 237. This view was put forward most consistently by Redmond's earliest biographers. See W.B. Wells, *John Redmond: a biography* (London, 1919), pp. 165–6; Denis Gwynn, *The life of John Redmond* (London, 1932), pp. 391–2.

116   Conor Mulvagh, '"Wherever the firing line extends ...": John Redmond's call to arms' http://www.rte.ie/centuryireland/index.php/watch/wherever-the-firing-line-extends [Accessed 14 June 2016].

117   Daithí Ó Corráin, 'A most public spirited and unselfish man', p. 97.

118   Alvin Jackson, *Ireland, 1798–1998: politics and war* (Oxford, 1999), pp. 197–9.

119   Paul Bew, *John Redmond* (Dundalk, 1996), p. 38.

120   Joseph P. Finnan, *John Redmond and Irish unity*, pp. 86–7.

121   Michael Wheatley, *Nationalism and the Irish Party*, pp. 209–12.

122   The numbers who went with the National Volunteers have been variously cited as between 100,000 and 145,000. The Irish Parliamentary Party themselves discerned 120,000 of 128,000 Volunteers to be Redmondite: Daithí Ó Corráin, 'A most public spirited and unselfish man', p. 98.

123   Michael Wheatley, *Nationalism and the Irish Party*, pp. 213–18. The Ancient Order of Hibernians, Wheatley points out, interestingly, maintained their pre-War levels of activity.

124 Daithí Ó Corráin, 'A most public spirited and unselfish man', p. 102.

125 F.S.L. Lyons, *John Dillon: a biography* (London, 1968), pp. 360–2.

126 James McConnel, *The Irish Parliamentary Party*, pp. 302–7.

127 Dermot Meleady, *John Redmond*, p. 310.

128 David Fitzpatrick, 'Militarism in Ireland, 1900–1922' in Thomas Bartlett and Keith Jeffery (eds), *A military history of Ireland* (Cambridge, 1997), pp. 386–8. Keith Jeffery has offered a figure of 210,000 for overall Irish enlistment: Keith Jeffery, *Ireland and the Great War* (Cambridge, 2000), p. 7.

129 James McConnel, *The Irish Parliamentary Party*, p. 297.

130 David Fitzpatrick, 'The logic of collective sacrifice: Ireland and the British Army, 1914–1918' in *Historical Journal*, xxxviii (1995), pp. 1018, 1029.

131 Catriona Pennell, *A Kingdom United: popular responses to the outbreak of the First World War in Britain and Ireland* (Oxford, 2012), pp. 189–97; Catriona Pennell, 'Presenting the war in Ireland, 1914–1918', in Troy R.E. Paddock (ed.), *World War I and propaganda* (Leiden, 2014), pp. 42–54.

132 Jérôme aan De Wiel, *The Catholic Church in Ireland, 1914–1918: war and politics* (Dublin, 2003), p. 27.

133 Denis Gwynn, *The life of John Redmond*, p. 423.

134 Alvin Jackson, *Home Rule*, p. 150; Paul Bew, *Ireland: the politics of enmity, 1789–2006* (Oxford, 2007), p. 372.

135 Dermot Meleady, *John Redmond*, p. 333.

136 *Freeman's Journal*, 26 May 1915.

137 Lawrence McBride, *The greening of Dublin Castle: the transformation of bureaucratic and judicial personnel in Ireland, 1892–1922* (Washington, 1991), pp. 193–221.

138 Michael Finn, 'Local heroes: war news and the construction of "community" in Britain, 1914–18' in *Historical Research*, lxxxiii (2010), pp. 520–38.

139 Michael Wheatley, *Nationalism and the Irish Party*, pp. 239–40.

140 Charles Townshend, *Easter 1916*, pp. 81–5.

141 Leon Ó Bróin, *Dublin Castle and the 1916 Rising: the story of Sir Matthew Nathan* (Dublin, 1966), pp. 37–42.

142 Eunan O'Halpin, *The decline of the Union: British government in Ireland, 1892–1920* (Dublin, 1987), pp. 107–8.

143 F.S.L. Lyons, *John Dillon*, pp. 362, 366.

144 See T. Desmond Williams, 'Eoin MacNeill and the Irish Volunteers' in F.X. Martin (ed.), *Leaders and men of the Easter Rising* (London, 1967), pp. 151–63; Robert Kee, *The Green Flag: a history of Irish nationalism* (London, 1972), pp. 224–5.

145 Fearghal McGarry, *The Rising*, p. 86; Charles Townshend, *Easter 1916*, pp. 91–2.

146 Joost Augusteijn, *Patrick Pearse: the making of a revolutionary* (Basingstoke, 2010), pp. 293–5.

147 Michael Tierney, *Eoin MacNeill*, p. 147.

148 Marnie Hay, *Bulmer Hobson and the nationalist movement in twentieth-century Ireland* (Manchester, 2009), p. 165.

149 F.X. Martin, 'The 1916 Rising: a "coup d'État" or a "Bloody Protest"?' in *Studia Hibernica*, viii (1968), p. 132.

150 P.S. O'Hegarty, *The victory of Sinn Féin: how it won it, and how it used it* (Dublin, 1924), p. 2.

151 Angus Mitchell (ed.), *One bold deed of open treason: the Berlin diary of Roger Casement, 1914–1916* (Sallins, 2016), pp. 32–5.

152 Marnie Hay, *Bulmer Hobson*, pp. 163, 165.

153 F.X. Martin and Eoin MacNeill, 'Eoin MacNeill on the 1916 Rising' in *IHS*, xii (1961), pp. 234–5. Martin's publication of MacNeill's contemporary memoranda on the 1916 Rising was an attempt to set the historical record straight on the MacNeillite position.

154 Ed Mulhall, 'Planning a Rising for Ireland' http://www.rte.ie/centuryireland/index.php/articles/coldly-and-deliberately-planned [Accessed 11 July 2016]. Seán T. O'Kelly's account also indicated the attendance of Seán McGarry and Seán Tobin although William O'Brien did not record their names in his memoir.

155 Diarmuid Lynch, *The IRB and the 1916 Rising*, p. 25.

156 Marnie Hay, *Bulmer Hobson*, p. 169.

157 Diarmuid Lynch, *The IRB and the 1916 Rising*, p. 25.

158 F.X. Martin (ed.), *The Irish Volunteers, 1913–15: recollections and documents* (Dublin, 2013), p. 203.

159 R.F. Foster, *W.B. Yeats: A life, II: the arch-poet, 1915–1939* (Oxford, 2003), p. 46.

160 Joost Augusteijn, *Patrick Pearse*, pp. 289–96; Ruth Dudley Edwards, *Patrick Pearse*, pp. 232–3; Charles Townshend, *Easter 1916*, p. 114.

161 Ruth Dudley Edwards, *Patrick Pearse*, pp. 230–2, 251–62.

162 Patrick Pearse, *The Coming Revolution: political writings and speeches of Patrick Pearse* (Cork, 2012), p. 170.

163 Ruth Dudley Edwards, *Patrick Pearse*, p. 225.

164 Joost Augusteijn, *Patrick Pearse*, pp. 293–5.

165 Patrick Pearse, *The Coming Revolution*, p. 170.

166 Fearghal McGarry, *The Rising*, pp. 96–101.

167 William O'Brien, *Forth the banners go: reminiscences of William O'Brien* (Dublin, 1969) p. 270.

168 Mary Gallagher, *Éamonn Ceannt*, p. 170.

169 Diarmuid Lynch, *The IRB and the 1916 Rising*, p. 25.

170 See Joost Augusteijn, *Patrick Pearse*, p. 283.

171 P.S. O'Hegarty, *The victory of Sinn Féin*, p. 11; Diarmuid Lynch, *The IRB and the 1916 Rising*, p. 25.

172 P.S. O'Hegarty, *The victory of Sinn Féin*, p. 11.

173 P.S. O'Hegarty, *The victory of Sinn Féin*, p. 11; Charles Townshend, *Easter 1916*, p. 100.

174 Charles Townshend, *Easter 1916*, p. 93.

175 Ruth Dudley Edwards, *The Seven: the lives and legacies of the founding fathers of the Irish Republic* (London, 2016), pp. 65–6, 143–4.

176 Charles Townshend, *Easter 1916*, p. 100.

177 Michael Tierney and F.X. Martin, *Eoin MacNeill: scholar and man of action*, p. 182.

178 Charles Townshend, *Easter 1916*, p. 99.

179 Donal Nevin, *James Connolly: a full life* (Dublin, 2005), pp. 557–71.

180 Charles Townshend, *Easter 1916*, p. 98.

181 Marnie Hay, *Bulmer Hobson*, pp. 170–1.

182 Matthew Kelly, *The Fenian ideal*, p. 233; Fearghal McGarry, *The Rising*, pp. 86–7.

183 Joost Augusteijn, *Patrick Pearse*, p. 286.

184 Charles Townshend, *Easter 1916*, p. 104.

185 Michael Foy and Brian Barton, *The Easter Rising* (Stroud, 1999), pp. 21–8.

186 Ibid, p. 28.

187 Charles Townshend, *Easter 1916*, p. 107.

188 Joost Augusteijn, *Patrick Pearse*, p. 296.

189 Diarmuid Lynch, *The IRB and the 1916 Rising*, p. 28.

190 Charles Townshend, *Easter 1916*, p. 117.

191 J.J. Lee, *Ireland, 1912–85*, p. 24.

192 Shane Kenna, *Thomas MacDonagh* (Dublin, 2014), p. 175.

193 Fearghal McGarry, *The Rising*, p. 92.

194 *Freeman's Journal*, 2 Aug. 1915; *Irish Times*, 2 Aug. 1915.

195 Michael Foy, *Tom Clarke*, p. 169.

196 Shane Kenna, *Jeremiah O'Donovan Rossa: unrepentant Fenian* (Sallins, 2015), pp. 251–2.

197 Michael Tierney, *Eoin MacNeill*, p. 178.

198 Ruth Dudley Edwards, *James Connolly* (Dublin, 1981), p. 124.

199 Donal Nevin, *James Connolly: a full life* (Dublin, 2005), p. 507.

200 C. Desmond Greaves, *The life and times of James Connolly* (London, 1972), p. 358.

201 Ann Matthews, *The Irish Citizen Army* (Cork, 2014), p. 188.

202 Donal Nevin, *James Connolly*, p. 702.

203 Lorcan Collins, *James Connolly* (Dublin, 2012), p. 230.

204 Charles Townshend, *Easter 1916*, p. 126.

205 Donal Nevin, *James Connolly*, p. 702.

206 Michael Tierney, *Eoin MacNeill*, pp 184–6.

207 Charles Townshend, *Easter 1916*, p. 119; Joost Augusteijn, *Patrick Pearse*, p. 299.

208 Geraldine Plunkett Dillon, Honor O'Brolchain (ed.), *All in the blood: a memoir* (Dublin, 2006), pp. 197–9.

209 Charles Townshend, *Easter 1916*, p. 124.

210 Joost Augusteijn, *Patrick Pearse*, p. 297.

211 Charles Townshend, *Easter 1916*, p. 118; Fearghal McGarry, *The Rising*, pp. 211–2; Michael Foy and Brian Barton, *The Easter Rising*, pp. 42–4.

212 Fearghal McGarry, *The Rising*, pp. 215–6, 221–2.

213 Charles Townshend, *Easter 1916*, pp. 123–5.

214 Michael Foy and Brian Barton, *The Easter Rising*, p. 48.

215 For a discussion of the radicalisation of the London-Irish 'refugees' see Darragh Gannon, 'London-Ireland and the 1916 Rising' http://www.rte.ie/centuryireland/index.php/articles/london-ireland-and-the-1916-rising [Date accessed 21 July 2016].

216 Ann Matthews, *The Kimmage garrison, 1916: making billy-can bombs at Larkfield* (Dublin, 2010), pp. 24–6.

217 Peter Hart, *Mick: the real Michael Collins* (London, 1995), pp. 82–8.

218 Diarmuid Lynch, *The IRB and the 1916 Rising*, pp. 61, 132.

219 Michael Foy and Brian Barton, *The Easter Rising*, pp. 55–6.

220 Marnie Hay, *Bulmer Hobson*, pp. 184–6. See also Charles Townshend, *Easter 1916*, p. 134.

221 F.X. Martin and Eoin MacNeill, 'Eoin MacNeill on the 1916 Rising', pp. 234–40.

222 Charles Townshend, *Easter 1916*, pp. 126–40 *passim*.

Chapter 3

1 William O'Brien, *Forth the banners go: reminiscences of William O'Brien* (Dublin, 1969), p. 288.

2 F.X. Martin, '1916: myth, fact, and mystery' in *Studia Hibernica* (1967), pp. 9–12; William Irwin Thompson, *Imagination of an insurrection, Dublin, Easter 1916: a study of an ideological movement* (Oxford, 1967), pp. 97–9.

3 Charles Townshend, *Easter 1916*, p. 181.

4 Ibid, pp. 169–80 *passim*.

5 W.J. Brennan-Whitmore, *Dublin burning: the Easter Rising from behind the barricades* (Dublin, 2013), p. 50.

6 Charles Townshend, *Easter 1916*, p. 159.

7 Fearghal McGarry, *The Rising*, p. 136.

8 Seán T. O'Kelly statement (M.A.I., Bureau of Military History, BMH/WS 1765).

9 Éamonn Bulfin statement (M.A.I., Bureau of Military History, BMH/WS 497).

10 Harry Walpole statement (M.A.I., Bureau of Military History, BMH/WS 218).

11 Frank Thornton statement (M.A.I., Bureau of Military History, BMH/WS 510).

12 Iver Neumann, 'Afterword' in Thomas Hylland Eriksen and Richard Jenkins (eds), *Flag, nation and symbolism in Europe and America* (London, 2007), p. 174.

13 Charles Saurin statement (M.A.I., Bureau of Military History, BMH/WS 288).

14 Patrick Caldwell statement (M.A.I., Bureau of Military History, BMH/WS 638).

15 Iver Neumann, 'Afterword', p. 174.

16 Seán MacEntee statement (M.A.I., Bureau of Military History, BMH/WS 1052).

17 Fearghal McGarry, *The Rising*, pp 161–2.

18 Michael Foy and Brian Barton, *The Easter Rising*, p. 85.

19 William Oman statement (M.A.I., Bureau of Military History, BMH/WS 421); Ruadhri Henderson statement (M.A.I., Bureau of Military History, BMH/WS 1686).

20 Fearghal McGarry, *The Rising*, p. 141.

21 Charles Townshend, *Easter 1916*, p. 166; Paul O'Brien, *Shootout: the battle for St. Stephen's Green, 1916* (Dublin, 2013), xii.

22 Frank Robbins statement (M.A.I., Bureau of Military History, BMH/WS 585).

23 Michael Foy and Brian Barton, *The Easter Rising*, p. 90; Charles Townshend, *Easter 1916*, p. 167.

24 Brian Hughes, *Michael Mallin* (Dublin, 2012), p. 194.

25 F.X. Martin, 'The 1916 Rising: a "Coup d'État" or a "Bloody Protest"?', p. 113.

26 Ann Matthews, *The Irish Citizen Army* (Cork, 2014), p. 94. Private Brady of the Royal Irish Fusiliers was also shot but survived.

27 James Stephens, *The insurrection in Dublin*, pp. 16–8.

28 Adrian and Sally Warwick-Haller (eds), *Letters from Dublin, 1916: Alfred Fannin's diary of the Rising* (Dublin, 1995), p. 21.

29 *Irish Times*, 25 April 1916.

30 Max Caulfield, *The Easter rebellion* (New York, 1963), p. 66.

31 Diana Norman, *Terrible beauty: a life of Constance Markievcz* (Swords, 1991), pp. 138–40.

32 Alexander Malcolm diary, 25 April 1916 (N.L.I., Alexander Malcolm papers, MS 46,081); Mick O'Farrell, *1916: what the people saw*, p. 275.

33 John McDonagh statement (M.A.I., Bureau of Military History, BMH/WS 532); Martin Conlon statement (M.A.I., Bureau of Military History, BMH/WS 419); Garry Holohan statement (M.A.I., Bureau of Military History, BMH/WS 328).

34   Helena Molony statement (M.A.I., Bureau of Military History, BMH/WS 391); Nancy Wyse-Power statement (M.A.I., Bureau of Military History, BMH/WS 541).

35   Mick O'Farrell, *1916: what the people saw*, pp. 118, 204.

36   Michael Foy and Brian Barton, *The Easter Rising*, pp. 117–18.

37   Fearghal McGarry, *The Rising*, pp. 219–22.

38   Adhamhnán Ó Súilleabháin, *Domhnall ua Buachalla: rebellious nationalist, reluctant governor* (Sallins, 2015), pp. 61–6.

39   Mick O'Farrell, *1916: what the people saw*, p. 141.

40   Ibid, pp. 271–2.

41   Fearghal McGarry, *The Rising*, pp. 142–3.

42   James Stephens, *The insurrection in Dublin*; Mick O'Farrell, *1916: what the people saw*, pp. 140–2, 158–9.

43   James Stephens, *The insurrection in Dublin*, p. 18.

44   Katharine Tynan, *The years of the shadow*, p. 197.

45   Mick O'Farrell, *1916: what the people saw*, p. 271.

46   Ibid, p. 39.

47   Ernie O'Malley, *On another man's wound*, p. 33.

48   Mick O'Farrell, *1916: what the people saw*, p. 112.

49   Ibid, p. 27.

50   Ibid, p. 228.

51   Ibid, pp. 228, 269; James Stephens, *The insurrection in* Dublin, pp. 19–20.

52   *Irish Times*, 25 April 1916.

53   Mick O'Farrell, *1916: what the people saw*, p. 132.

54   Ibid, p. 26.

55   William Cant, 'My experiences during the Rising in Dublin, Easter Week 1916' (N.L.I., Cant family papers, MS 49,854/9).

56   Charles Walker statement (M.A.I., Bureau of Military History, BMH/WS 241).

57   *Irish War News*, 25 April 1916.

58   Fearghal McGarry, *The Rising*, p. 153.

59   Fintan Murphy statement (M.A.I., Bureau of Military History, BMH/WS 370).

60   Fearghal McGarry, *The Rising*, pp. 222–30.

61   Michael Molloy statement (M.A.I., Bureau of Military History, BMH/WS 716).

62   Seosamh de Brun statement (M.A.I., Bureau of Military History, BMH/WS 312); Seamus Pounch statement (M.A.I., Bureau of Military History, BMH/WS 1686).

63   Michael Walker statement (M.A.I., Bureau of Military History, BMH/WS 1686).

64   Mick O'Farrell, *1916: what the people saw*, pp. 99, 210; William Cant, 'My experiences during the Rising in Dublin, Easter Week 1916' (N.L.I., Cant family papers, MS 49,854/9).

65   Fearghal McGarry, *The Rising*, p. 146.

66   Joe Duffy, *Children of the Rising: the untold story of the young lives lost during Easter 1916* (Castleknock, 2015), pp. 74–86.

67   *The Cork Examiner*, 27 April 1916; *Belfast Newsletter*, 29 April 1916.

68   Ruth Dudley Edwards, *Patrick Pearse*, pp. 290–1.

69   Desmond Ryan statement (M.A.I., Bureau of Military History, BMH/WS 724); William Whelan statement (M.A.I., Bureau of Military History, BMH/WS 369).

70   Michael O'Flanagan statement (M.A.I., Bureau of Military History, BMH/WS 800).

71   James Stephens, *The insurrection in Dublin* (Dublin, 1916), p. 25.

72   Alexander Malcolm diary, 25 April 1916 (N.L.I., Alexander Malcolm papers, MS 46,081).

73   Mick O'Farrell, *1916: what the people saw*, pp. 113, 212.

74   Ibid, p. 209.

75   Ibid, p. 56.

76   Ibid, pp. 18, 101, 113.

77   Jeremiah O'Leary statement (M.A.I., Bureau of Military History, BMH/WS 1108).

78   James Stephens, *The insurrection in* Dublin, p. 34.

79   Keith Jeffery (ed.), *The Sinn Fein rebellion as they saw it*, p. 43.

80   Joe Good (Maurice Good ed.), *Enchanted by dreams: the journal of a revolutionary* (Dingle, 1996), p. 36.

81   Ibid, p. 38.

82   Ibid, p. 37.

83   John Gibney, *16 lives: Seán Heuston* (Dublin, 2013), p. 142.

84   Charles Townshend, *Easter 1916*, p. 204.

85   Sean McLoughlin statement (M.A.I., Bureau of Military History, BMH/WS 290).

86   Charles Townshend, *Easter 1916*, p. 205.

87   Fearghal McGarry, *The Rising*, p. 169.

88   William Christian statement (M.A.I., Bureau of Military History, BMH/WS 646).

89   Mick O'Farrell, *1916: what the people saw*, pp. 145–6.

90   William Cant, 'My experiences during the Rising in Dublin, Easter Week 1916' (N.L.I., Cant family papers, MS 49,854/9).

91   Mick O'Farrell, *1916: what the people saw*, p. 125.

92   James Stephens, *The insurrection in Dublin*, p. 39.

93   Ibid, p. 41.

94   Ernie O'Malley, *On another man's wound*, p. 38.

95   Mick O'Farrell, *1916: what the people saw*, p. 118.

96   James Cullen statement (M.A.I., Bureau of Military History, BMH/WS 1343); Thomas Doyle statement (M.A.I., Bureau of Military History, BMH/WS 1041).

97   John O'Reilly statement (M.A.I., Bureau of Military History, BMH/WS 1031); Martin Dunbar statement (M.A.I., Bureau of Military History, BMH/WS 988); James Gleeson statement (M.A.I., Bureau of Military History, BMH/WS 1012).

98   Peter Paul Galligan statement (M.A.I., Bureau of Military History, BMH/WS 170).

99   James Cullen statement (M.A.I., Bureau of Military History, BMH/WS 1343).

100   Thomas Doyle statement (M.A.I., Bureau of Military History, BMH/WS 1041).

101   Maire Fitzpatrick statement (M.A.I., Bureau of Military History, BMH/WS 1345).

102   Thomas Doyle statement (M.A.I., Bureau of Military History, BMH/WS 1041).

103   Patrick Murphy statement (M.A.I., Bureau of Military History, BMH/WS 1216).

104   Joe Good, *Enchanted by Dreams*, p. 44; Sean Nunan statement (M.A.I., Bureau of Military History, BMH/WS 1744); Seán MacEntee statement (M.A.I., Bureau of Military History, BMH/WS 1052).

105   Oscar Traynor statement (M.A.I., Bureau of Military History, BMH/WS 340).

106   Fearghal McGarry, *The Rising*, p. 188.

107   Michael Foy and Brian Barton, *The Easter Rising*, pp. 154–64.

108 Charles Townshend, *Easter 1916*, pp. 169–70, 205–6.

109 Eilis Ui Chonaill statement (M.A.I., Bureau of Military History, BMH/WS 568).

110 *Irish Times*, 27 April 1916.

111 Mick O'Farrell *1916: what the people saw*, p. 147.

112 James Stephens, *The insurrection in Dublin*, pp. 50–2; Alexander Malcolm diary, 27 April 1916 (N.L.I., Alexander Malcolm papers, MS 46,081).

113 Fearghal McGarry, *The Rising*, p. 204.

114 Michael Foy and Brian Barton, *The Easter Rising*, p. 169.

115 Ibid, pp. 183–6.

116 Charles Townshend, *Easter 1916*, pp. 215, 217.

117 Fearghal McGarry, *The Rising*, p. 237.

118 Sean McLoughlin statement (M.A.I., Bureau of Military History, BMH/WS 290).

119 Donal Nevin, *James Connolly*, p. 656.

120 Thomas Devine statement (M.A.I., Bureau of Military History, BMH/WS 428).

121 Seán MacEntee statement (M.A.I., Bureau of Military History, BMH/WS 1052).

122 James Stephens, *The insurrection in Dublin*, p. 57; Alexander Malcolm diary, 28 April 1916 (N.L.I., Alexander Malcolm papers, MS 46,081).

123 James Stephens, *The insurrection in Dublin*, p. 57.

124 Alexander Malcolm diary, 28 April 1916 (N.L.I., Alexander Malcolm papers, MS 46,081).

125 Mick O'Farrell, *1916: what the people saw*, p. 21.

126 James Stephens, *The insurrection in Dublin*, p. 62.

Chapter 4

1 Fearghal McGarry, *The Rising*, p. 205.

2 Desmond FitzGerald, *Memoirs of Desmond FitzGerald, 1913–16* (London, 1968), p. 152.

3 Thomas Devine statement (M.A.I., Bureau of Military History, BMH/WS 428).

4 John Kenny statement (M.A.I., Bureau of Military History, BMH/WS 1693).

5 Dennis Daly statement (M.A.I., Bureau of Military History, BMH/WS 110).

6 Cormac O'Malley and Tim Horgan (eds), *The men will talk to me: Kerry interviews* (Cork, 2012), p. 321.

7 Thomas Devine statement (M.A.I., Bureau of Military History, BMH/WS 428); Patrick Rankin statement, (M.A.I., Bureau of Military History, BMH/WS 163).

8 Fintan Murphy statement (M.A.I., Bureau of Military History, BMH/WS 370); James Carrigan statement (M.A.I., Bureau of Military History, BMH/WS 613).

9 Eamon Bulfin statement (M.A.I., Bureau of Military History, BMH/WS 497).

10 Sean McLoughlin statement (M.A.I., Bureau of Military History, BMH/WS 290).

11 Julia Grennan, 'Miss Julia Grennan's story of the surrender' in *Catholic Bulletin*, xii (1917), p. 396.

12 Sean McGarry statement (M.A.I., Bureau of Military History, BMH/WS 368).

13 Joe Good statement (M.A.I., Bureau of Military History, BMH/WS 388).

14 Desmond Ryan statement (M.A.I., Bureau of Military History, BMH/WS 724).

15 Desmond Ryan, *The Rising* (Dublin, 1949), p. 253.

16 Seamus Doyle statement (M.A.I., Bureau of Military History, BMH/WS 315); Fr Augustine statement (M.A.I., Bureau of Military History, BMH/WS 920).

17 Sean McEntee statement (M.A.I., Bureau of Military History, BMH/WS 1052).

18 Joe Good statement (M.A.I., Bureau of Military History, BMH/WS 388).

19 Oscar Traynor statement (M.A.I., Bureau of Military History, BMH/WS 340).

20 Thomas Leahy statement (M.A.I., Bureau of Military History, BMH/WS 660); Eamon Bulfin statement (M.A.I., Bureau of Military History, BMH/WS 497).

21 Barry Kennerk, *Moore Street: the story of Dublin's market district* (Cork, 2012), p. 46.

22 Fearghal McGarry, *The Rising*, p. 188.

23 Desmond Ryan, *The Rising*, pp. 256–7.

24 Ibid, p. 256.

25 Thomas Leahy statement (M.A.I., Bureau of Military History, BMH/WS 660).

26 Charles Saurin statement (M.A.I., Bureau of Military History, BMH/WS 288).

27 Joe Good, *Enchanted by dreams* (Dingle, 1996), p. 69.

28 Paul O'Brien, *Crossfire: the battle of the Four Courts, 1916* (Dublin, 2012), pp. 92–8; Fearghal McGarry, *The Rising*, p. 187.

29 Charles Townshend, *Easter 1916*, p. 207.

30 Fearghal McGarry, *The Rising*, pp. 187–8.

31 See *The Dead of Easter Week* graphic in 'Proclaiming a Republic: The 1916 Rising' exhibition at the National Museum of Ireland.

32 Elizabeth O'Farrell, 'Miss Elizabeth O'Farrell's story of the surrender' in *Catholic Bulletin*, xii (1917), pp. 266–70; Alex Findlater (ed.), *1916 Surrenders: Captain H.E. De Courcy-Wheeler's eyewitness account* (Dublin, 2016), pp. 25–33.

33 Frank Shouldice statement (M.A.I., Bureau of Military History, BMH/WS 162).

34 Fr T. O'Donoghue statement (M.A.I., Bureau of Military History, BMH/WS 1666); Frank Robbins statement (M.A.I., Bureau of Military History, BMH/WS 585).

35 Elizabeth O'Farrell, 'Miss Elizabeth O'Farrell's story of the surrender', pp. 329–33; Alex Findlater, *1916 Surrenders*, pp. 35–53.

36 Bernard McAllister statement (M.A.I., Bureau of Military History, BMH/WS 147).

37 Seamus Doyle statement (M.A.I., Bureau of Military History, BMH/WS 315).

38 Fred Murray statement (M.A.I., Bureau of Military History, BMH/WS 15).

Chapter 5

1 F.S.L. Lyons, *Ireland since the Famine* (London, 1971), p. 375.

2 Brian Barton and Michael Foy, *The Easter Rising*, p. 210; Charles Townshend, *Easter 1916*, pp. 265–6.

3   Charles Saurin statement (M.A.I., Bureau of Military History, BMH/WS 288).

4   Michael O'Reilly statement (M.A.I., Bureau of Military History, BMH/WS 886).

5   Thomas Devine statement (M.A.I., Bureau of Military History, BMH/WS 428).

6   Most rebels, in fact, did not comment on antagonistic crowds. See for example Eamon Bulfin statement (M.A.I., Bureau of Military History, BMH/WS 497); Sean Nunan statement (M.A.I., Bureau of Military History, BMH/WS 1744); Charles Donnelly statement (M.A.I., Bureau of Military History, BMH/WS 428).

7   Seán MacEntee statement (M.A.I., Bureau of Military History, BMH/WS 1052).

8   Robert Cecil Le Cren diary, 30 April 1916 (N.L.I, Robert Cecil Le Cren papers, MS 36, 172).

9   Frank Robbins statement (M.A.I., Bureau of Military History, BMH/WS 585).

10 Fr T. O'Donoghue statement (M.A.I., Bureau of Military History, BMH/WS 1666).

11 Seamus Kavanagh statement (M.A.I., Bureau of Military History, BMH/WS 1670).

12 William Oman statement (M.A.I., Bureau of Military History, BMH/WS 421).

13 William Cant, 'My experiences during the Rising in Dublin, Easter Week 1916' (N.L.I., Cant family papers, MS 49,854/9); Robert Cecil Le Cren diary, 30 April 1916 (N.L.I, Robert Cecil Le Cren papers, MS 36, 172); Mick O'Farrell, *1916: What the people saw*, p. 35.

14 Katharine Tynan, *The years of the shadow*, p. 232.

15 Alexander Malcolm diary, 1 May 1916 (N.L.I., Alexander Malcolm papers, MS 46, 081).

16 James Stephens, *The Insurrection in Dublin*, p. 96.

17 Mick O'Farrell, *1916: What the people saw*, p. 35.

18 Robert Cecil Le Cren diary, 30 April 1916 (N.L.I, Robert Cecil Le Cren papers, MS 36, 172).

19 *Irish Times*, 3 May 1916.

20 Katharine Tynan, *The years of the shadow*, p. 209.

21 See Daithi O'Corrain, '"They blew up the best portion of our city and … it is their duty to replace it": compensation and reconstruction in the aftermath of the 1916 Rising' in I.H.S., xxxvix (2014), pp. 272–95.

22 Michael Laffan, *The resurrection of Ireland*, p. 51.

23 See Chapter 6.

24 Seán Enright, *The trials*, pp. 47–56.

25 David Foxton, *Revolutionary lawyers: Sinn Féin and crown courts in Ireland and Britain, 1916–1923* (Dublin, 2008), pp. 68–70.

26 Charles Townshend, *Easter 1916*, p. 276.

27 David Foxton, *Revolutionary lawyers*, pp. 70–1.

28 Seán Enright, *The trials*, p. 45.

29 Seán McConville, *Irish political prisoners, 1848–1922*, p. 431.

30 Brian Barton, *From behind a closed door: secret court martial records of the 1916 Easter Rising* (Belfast, 2002), p. 29.

31 *The Times*, 25 April 1916; ibid, 26 April 1916; ibid, 27 April 1916.

32 *The Times*, 26 April 1916.

33 *Liverpool Daily Post*, 26 April 1916.

34 *Manchester Evening News*, 27 April 1916.

35 *Birmingham Daily Gazette*, 28 April 1916.

36 *Edinburgh Evening News*, 29 April 1916.

37 *Cambria Daily Leader*, 1 May 1916.

38 See David Foxton, *Revolutionary lawyers*, p. 65.

39 Eunan O'Halpin, *The decline of the Union, 1892–1920* (Dublin, 1987), pp. 119–21; Ronan Fanning, *Fatal path*, p. 141.

40 Charles Townshend, *Easter 1916*, p. 208.

41 Ibid, pp. 272–4.

42 F.S.L. Lyons, *John Dillon*, p. 377.

43 Charles Townshend, *Easter 1916*, p. 296.

44 Seán Enright, *The Trials*, p. 2.

45 Ibid, p. 91.

46 Brian Barton, *From behind a closed door*, p. 108.

47 León Ó Broin, *W.E. Wylie and the Irish revolution, 1916–1921* (Dublin, 1989), p. 21.

48 Seán Enright, *The Trials*, pp. 91–2.

49 Brian Barton, *From behind a closed door*, p. 111.

50 Countess of Fingall, *Seventy years young: memories of Elizabeth, Countess of Fingall* (Dublin, 1971), p. 36.

51 Brian Barton, *From behind a closed door*, p. 111. Seán Enright has suggested that Ceannt's calling of MacDonagh was a tactical ploy to gain more time as he may well have known of that morning's execution: Seán Enright, *The Trials*, p. 165.

52 Brian Barton, *From behind a closed door*, p. 292.

53 León Ó Broin, *W.E. Wylie and the Irish revolution*, p. 23.

54 Seán Enright, *The Trials*, p. 186.

55 León Ó Broin, *W.E. Wylie and the Irish revolution*, p. 27.

56 Brian Barton, *From behind a closed door*, p. 80.

57 Charles Townshend, *Easter 1916*, p. 395.

58 See Brian Barton, *From behind a closed door*, p. 80; Seán Enright, *The Trials*, p. 187.

59 Some have suggested Maxwell was not inclined to spare Markievicz the death sentence. See Seán Enright, *The Trials*, pp. 72–3.

60 Charles Townshend, *Easter 1916*, p. 283.

61 Brian Barton, *From behind a closed door*, pp. 175–6.

62 Ibid, pp. 247–8.

63 Ibid, pp. 232–3.

64 On this wider point see Charles Townshend, *Easter 1916*, pp. 282–3.

65 Brian Barton, *From behind a closed door*, pp. 164–5.

66 See Ruth Dudley Edwards, *The Seven: the lives and legacies of the founding fathers of the Irish Republic* (London, 2016).

67 Brian Barton, *From behind a closed door*, pp. 221–2.

68 D.P. McCracken, *MacBride's brigade* (Dublin, 1997), p. 163.

69 Brian Barton, *From behind a closed door*, pp. 221–2.

70 Ibid, pp. 272–3.

71 Seán Enright, *The Trials*, p. 193.

72 Brian Barton, *From behind a closed door*, pp. 74–7.

73 For treatments of this rather sensitive subject see Seán Enright, *The Trials*, pp. 200–3.

74 León Ó Broin, *W.E. Wylie and the Irish revolution*, p. 32.

75 Brian Barton, *From behind a closed door*, pp. 63–71.

76 Fr Aloysius statement (M.A.I., Bureau of Military History, BMH/WS 207); Piaras Mac Lochlainn, *Last words: letters and statements of the leaders executed after the Rising at Easter 1916* (Dublin, 1971), p. 79.

77   Kathleen Clarke, *Revolutionary woman, 1878–1972* (Dublin, 1991), pp. 93–6; Michael Soughley statement (M.A.I., Bureau of Military History, BMH/WS 189).

78   Áine Ceannt statement (M.A.I., Bureau of Military History, BMH/WS 264); Fr Aloysius statement (M.A.I., Bureau of Military History, BMH/WS 207); Alfred Bucknill statement (M.A.I., Bureau of Military History, BMH/WS 1019); Mary (Sister Francesca) MacDonagh to Jim MacDonagh, 9 May 1916 (N.L.I., Thomas MacDonagh family papers, MS 44, 322/5).

79   Grace Plunkett statement (M.A.I., Bureau of Military History, BMH/WS 257); 'An account from Fr Sebastian' in *Catholic Bulletin*, July 1916.

80   Kathleen Clarke, *Revolutionary woman, 1878–1972* (Dublin, 1991), pp. 117–19; Michael Soughley statement (M.A.I., Bureau of Military History, BMH/WS 189).

81   Eily O'Hanrahan Reilly statement (M.A.I., Bureau of Military History, BMH/WS 270); Fr Augustine statement (M.A.I., Bureau of Military History, BMH/WS 920); Áine Ceannt statement (M.A.I., Bureau of Military History, BMH/WS 264).

82   Piaras Mac Lochlainn, *Last words*, p. 79; Fr Aloysius statement (M.A.I., Bureau of Military History, BMH/WS 207).

83   Fr Augustine statement (M.A.I., Bureau of Military History, BMH/WS 920).

84   Áine Ceannt statement (M.A.I., Bureau of Military History, BMH/WS 264); Fr Augustine statement (M.A.I., Bureau of Military History, BMH/WS 920).

85   Thomas Mallin statement (M.A.I., Bureau of Military History, BMH/WS 382).

86   Piaras Mac Lochlainn, *Last words*, pp. 109–16.

87   Ibid, pp. 146–53.

88   Ibid, pp. 155–7.

89   Min Ryan statement, 1966 (RTE Archives, Easter Rising, Portraits 1916).

90   Nora O'Brien statement (M.A.I., Bureau of Military History, BMH/WS 286); Fr Aloysius statement (M.A.I., Bureau of Military History, BMH/WS 207); Alfred Bucknill statement (M.A.I., Bureau of Military History, BMH/WS 1019); Peter Paul Galligan statement (M.A.I., Bureau of Military History, BMH/WS 170).

91   William Cant, 'My experiences during the Rising in Dublin, Easter Week 1916' (N.L.I., Cant family papers, MS 49,854/9); Keith Jeffery (ed.), *The Sinn Fein rebellion as they saw it* (Dublin, 1999), p. 64.

92   *Irish Times*, 2 May 1916.

93   *Irish Times*, 3 May 1916.

94   Fergus Pyle and Owen Dudley Edwards, 'The *Irish Times* on the Easter Rising' in idem, *1916: the Easter Rising* (London, 1968), p. 242.

95   Adrian and Sally Warwick-Haller (eds), *Letters from Dublin, 1916: Alfred Fannin's diary of the Rising* (Dublin, 1995), p. 45.

96   F.S.L. Lyons, *John Dillon*, p. 377.

97   *Irish Times*, 2 May 1916.

98   J.J. Lee, *Ireland, 1912–85*, p. 29.

99   Fearghal McGarry, *The Rising*, p. 202; Charles Townshend, *Easter 1916*, p. 307.

100 *Irish Times*, 2 May 1916; ibid, 3 May 1916; ibid, 4 May 1916.

101 *Freeman's Journal*, 5 May 1916; *Irish Independent*, 5 May 1916.

102 See for example: *Anglo-Celt*, 6 May 1916; *Kildare Observer*, 6 May 1916; *Connacht Telegraph*, 6 May 1916; *Southern Star*, 6 May 1916.

103 Seán Enright, *The Trials*, p. 26.

104 *Irish Times*, 4 May 1916.

105 Ernie O'Malley, *On another man's wound*, p. 42.

106 *Freeman's Journal*, 5 May 1916.

107 *Irish Independent*, 6 May 1916.

108 *Ulster Herald*, 6 May 1916.

109 *Kerry Weekly Reporter*, 6 May 1916.

110 *Freeman's Journal*, 9 May 1916.

111 See Robert Kee, *The Green flag: ourselves alone*, iii (London, 1976), pp. 1–8; F.S.L. Lyons, 'The Rising and after' in W.E. Vaughan (ed.), *A new history of Ireland, vi: Ireland under the Union, 1870–1921* (Oxford, 1996), 218–19.

112 J.J. Lee, *Ireland, 1912–85*, p. 32.

113 See Fearghal McGarry, *The Rising*, p. 202; Charles Townshend, *Easter 1916*, p. 307.

114 *Freeman's Journal*, 5 May 1916.

115 *Irish Independent*, 6 May 1916.

116 *Kildare Observer*, 6 May 1916.

117 *Nenagh News*, 6 May 1916.

118 *Hansard 5* (Commons), lxxxii, col. 948 (11 May 1916).

119 Ernie O'Malley, *On another man's wound*, p. 42.

120 Adrian and Sally Warwick-Haller (eds), *Alfred Fannin's diary of the Rising*, pp. 48–9; Alexander Malcolm diary, 4 May 1916 (N.L.I., Alexander Malcolm papers, MS 46, 081).

121 See *Kildare Observer*, 29 April 1916; *Leitrim Observer*, 6 May 1916, *Nenagh Guardian*, 29 April 1916.

122 James Stephens, *The insurrection in Dublin*, p. 94.

123 Ernie O'Malley, *On another man's wound*, p. 44.

124 See RIC confidential reports for the month of May 1916 in Co. Waterford and Co. Wicklow.

125 *Freeman's Journal*, 9 May 1916.

126 *Freeman's Journal*, 9 May 1916; ibid, 13 May 1916.

127 Despite the fact that the executions were promulgated under DORA, the Irish Law Office revealed 'undoubtedly the average citizen has an extraordinary belief in the magic term "Martial Law" … the very indefinite knowledge of its powers spreads terror among the disaffected': Charles Townshend, *Easter 1916*, p. 303.

128 *Freeman's Journal*, 8 May 1916; *Irish Independent*, 9 May 1916.

129 John Dillon to John Redmond, 7 May 1916 (N.L.I., John Redmond papers, MS 15,262/5).

130 *Freeman's Journal*, 9 May 1916; *Irish Independent*, 10 May 1916.

131 Seán McConville, *Irish political prisoners, 1848–1922*, p. 430.

132 *Hansard 5* (Commons), lxxxii, col. 948 (11 May 1916).

133 See *Anglo-Celt*, 13 May 1916; *Kildare Observer*, 13 May 1916; *Southern Star*, 20 May 1916; *Connacht Telegraph*, 20 May 1916.

134 Alvin Jackson, *Home Rule: an Irish history, 1800–2000* (London, 2003), pp. 154–5.

135 Charles Townshend, *Easter 1916*, p. 299.

136 RIC Inspector General's report, 15 June 1916 (N.L.I., RIC County reports, P8541).

137 See RIC confidential reports for the month of May 1916 in counties Galway, Meath, Monaghan and Tyrone.

138 Katharine Tynan, *The years of the shadow* (Boston, 1919), p. 204.

Chapter 6

1 Michael Kelly statement (M.A.I., Bureau of Military History, BMH/WS 564).

2 Fintan Murphy statement (M.A.I., Bureau of Military History, BMH/WS 370).

3 William Daly statement (M.A.I., Bureau of Military History, BMH/WS 291); James Kavanagh statement (M.A.I., Bureau of Military History, BMH/WS 889); Joseph Lawless statement (M.A.I., Bureau of Military History, BMH/WS 1043).

4 Michael Kelly statement (M.A.I., Bureau of Military History, BMH/WS 564); Michael Brennan statement (M.A.I., Bureau of Military History, BMH/WS 1068).

5 Michael Brennan statement (M.A.I., Bureau of Military History, BMH/WS 1068).

6 Seán McConville, *Irish political prisoners, 1848–1922*, p. 455.

7 Ibid, pp. 455–6.

8 Seán Prendergast statement (M.A.I., Bureau of Military History, BMH/WS 755); Daniel Tuite statement (M.A.I., Bureau of Military History, BMH/WS 337).

9 Liam Tannam statement (M.A.I., Bureau of Military History, BMH/WS 242).

10 Michael Brennan statement (M.A.I., Bureau of Military History, BMH/WS 1068).

11 Michael Lynch statement (M.A.I., Bureau of Military History, BMH/WS 511).

12 Michael Lynch statement (M.A.I., Bureau of Military History, BMH/WS 511); Frank Robbins statement (M.A.I., Bureau of Military History, BMH/WS 585).

13 Michael Lynch statement (M.A.I., Bureau of Military History, BMH/WS 511).

14 Darrell Figgis, *A chronicle of jails* (Dublin, 1918), pp. 76–7.

15 Daniel Tuite statement (M.A.I., Bureau of Military History, BMH/WS 337).

16 Liam Tannam statement (M.A.I., Bureau of Military History, BMH/WS 242).

17 Charles Weston statement (M.A.I., Bureau of Military History, BMH/WS 149).

18 Joseph Lawless statement (M.A.I., Bureau of Military History, BMH/WS 1043).

19 See Adolf Vischer, *Barbed wire disease: a psychological study of the prisoner of war* (London, 1919).

20 Séamus Kavanagh statement (M.A.I., Bureau of Military History, BMH/WS 1053).

21 Thomas Leahy statement (M.A.I., Bureau of Military History, BMH/WS 660).

22 Seán Prendergast statement (M.A.I., Bureau of Military History, BMH/WS 755).

23 William Murphy, 'Narratives of confinement: Fenians, prisons and writing, 1867–1916' in Fearghal McGarry and James McConnel (eds), *The black hand of republicanism: Fenianism in modern Ireland* (Dublin, 2009), p. 160.

24 Sean O'Duffy statement (M.A.I., Bureau of Military History, BMH/WS 618); Michael Lynch statement (M.A.I., Bureau of Military History, BMH/WS 511).

25 Michael Lynch statement (M.A.I., Bureau of Military History, BMH/WS 511).

26 James Kavanagh statement (M.A.I., Bureau of Military History, BMH/WS 889).

27 Frank Robbins statement (M.A.I., Bureau of Military History, BMH/WS 585).

28 William Murphy, *Political imprisonment and the Irish, 1912–1921* (Oxford, 2014), p. 58.

29 Daniel Tuite statement (M.A.I., Bureau of Military History, BMH/WS 337).

30 Thomas Leahy statement (M.A.I., Bureau of Military History, BMH/WS 660).

31 Darrell Figgis, *A chronicle of jails*, p. 89.

32 Harold Mytum, 'Materiality matters: the role of things in coping strategies at Cunningham's Camp, Douglas during World War I' in Harold Mytum and Gilly Carr (eds), *Prisoners of War: archaeology, memory, and heritage of 19th- and 20th- century mass internment* (London, 2013), pp. 169–88; Gillian Carr, '"My home was the area round my bed" experiencing and negotiating space at civil internment camps in Germany, 1942–1945' in Harold Mytum and Gilly Carr (eds), *Prisoners of War: archaeology, memory, and heritage of 19th- and 20th- century mass internment* (London, 2013), pp. 189–204.

33 Darragh Gannon, 'The rise of the rainbow chasers: advanced Irish political nationalism in Britain, 1916–22' in *Éire-Ireland*, xlix (2014), p. 118.

34 Seán T. O'Kelly to Art O'Brien, 1916 (N.L.I., Art Ó Briain papers, MS 8428/24).

35 Sean O Mahony, *Frongoch*, p. 21.

36 Joseph McCarthy statement (M.A.I., Bureau of Military History, BMH/WS 1497).

37 Sean O Mahony, *Frongoch: university of revolution* (Dublin, 1987), p. 23.

38 W.J. Brennan-Whitmore, *With the Irish in Frongoch* (Dublin, 1917), p. 20.

39 Sean O Mahony, *Frongoch*, pp. 24–5.

40 William Murphy, *Political imprisonment and the Irish*, p. 60.

41 Peter Hart, *Mick: the real Michael Collins* (London, 2005), p. 101.

42 Sean O Mahony, *Frongoch*, pp. 60–1.

43 Daniel Tuite statement (M.A.I., Bureau of Military History, BMH/WS 337).

44 Frank Robbins statement (M.A.I., Bureau of Military History, BMH/WS 585).

45 Daniel Tuite statement (M.A.I., Bureau of Military History, BMH/WS 337); Sean O Mahony, *Frongoch*, pp. 43–4, 61–2.

46 W.J. Brennan-Whitmore, *With the Irish in Frongoch*, p. 46.

47 See John Davidson Ketchum, *Ruhleben: a prison camp society* (Toronto, 1965).

48 W.J. Brennan-Whitmore, *With the Irish in Frongoch*, p. 36.

49 William Daly statement (M.A.I., Bureau of Military History, BMH/WS 291).

50 Lyn Ebenezer, *Frongoch camp 1916 and the birth of the IRA* (Llanrwst, 2006), p. 120.

51 Sean O Mahony, *Frongoch*, pp. 41, 73; Michael Lynch statement (M.A.I., Bureau of Military History, BMH/WS 511).

52 Sean O Mahony, *Frongoch*, pp. 99–101.

53   Ibid, p. 73.

54   W.J. Brennan-Whitmore, *With the Irish in Frongoch*, pp. 56–7; Patrick Kelly statement (M.A.I., Bureau of Military History, BMH/WS 781); Thomas Leahy statement (M.A.I., Bureau of Military History, BMH/WS 660).

55   Panikos Panayi, '"Barbed wire disease" or a "Prison Camp Society": the everyday lives of German internees on the Isle of Man, 1914–1919' in idem (ed.), *Germans as minorities during the First World War* (Farnham, 2014), p. 121.

56   William Daly statement (M.A.I., Bureau of Military History, BMH/WS 291); Liam Tannam statement (M.A.I., Bureau of Military History, BMH/WS 242); W.J. Brennan-Whitmore, *With the Irish in Frongoch*, pp. 50–1.

57   Joseph McCarthy statement (M.A.I., Bureau of Military History, BMH/WS 1497).

58   Seán McConville, *Irish political prisoners*, pp. 462–3.

59   Panikos Panayi, *Prisoners of Britain: German civilian and combatant internees during the First World War* (Manchester, 2012); Matthew Stibbe, *British civilians in Germany: the Ruhleben camp, 1914–1918* (Manchester, 2008).

60   Sean O Mahony, *Frongoch*, p. 38.

61   Thomas Pugh statement (M.A.I., Bureau of Military History, BMH/WS 397).

62   Seán Prendergast statement (M.A.I., Bureau of Military History, BMH/WS 755).

63   Sean O Mahony, *Frongoch*, p. 132.

64   Gilly Carr and Harold Mytum, 'The importance of creativity behind barbed wire: setting a research agenda' in idem, *Cultural heritage and prisoners of war: creativity beyond barbed wire* (New York, 2012), p. 3.

65   Joseph Lawless statement (M.A.I., Bureau of Military History, BMH/WS 1043); Joseph McCarthy statement (M.A.I., Bureau of Military History, BMH/WS 1497); Joe Good, *Enchanted by dreams*, p. 98.

66   Nicholas Saunders, *Trench art: a brief history and guide, 1914-1939* (Barnsley, 2011), p. 117. See also Joanna Brück, '"A good Irishman should blush every time he sees a penny": gender, nationalism and memory in Irish internment camp craftwork, 1916-1923' in *Journal of material culture*, xx (2015), pp. 155–7.

67   Joseph Lawless statement (M.A.I., Bureau of Military History, BMH/WS 1043).

68   Seamus Fitzgerald statement (M.A.I., Bureau of Military History, BMH/WS 1737).

69   Sean O Mahony, *Frongoch*, p. 62.

70   William Mullins statement (M.A.I., Bureau of Military History, BMH/WS 801); Seamus Fitzgerald statement (M.A.I., Bureau of Military History, BMH/WS 1737); William Stapleton statement (M.A.I., Bureau of Military History, BMH/WS 822).

71   Seán Prendergast statement (M.A.I., Bureau of Military History, BMH/WS 755).

72   William Murphy, *Political imprisonment*, p. 67.

73   Peter Hart, *Mick*, pp. 108–9.

74   Sean O Mahony, *Frongoch*, pp. 119–21.

75   William Murphy, *Political imprisonment*, pp. 64–5, 69.

76   Peter Hart, *Mick*, p. 105.

77   William Murphy, *Political imprisonment*, p. 61.

78   Seán McConville, *Irish political prisoners*, pp. 537–49.

79   Ibid, p. 523.

80   Robert Brennan statement (M.A.I., Bureau of Military History, BMH/WS 779).

Chapter 7

1   J.J. Lee, *Ireland: 1912–1985*, pp. 37–8; F.S.L. Lyons, 'The Rising and after', pp. 219–20.

2   Charles Townshend, *Easter 1916*, pp. 300–23 *passim*; Fearghal McGarry, *The Rising*, pp. 277–86 *passim*.

3   *The Times*, 28 April 1916.

4   Ibid, 29 April 1916.

5   F.S.L. Lyons, *John Dillon*, p. 373.

6   Conor Mulvagh, 'A souring of friendships? Internal divisions in the leadership of the Irish parliamentary party in the aftermath of the Easter Rising' in Diarmaid Ferriter and Susannah O'Riordan (eds), *Years of turbulence: the Irish revolution and its aftermath* (Dublin, 2015), p. 88.

7   Dermot Meleady, *John Redmond*, p. 370.

8   W.B. Wells, *John Redmond*, p. 181; Stephen Gwynn, *John Redmond's last years* (London, 1919), p. 226; Joseph P. Finnan, *John Redmond and Irish unity*, p. 196.

9   Joseph P. Finnan, *John Redmond and Irish unity*, p. 196.

10   Dermot Meleady, *John Redmond*, p. 371.

11   *Hansard 5* (Commons), lxxxii, col. 37 (3 May 1916).

12   Dermot Meleady, *John Redmond*, p. 371.

13   *Manchester Guardian*, 5 May 1916; *Daily Chronicle*, 5 May 1916.

14   *Liverpool Echo*, 6 May 1916; *Lincolnshire Echo*, 6 May 1916.

15   *Hansard 5* (Commons), lxxxii, col. 283 (8 May 1916).

16   *Aberdeen Evening Express*, 12 May 1916; *Birmingham Mail*, 12 May 1916; *Newcastle Journal*, 13 May 1916.

17   Stephen Gwynn, *John Redmond's last years*, p. 231.

18   Alvin Jackson, *Home Rule*, pp. 155–70 *passim*.

19   Stephen Gwynn, *John Redmond's last years*, p. 234; Denis Gwynn, *The life of John Redmond*, pp. 390–2.

20   Dermot Meleady, *John Redmond*, pp. 390–3. The Redmond papers in the National Library of Ireland remarkably contain no correspondence with Dillon, Devlin or O'Connor during this period. (N.L.I., John Redmond papers, MS 15,262/6–8).

21   Paul Bew, *Ideology and the Irish Question*, pp. 144–52; Patrick Maume, *The long gestation: Irish nationalist life, 1891–1918* (Dublin, 1999), p. 171; Alan O'Day, *Irish Home Rule*, pp. 281–3.

22   RIC Inspector General's monthly report for June 1916, 15 July 1916 (N.L.I., RIC County Inspectors' reports, P 8541).

23   Michael Laffan, *The resurrection of Ireland*, pp. 62–4.

24   Fearghal McGarry, *The Rising*, pp. 264–5.

25   Charles Townshend, *Easter 1916*, p. 275.

26   *Irish Times*, 31 May 1916.

27   *Kerry Sentinel*, 30 May 1916; *Leitrim Observer*, 3 June 1916; *Kilkenny People*, 3 June 1916.

28   *Southern Star*, 13 May 1916; *Longford Leader*, 20 May 1916; *Anglo-Celt*, 20 May 1916.

29   Caoimhe Nic Dháibhéid, 'The Irish National Aid Association and the radicalization of public opinion in Ireland, 1916–1918' in *Historical Journal*, lxxxvi (2012), pp. 707–8.

30   William Murphy, *Political imprisonment and the Irish*, p. 73.

31   Caoimhe Nic Dháibhéid, 'The Irish National Aid Association', pp. 714–15.

32   Senia Pašeta, *Irish nationalist women*, p. 207.

33   Caoimhe Nic Dháibhéid, 'The Irish National Aid Association', pp. 709, 727–9.

34   Senia Pašeta, *Irish nationalist women*, pp. 208–10.

35   R.F. Foster, *Modern Ireland*, p. 487.

36   RIC Inspector General's monthly report for June 1916, 15 July 1916 (N.L.I., RIC County Inspectors' reports, P 8541).

37   Orla Fitzpatrick, 'Portraits and propaganda: photographs of the widows and children of the 1916 leaders in the *Catholic Bulletin*' in Lisa Godson and Joanna Brück (eds), *Making 1916*, pp. 82–90.

38   Richard English, *Irish freedom*, pp. 266–8.

39   Ernie O'Malley, *On another man's wound*, p. 51.

40   C.S. Andrews, *Dublin made me: an autobiography* (Dublin, 1979), p. 92.

41   RIC Inspector General's monthly report for July 1916, 14 Aug 1916 (N.L.I., RIC County Inspectors' reports, P 8541).

42   T.H. Breen, *The marketplace of revolution: how consumer politics shaped American independence* (Oxford, 2004), xv–xvii.

43   Seán Prendergast statement (M.A.I., Bureau of Military History witness statements, BMH/WS 755).

44   Peter Hart, *Mick: the real Michael Collins*, p. 118.

45   See the I.N.A.A.V.D.F. ledgers and registers, Mar. 1917–Mar. 1918 (N.L.I., I.N.A.A.V.D.F. papers, MS 23,465–23,467).

46   Peter Hart, *Mick: the real Michael Collins*, p. 118.

47   Maryann Valiulis, *Portrait of a revolutionary*, p. 20; Joost Augusteijn, *From public defiance to guerrilla warfare: the experience of ordinary volunteers in the Irish War of Independence, 1916–21* (Dublin, 1996), pp. 56–62.

48   Michael Laffan, *The resurrection of Ireland*, pp. 80–4.

49   Kevin O'Shiel statement (MAI, Bureau of Military History witness statements, BMH/WS 1770); *Irish Independent*, 8 February 1917; *Kerryman*, 10 February 1917.

50   Dermot Meleady, *John Redmond*, p. 409.

51   F.S.L. Lyons, *John Dillon*, p. 411.

52   *Hansard 5* (Commons), xc, col. 1786 (26 Feb. 1917).

53   Michael Laffan, *The resurrection of Ireland*, pp. 96–7.

54   Marie Coleman, 'Mobilisation: the South-Longford by-election and its impact on political mobilisation' in Joost Augusteijn (ed.), *The Irish revolution, 1913–1923* (Basingstoke, 2002), pp. 56–7.

55   *Evening Herald*, 28 April 1917; ibid, 30 April 1917; *Belfast Newsletter*, 30 April 1917.

56   Michael Laffan, *The resurrection of Ireland*, p. 94.

57   Dermot Meleady, *John Redmond*, p. 420.

58   T.P. O'Connor to John Dillon, 24 May 1917 (T.C.D.M.D., John Dillon papers, MSS 6741/376); John Dillon to T.P. O'Connor, 25 May 1917 (ibid, MSS 6741/382).

59   Ronan Fanning, *Fatal Path*, p. 164.

60   Conor Mulvagh, 'A souring of friendships?', pp. 88, 99–101.

61   R.B. McDowell, *The Irish Convention, 1917–18* (London, 1970), vii.

62   John Dillon to T.P. O'Connor, 7 June 1917 (T.C.D.M.D., John Dillon papers, MSS 6741/407).

63   Simon Donnelly statement (M.A.I., Bureau of Military History witness statements, BMH/WS 113).

64   David Fitzpatrick, 'De Valera in 1917: the undoing of the Easter Rising' in J.P. O'Carroll and J.A. Murphy (eds), *De Valera and his times* (Cork, 1983), pp. 102–3.

65   Michael Laffan, *The resurrection of Ireland*, p. 110.

66   Frank Pakenham and T.P. O'Neill, *Éamon de Valera* (London, 1970), p. 70.

67   David Fitzpatrick, *Politics and Irish life*, p. 107.

68   Marie Coleman, *County Longford and the Irish revolution, 1910–1923* (Dublin, 2003), p. 78; David Fitzpatrick, *Politics and Irish life*, pp. 119–20.

69   Marie Coleman, *County Longford*, pp. 78–9; John Borgonovo, *The dynamics of war and revolution: Cork city, 1916–1918* (Cork, 2013), pp. 81–2; Fergus Campbell, *Land and revolution: nationalist politics in the west of Ireland, 1891–1921* (Oxford, 2005), pp. 222–3.

70   Peter Hart, 'On the necessity of violence in the Irish revolution' in Danine Farquharson and Sean Farrell (eds), *Shadows of the gunmen: violence and culture in modern Ireland* (Cork, 2008), pp. 22, 37.

71   David Fitzpatrick, 'Militarism in Ireland, 1900–22', p. 379.

72   Seumas Robinson statement (M.A.I., Bureau of Military History witness statements, BMH/WS 1721).

73   Frank Thornton statement (M.A.I., Bureau of Military History witness statements, BMH/WS 510).

74   Leon O'Broin, *Revolutionary underground: the story of the Irish Republican Brotherhood, 1858–1924* (Dublin, 1976), pp. 176–7.

75   Joost Augusteijn, *From public defiance to guerrilla warfare*, p. 63.

76   Peter Hart, *Mick*, p. 151.

77   Ronan Fanning, *Éamon de Valera: a will to power* (London, 2015), pp. 56–7.

78   Joost Augusteijn, *From public defiance to guerrilla warfare*, p. 64.

79   *Irish Independent*, 26 October 1917; ibid, 27 October 1917.

Chapter 8

1   L.P. Hartley, *The Go-Between* (London, 1953), p. 1.

2   See Mary Daly and Margaret O'Callaghan (eds), *1916 in 1966: commemorating the Easter Rising* (Dublin, 2007); Richard S. Grayson and Fearghal McGarry (eds), *Remembering 1916: the Easter Rising, the Somme and the politics of memory* (Cambridge, 2016).

3   See Jay Winter, 'The generation of memory: reflections on the "Memory Boom" in contemporary historical studies', *Canadian Military History*, x (2001), pp. 57–66.

4   See Inspiring Ireland: http://www.inspiring-ireland.ie/.

5   Mark McCarthy, *Ireland's 1916 Rising: explorations of history-making, commemoration and heritage in modern times* (Farnham, 2012), pp. 140–1.

6   *Irish Independent*, 5 May 1924; ibid, 10 May 1928; ibid, 7 May 1930.

7   *Irish Independent*, 3 May 1933; ibid, 3 May 1934.

8   Diarmaid Ferriter, 'Commemorating the Rising, 1922–65: "a figurative scramble for the bones of the patriot dead"?' in Mary Daly and Margaret O'Callaghan (eds), *1916 in 1966: commemorating the Easter Rising* (Dublin, 2007), p. 198.

9   Jay Winter, *Sites of memory, sites of mourning* (Cambridge, 1995), p. 80.

10 *Irish Independent*, 5 May 1926; ibid, 5 May 1932.

11 *Irish Press*, 3 May 1933.

12 Paul Connerton, *How societies remember* (Cambridge, 1989), p. 44.

13 Mark McCarthy, *Ireland's 1916 Rising*, p. 141.

14 Roisin Higgins, *Transforming 1916: meaning, memory and the fiftieth anniversary of the Easter Rising* (Cork, 2012), p. 14.

15 See Eric Hobsbawm and Terence Ranger (eds), *The Invention of Tradition* (Cambridge, 1992).

16 Mary Daly, 'Less a commemoration of the actual achievements and more a commemoration of the hopes of the men of 1916' in Mary Daly and Margaret O'Callaghan (eds), *1916 in 1966: commemorating the Easter Rising* (Dublin, 2007), p. 22.

17 Pierre Nora, 'From lieux de mémoire to realms of memory' in idem, *Realms of Memory: rethinking the French Past: conflicts and divisions*, i (Columbia, 1996), xvii.

18 Pierre Nora, 'Between memory and history: les lieux de mémoire' in *Representations*, xxvi (1989), p. 7.

19 *Irish Independent*, 11 April 1935; ibid, 17 April 1935.

20 *Irish Times*, 22 April 1935.

21 *Irish Independent*, 22 April 1935.

22 Paul Connerton, *How societies remember*, p. 61.

23 See R.F. Foster, *The Irish Story: telling tales and making it up in Ireland* (London, 2002).

24 *Irish Independent*, 22 April 1935.

25 See Dermot Keogh, *Twentieth-century Ireland* (Dublin, 2005).

26 Diarmaid Ferriter, 'Commemorating the Rising, 1922–65', p. 198.

27 *Irish Independent*, 14 April 1941; *Irish Press*, 14 April 1941.

28 Dermot Bolger (ed.), *Letters from the New Island* (Dublin, 1991), p. 10.

29 Maurice Halbwachs, *On collective memory* (Chicago, 1992), pp. 38–40.

30 Mark McCarthy, *Ireland's 1916 Rising*, p. 195.

31 Department of External Affairs, *Cuimhneachán, 1916–1966: a record of Ireland's commemoration of the 1916 Rising* (Dublin, 1966), p. 24.

32 Roisin Higgins, *Transforming 1916*, pp. 40–3.

33 Carole Holohan, 'More than a revival of memories? 1960s youth and the 1916 Rising' in Mary Daly and Margaret O'Callaghan (eds), *1916 in 1966*, pp. 175–6.

34 Roisin Higgins, *Transforming 1916*, pp. 47–8.

35 Maurice Halbwachs, *On collective memory*, p. 38.

36 See Émile Durkheim, *The elementary forms of religious life* (Oxford, 2008).

37 Carole Holohan, 'More than a revival of memories?', p. 176.

38 Roisin Higgins, '"I am the narrator over-and-above … the caller up of the dead" pageant and drama in 1966' in Mary Daly and Margaret O'Callaghan (eds), *1916 in 1966*, p. 157.

39 Maurice Halbwachs, *On collective memory*, p. 40.

40 Ibid, pp. 23–6.

41 Mary Daly, 'Less a commemoration of the actual achievements', p. 27.

42 See Tom Garvin, *Judging Lemass: the measure of the man* (Dublin, 2009).

43 Mary Daly, 'Less a commemoration of the actual achievements', p. 36.

44 *Irish Independent*, 18 April 1966.

45 Conor Cruise O'Brien, *States of Ireland* (London, 1972), p. 150.

46 Roisin Higgins, *Transforming 1916*, pp. 1–2.

47 See Mary Daly and Margaret O'Callaghan, 'Irish modernity and the "patriot dead" in 1966' in idem, *1916 in 1966*, p. 5.

48 Diarmaid Ferriter, *A Nation and not a rabble: the Irish revolution, 1912–23* (London, 2015), p. 367.

49 John R. Gillis, 'Memory and identity: the history of a relationship' in idem *Commemorations: the politics of national identity* (Princeton, 1994), p. 13.

50 Diarmaid Ferriter, *Ambiguous republic: Ireland in the 1970s* (London, 2012), pp. 221–54.

51 See Benedict Anderson, *Imagined communities: reflections on the origins and spread of nationalism* (New York, 1991).

52 Margaret O'Callaghan, 'Reframing 1916 after 1969: Irish governments, a National Day of Reconciliation, and the politics of commemoration in the 1970s' in Richard S. Grayson and Fearghal McGarry (eds), *Remembering 1916*, pp. 215–19.

53 See Sigmund Freud, *The collected works of Sigmund Freud: psychoanalytic studies, theoretical essays and articles* (London, 2016).

54 Mark McCarthy, *Ireland's 1916 Rising*, pp. 317–18.

55 Sigmund Freud, *On metapsychology: the theory of psychoanalysis* (London, 1991), pp. 288–9.

56 Mark McCarthy, *Ireland's 1916 Rising*, pp. 361–3.

57 Battle of the Somme commemorative programme, 1 July 2006 http://www.taoiseach.gov.ie/eng/News/Archives/2006/Government_Press_Releases_2006/90th_Anniversary_Commemoration_of_the_Battle_of_the_Somme,.html [Accessed 28 June 2016].

58 Gabriel Doherty, 'The commemoration of the ninetieth anniversary of the Easter Rising' in Gabriel Doherty and Dermot Keogh (eds), *1916: the long revolution* (Cork, 2007), pp. 380–2.

59 President Mary McAleese speech at University College Cork, 27 January 2006 http://www.president.ie/en/media-library/speeches/remarks-by-president-mcaleese-at-the-conference-the-long-revolution-the-191 [Accessed 28 June 2016].

60 Mark McCarthy, *Ireland's 1916 Rising*, p. 414.

61 Speech by Taoiseach Bertie Ahern at the National Museum of Ireland, 9 April 2006 http://cain.ulst.ac.uk/issues/politics/docs/dott/ba090406.htm [Accessed 28 June 2016].

62 Pierre Nora, 'Comment écrire l'histoire de France' in idem, *Lieux de mémoires: les France, conflits et partages*, iii (Paris, 1992), 11–32.

63 Mark McCarthy, *Ireland's 1916 Rising*, pp. 375–6.

64 *Irish Times*, 3 July 2006.

65 Speech by President Mary McAleese at Áras an Uachtarán, 12 July 2006 http://www.president.ie/en/media-library/speeches/remarks-by-president-mcaleese-at-a-north-south-reception-to-mark-the-12th-o [Accessed 28 June 2016].

66 See Guy Beiner, 'Making sense of memory: coming to terms with conceptualisations of historical remembrance' in *Remembering 1916: the Easter Rising, the Somme and the politics of memory in Ireland* (Cambridge, 2016), pp. 20–1; *Astrid Erll* (transl. Sara Young), *Memory in Culture* (Basingstoke, 2011), pp. 30–1.

67 Jan Assmann, 'Communicative and cultural memory' in Astrid Erll and Ansgar Nünning (eds), *Cultural memory studies: an international and interdisciplinary handbook* (Berlin, 2008), p. 109.

68 See Sigmund Freud (transl. James Strachey), *The standard edition of the complete psychological works of Sigmund Freud: early psycho-analytic publications (1893–1899)* (London, 2001), pp. 287–322; Carl Gustav Jung (Aniela Jaffé ed.), *Memories, dreams, reflections* (New York, 1963).

69 See James Fentress and Chris Wickham, *Social memory* (London, 1992), ix.

70 Jan Assmann, 'Communicative and cultural memory' in Astrid Erll and Ansgar Nünning (eds), *Cultural memory studies: an international and interdisciplinary handbook* (Berlin, 2008), p. 111.

71 Aleida Assmann, 'Memory, individual and collective' in Robert E. Goodin and Charles Tilly (eds), *The Oxford handbook of contextual political analysis* (Oxford, 2006), pp. 213–15, 220–1.

72 Lar Joye and Brenda Malone, 'Displaying the nation', pp. 182–4.

73 *Irish Independent*, 8 June 1932.

74 *Irish Independent*, 22 June 1932; *Irish Press*, 25 June 1932; *Irish Times*, 22 June 1932.

75 Nellie Gifford-Donnelly military pension application (M.A.I., Military Pension records, MSP34REF1386). See also *Irish Press*, 19 October 1935.

76 *Irish Press*, 25 June 1932.

77 Lar Joye and Brenda Malone, 'Displaying the nation', p. 184.

78 Nellie Gifford-Donnelly military pension application (M.A.I., Military Pension records, MSP34REF1386).

79 *Irish Press*, 19 October 1935.

80 Lar Joye and Brenda Malone, 'Displaying the nation', pp 186–7. Over one hundred objects were received within one week of the public announcement. See *Irish Press*, 28 January 1935.

81 *Irish Times*, 16 April 1935; *Irish Press*, 16 April 1935.

82 *Irish Independent*, 16 April 1935; *Irish Times*, 16 April 1935; *Irish Press*, 16 April 1935; *Irish Press*, 17 April 1935.

83 *Irish Press*, 17 April 1935.

84 *Irish Times*, 16 April 1935.

85 *Irish Independent*, 16 April 1935.

86 *Irish Press*, 17 April 1935.

87 *Irish Independent*, 19 March 1941. See also *Irish Press*, 19 March 1941.

88 Lar Joye and Brenda Malone, 'Displaying the nation', p. 187.

89 *Irish Independent*, 3 April 1941; *Irish Press*, 5 May 1941; *Irish Press*, 14 May 1941.

90 *Irish Press*, 14 April 1941.

91 *Irish Independent*, 19 April 1941.

92 *Irish Independent*, 15 April 1966.

93 'Historical collection – National Museum' statement, 1966 (N.M.I.A.S., 1966 Golden Jubilee of the Rising papers, D4-D6/331 (ii)).

94 Oliver Snoddy, *Guide to the historical exhibition commemorative of the Rising of 1916* (Dublin, 1966), pp. 5–25.

95 A.T. Lucas note on 'Guide to 1916 exhibition', 31 May 1966 (N.M.I.A.S., 1966 Golden Jubilee of the Rising papers, D4-D6/331 (i)).

96 *Irish Times*, 13 April 1966; *Evening Press*, 22 April 1966.

97 A.T. Lucas memorandum on 'Order of ceremony: 12 April 1966', 7 April 1966 (N.M.I.A.S, 1966 Golden Jubilee of the Rising papers, D4-D6/331 (ii)).

98 *Irish Press*, 12 April 1966.

99 John Teahan to Secretary to the Department of the Taoiseach, 26 July 1988 (N.M.I.A.S., 1991 Commemoration Exhibition, AI.ELIEX.0090.03.001).

100 *Irish Independent*, 11 April 1935; ibid, 17 April 1935.

101 John Teahan memorandum 'general suggestions on 1916 exhibition/audio visuals', 26 September 1990 (N.M.I.A.S., 1991 Commemoration Exhibition, AI.ELIEX.0090.03.001 (23)).

102 See *Irish Times*, 25 April 1991.

103 '1916 Room', n.d. (N.M.I.A.S., 1991 Commemoration Exhibition, AI.ELIEX.0090.03.001 (6)).

104 Michael Kenny to Pat Wallace, 16 August 1990 26 September 1990 (N.M.I.A.S., 1991 Commemoration Exhibition, AI.ELIEX.0090.03.001 (14)).

105 '1916 Room', n.d. (N.M.I.A.S., 1991 Commemoration Exhibition, AI.ELIEX.0090.03.001 (9)).

106 *Irish Times*, 25 April 1991.

107 Michael Kenny to Mr Lynch, January [1992?] (N.M.I.A.S., 1991 Commemoration Exhibition, AI.ELIEX.0090.03.001 (25)).

108 See Sandra Heise, 'Leabhar na hAiséirghe' in *Irish Arts Review*, xxix (2012), pp. 98–103.

109 *Irish Independent*, 10 April 2006; *Irish Times*, 10 April 2006.

110 *Irish Press*, 16 April 1935; ibid, 5 May 1941.

111 James Fentress and Chris Wickham, *Social memory* (London, 1992), ix–x.

112 Ibid, p. 7.

113 Jan Assmann, 'Communicative and cultural memory', pp. 111–12, 114; Aleida Assmann, 'Memory, individual and collective', pp. 213–15.

114 Rose McNamara statement, 1941 (N.M.I.A.S., Easter Week donations, 1941, EWD. 0091. 007. 00008 (4)).

115 Madge Daly to Tomás Ó Cléirigh, 10 February 1935 (N.M.I.A.S., Easter Week donations, 1933-35, EWD. 0091. 001. 00045(1)).

116 Sean Doyle to Tomás Ó Cléirigh, 12 May 1937 (N.M.I.A.S., Easter Week donations, 1933-35, EWD. 0091. 003. 00032(6)).

117 John Reynolds to the Curator (National Museum of Ireland), 7 March 1938 (N.M.I.A.S., Easter Week donations, 1933–35, EWD. 001. 004. 00024(1)).

118 Máire Ní Maicín to National Museum of Ireland, 15 June 1943 (N.M.I.A.S., Easter Week donations, 1935–36, EWD. 0091. 002. 00006 (1)).

119 Doran Hurley to the Director (National Museum of Ireland), 10 October 1948 (N.M.I.A.S., Easter Week donations, 1947–49/50, EWD. 0092. 004. 00027 (2)).

120 List of objects donated through medium of S.D. Markievicz, 29 October 1939 (N.M.I.A.S., Easter Week donations, ELID. 0091. 005); Stanislas Dunin-Markievicz to Liam Gogan, 28 April 1943 (N.M.I.A.S., Easter Week donations, EWD. 0091. 005. 00013 (33)).

121 Keeper of the National Museum of Ireland to Brigid Pearse, 22 January 1937 (N.M.I.A.S., Easter Week donations, EWD. 0091. 003. 00010 (1)).

122 P. Twanley to Liam Gogan, 16 March 1937 (N.M.I.A.S., Easter Week donations, EWD. 0091. 003. 00010 (10)).

123 R.F. Foster, *Vivid Faces*, pp. 294–306.

124 Diarmuid Lynch to Tomás Ó Cléirigh, 8 March 1935 (N.M.I.A.S., Easter Week donations, 1933–35, EWD. 0091. 001. 00043 (6)).

125 Molly Childers to Tomás Ó Cléirigh, 4 April 1935 (N.M.I.A.S., Easter Week donations, 1933–35, EWD. 0091. 001. 00047).

126 W.T. Cosgrave to Alderman P.S. Doyle, 18 June 1937 (N.M.I.A.S., Easter Week donations, EWD. 0091. 006. 00032 (3)).

127 List of material donated to the National Museum of Ireland by Éamon de Valera, April 1941 (N.M.I.A.S., Easter Week donations, 1941, EWD. 0091. 007. 00028).

128 *Irish Press*, 15 April 1966; ibid, 19 April 1966.

129 Walter Benjamin, *Theses on the philosophy of history* (1940).

130 A notable exception to this Civil War by proxy was W. Alison Phillips, *The revolution in Ireland, 1906–1923* (London, 1926).

131 P.S. O'Hegarty, *The victory of Sinn Féin: how it won, and how it used it* (London, 1924); Piaras Béaslaí, *Michael Collins and the making of a new Ireland* (2 vols, London, 1926).

132 Dorothy Macardle, *The Irish Republic* (Dublin, 1937).

133 See Alvin Jackson, 'Irish history in the twentieth and twenty-first centuries' in idem *The Oxford handbook of modern Irish history* (Oxford, 2014), pp. 3–21.

134 F.S.L. Lyons, *Ireland since the Famine* (London, 1971), p. 359.

135 J.C. Beckett's survey of Ireland, published five years earlier, established the 1914–23 framework but offered more sequential narrative of the Rising than analytical focus: J.C. Beckett, *The making of modern Ireland, 1603–1923* (London, 1966), pp. 435–41.

136 Oliver MacDonagh had first presented this Yeatsian schema in his *Ireland: the Union and its aftermath*, published in 1968. However, in the same volume, MacDonagh had also suggested a deeper chronology dating back to the Acts of Union: 'the significance of the Rising is missed unless the long past is taken into account'. See Oliver MacDonagh, *Ireland: the Union and its aftermath* (Dublin, 1968), p. 74.

137 J. Lee, *The modernisation of Irish society, 1848–1918* (Dublin, 1973), pp. 137–63.

138 Alvin Jackson, *Ireland, 1798–1998: politics and war* (Oxford, 1999), pp. 142–274. Jackson's subsequent *Ireland, 1798–1998: war, peace and beyond* adheres to the same interpretative framework.

139 Paul Bew, *Ireland: the politics of enmity*.

140 Diarmaid Ferriter, *The transformation of Ireland, 1900–2000* (London, 2004).

141 R.F. Foster, *Modern Ireland*, p. 471.

142 D. George Boyce, *Nineteenth-century Ireland: the search for stability* (Dublin, 1990).

143 Charles Townshend, *Ireland: the twentieth century*.

144 R.V. Comerford, *Ireland* (London, 2003), p. 42.

145 Richard English, *Irish Freedom*; Thomas Bartlett, *Ireland: a history* (Cambridge, 2010).

146 Desmond Ryan, *The Rising*; for the research notes on this volume see the Desmond Ryan papers (LA10 351) at the University College Dublin archives.

147 Max Caulfield, *The Easter Rebellion*, p. 13.

148 Michael Foy and Brian Barton, *The Easter Rising*.

149 Claire Wills, *Dublin 1916: the siege of the GPO* (London, 2009).

150 See Paul O'Brien, *Crossfire: the battle of the Four Courts, 1916* (Dublin, 2012); Paul O'Brien, *Blood on the streets: 1916 and the battle for Mount Street Bridge* (Dublin, 2008).

151 Charles Townshend, *Easter Rising*.

152 Fearghal McGarry, *The Rising*, p. 4.

153 F.X. Martin (ed.), *Leaders and men of the Easter Rising* (London, 1967).

154 Louis Le Roux (Desmond Ryan transl.), *The life of Patrick H. Pearse* (Dublin, 1932). See also Desmond Ryan's earlier volume from which Le Roux quoted: Desmond Ryan, *The man called Pearse* (Dublin, 1919).

155 Ruth Dudley Edwards, *Patrick Pearse*.

156 Seán Farrell Moran, *Patrick Pearse and the politics of redemption: the mind of the Easter Rising, 1916* (Washington, 1994).

157 Joost Augusteijn, *Patrick Pearse*.

158 Roisín Higgins and Regina Uí Chollatáin (eds), *The life and afterlife of P.H. Pearse* (Dublin, 2009). See also Elaine Sisson, *Pearse's patriots: St. Enda's and the cult of boyhood* (Cork, 2004).

159 C. Desmond Greaves, *The life and times of James Connolly*.

160 Owen Dudley Edwards, *The mind of an activist*.

161 Austen Morgan, *James Connolly: a political biography* (Manchester, 1988).

162 Kieran Allen, *The politics of James Connolly* (London, 1990).

163 Donal Nevin, *James Connolly: 'a full life'*.

164 Denis Gwynn, *Traitor or Patriot, the life and death of Roger Casement* (London, 1931).

165 Brian Inglis, *Roger Casement* (London, 1973); Angus Mitchell, *Casement* (London, 2003); Angus Mitchell, *Roger Casement* (Dublin, 2013).

166 B.L. Reid, *The lives of Roger Casement* (Yale, 1976).

167 Séamus Ó Síocháin, *Roger Casement: imperialist, rebel, revolutionary* (Dublin, 2003); Mary Daly (ed.), *Roger Casement in world and Irish history* (Dublin, 2005).

168 Louis Le Roux, *Tom Clarke and the Irish freedom movement* (Dublin, 1936).

169 Michael Foy, *Tom Clarke*.

170 Gerard MacAtasney, *Sean Mac Diarmada: the mind of a revolution* (Manorhamilton, 2004).

171 Mary Gallagher, *Éamonn Ceannt*; Shane Kenna, *Thomas MacDonagh*; Honor O'Brolchain, *Joseph Plunkett* (Dublin, 2012).

172 G.A. Hayes-McCoy to Secretary to Department of Education, 7 August 1941 (N.M.I.A.S., 1916 Commemoration Exhibition, D4.D6/331(i)).

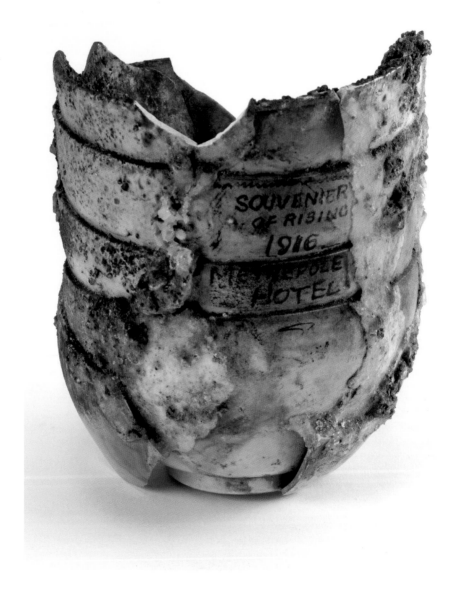

vii
Five sugar bowls
fused together by
the fires at the
Metropole Hotel
on Sackville Street
during Easter Week.
HE:EW.854

Index